TOWARD
COMMON GROUND

*This book is one of a series called
"Ethical Culture Publications"
published in collaboration
with the American Ethical Union*

TOWARD
COMMON GROUND

THE STORY
OF THE ETHICAL SOCIETIES
IN THE UNITED STATES

Howard B. Radest

Frederick Ungar Publishing Co.
New York

Acknowledgments

More than custom drives me to thank those who have helped with this work. I must accept responsibility for what is written but, in truth, so much was contributed by so many that this book would have been impossible without a massive and willing effort of cooperation.

First came the idea for developing an Ethical Culture archive from which a history could be drawn. Encouraged by my colleague and friend Jerome Nathanson, a proposal was made to the Board of the New York Society. Led by their chairman, Hugh Stern, and on a motion from Mr. Herbert Rothschild, that Society graciously and generously provided the place, the support, and the encouragement for the project. My appreciation for their confidence cannot be measured. The Ethical Culture Society in Bergen County which I then served was equally generous in releasing some of my time and in encouraging my work. Again, to a group of very good friends and co-workers my deepest sense of gratitude. Finally, the Fraternity of Ethical Leaders, who listened and responded critically to periodic reports, helped in ways too numerous to detail.

Several people gave unstintingly of their time, reading the manuscript in its early drafts, making comments and suggestions, offering advice. First among these was Horace Friess, whose patient, even temperament must often have been sorely tried by my less felicitous efforts. Bringing to the subject a wealth of knowledge, but more significantly a sensitivity all too rare, Professor Friess combined critical intelligence with the best arts of the teacher. Another colleague and teacher, Professor Joseph L. Blau, gave me the benefit of his wide knowledge and scholarship in the fields of religion and American studies. Both Jerome Nathanson and Algernon D. Black read and criticized the manuscript, one more instance of the help they have given me over the years. A continuing inspiration because she embodies so much of what I have tried to communicate in these pages was Florence Wolff Klaber.

Three dedicated hard-working women researched many of the documents for me, painstakingly copying out materials for my use. To Nellie Reichenbach, Alice Goldmark, and Anna Sachere I am greatly indebted. Frieda Moss, whose untimely death deprived us of a warm and competent friend, undertook nearly all of the interviews and oral histories. With the kindness and perceptiveness so necessary to her task she met with numbers of people seeking to recapture precious memories for the record. Ilse Sakheim and Nina Kimche did the hard work of transcribing often illegible material with a diligence that went far beyond ordinary secretarial skill.

Many individuals contributed clippings, photographs, letters. Others assisted by organizing materials in various localities around the country, and forwarding duplicates and files to us in New York. It is therefore with deep appreciation that I record my gratitude to: Margaret Adler, Bella Avrutik, Marilyn Baker, Inez Bordner, Howard Box, Freeman Champney, John Collins, Ann Courtway, Charles Deutsch, Harry Frankel, Ruth Friess, Myra Gallert, Helen Gluck, Rebecca Goldblum, Raphael Gould, Bella Gross, Bertha S. Gruenberg, Doreen Hartwig, Irene Hochheimer, James F. Hornback, Harold Houghton, Donald Jacoby, Berwin Kaiser, Mrs. John Kalbach, Stephen Kaufman, Dorothy Lockhart, Henry Lynn, Claudia Machol, L. D. MacIntyre, Ellen Malino, Margaret Michaelson, David Norton, Olivia Redfield, Michael Rosen, Samuel Sander, Sybil Shelton, Zelda Simon, Jerry Stern, Mr. and Mrs. Calvin Valensi, Victoria Wagner,

Mr. and Mrs. Harold Walker, James Wallerstein, Madeline Wamser, Fred Weinstein, Bea Werner, Mrs. Sol M. Wolffson.

Closest to the project, and a continuing source of materials and ideas, as well as an increasingly able researcher was Mrs. Natalie Koretz. Now Archivist for Ethical Culture, she showed remarkable ability to grasp what was needed and an intelligence equal to the complex task of creating, as well as maintaining, a disparate though fascinating record. If any one person deserves to be listed as coauthor of this work it is she.

Some people contribute support and inspiration by their presence. My wife, Rita, read nearly all of the pages as they came from my typewriter, listened to half-formed thoughts and phrases before they were set down, and in her quiet way helped to sharpen and clarify much of the content of this book. But more important, she provided the constant warmth of support and understanding without which any creative work is impossible. My sons, Robert and Michael, were a reminder to me that history is not merely past but future, and that the present is always responsible.

Many people gave time from busy lives for interviews; to them, my deepest thanks. And to the many whom I have not named, to members who listened appreciatively and critically when I shared a piece of this work from the Platform and to others who in conversation gave me benefit of their thinking, I owe a deep debt. If this story is worthy in any measure of the long and fruitful efforts that have created Ethical Culture, it will have more than repaid these years of work.

Howard B. Radest

Fair Lawn, New Jersey
January 1969

List of Those Interviewed

Altschul, Frieda
Anspacher, Florence
  (née Scholle-Sutro)
Baldwin, Roger
Berman, Hyman
Black, Algernon D.
Black, Elinor Goldmark
Blumberg, Mr. and Mrs. Bernard
Blumenthal, Mrs. Sidney
Brickner, Ruth
Burton, Fred
Carpenter, H. Daniel
Frank, Mrs. Henry
Frank, Walter
Friess, Horace L.
Friess, Ruth
Gruenberg, Sidonie
Goldwater, Edith

Gutman, James
Klaber, Florence
Herman, Henry
Jablonower, Mr. and Mrs. Joseph
Lemle, Edna
Lichterman, Joseph
Lindquist, Grace
Louis, Bertha
Miller, Marion
Miller, Spencer, Jr.
Mitchell, Lucy
Morgenstern, Clara
Moss, Jeanette
  (née Robbins)
Nathanson, Jerome
Naumberg, Mrs. Eliza Herzfeld
Neumann, Henry
Newton, Alberta

ix

Openhym, Wilfred
Pilpel, Robert
Politzer, Mrs. Alice
Robbins, Ira
Robbins, Janet
   (née McCloskey)
Robinson, Dr. and Mrs. Ormsby
Rothschild, Herbert and
   Nannette
Sanger, Eleanor
   (née Naumberg)

Silverberg, Dr. Mabel
   (née Gutman)
Stein, Clarence
Stein, Doris (née Blumenthal)
Strasser, Edna
Thayer, V. T.
Weis, Mr. and Mrs. Walter
Weinberg, Robert
Wells, Guy
Wolf, Ada (née DePinna)
Wolff, Herbert

Contents

xi

PART TWO   *Years of Hope and Fulfillment*

PART THREE   *Ethical Culture in the Twentieth Century*

Introduction

The U.S. Supreme Court ruled Bible reading and prayers in public schools unconstitutional. A young man refused military service on the grounds of higher moral obligation but denied belief in a Supreme Being. The Pope established a Vatican Secretariat for "Unbelievers." Theologians wrestled with the "death of God." And the favorite word in many places is *dialogue*. Clearly the upheavals of our age are not only political and economic, and everywhere questions loom larger than answers.

Still, the quest for certainty plagues us. Here and there a few voices say that it can never be satisfied in the old way, but that man must find certainty in change. One such voice is Ethical Culture. For more than ninety years now, the Ethical movement has recognized that man's most precious values, if they are to be preserved, must be separated from outworn myths and accreted metaphysics. The attempt to achieve such a separation, to preserve the worthwhile, to create new values, and to realize them in the daily life of men and women is the ongoing experiment called Ethical Culture. As with all experiments,

1

the conclusion of any one phase provides new puzzles along with tentative answers. Thus the élan of the movement (and its frustration,
too) is never-ending challenge.

   In some thirty cities and towns of this country small groups of people have formed Ethical Culture societies. Their children attend Sunday schools; in many ways they do as their church-going neighbors
do. Yet the Ethical Meeting is surrounded by no symbolic forms; and
the traditional worshipper would recognize little as ritual—no robes,
no colors, no candles. No specific text is referred to nor is some lesson
of the day read from one of the world's great scriptures. A reading is
as likely to come from a contemporary author as from an ancient
source; music may be sacred or secular. The focus of the Society is the
Ethical Platform, an address on themes drawn from the latest head-
lines or the perennial problems of men. The Sunday schools study
materials from many religious traditions and from the social, political,
and scientific life of man. The programs of the day announce activities of education and good works. It is both reminiscent of and yet
different from the common experience of religious organizations.

   Indeed, there will be some in the group who will bridle at being
called religious and insist that religion was left behind when they set
to working out a "philosophy of life" or a "way of life." They will tell
you, some of them, that they do not ask their children to follow in
their footsteps but hope their offspring will find Ethical Culture for
themselves. They will speak with pride of the works of the past; of
schools, social reform, race relations, and services to young people.
They will insist that theirs is a free faith but not an atheistic one, since
theist, deist, agnostic, and atheist are equally welcome. They will tell
you that there is no corporate prayer or congregational worship—that
the meeting would, if convenient, be at another time than Sunday.

   In many of the Societies the visitor will meet an Ethical Culture
Leader who performs functions usually regarded as ministerial, but
who has no sacramental sanctions. He may come to this work from
the law, the sciences, the schools, or from other ministries. The observer will be impressed with the major role played by laymen in
directing the life of the Society. He will, if he listens very closely, be
struck by the open self-criticism of the work of a particular Society or
the movement itself. He will learn that people are married here and
buried here. He will, in short, find a mixture of traditional religious

functions and secular interests, of ordinary cultic patterns and extraordinary individualism.

It is safe to predict that there will be resistance within Ethical Culture to an established tradition. Its adherents who have come out of other faiths look upon history and tradition with suspicion, for they have experienced the use of the past as authority, of tradition as legislation. But a human being cannot live only in the present; to even seek to do so is to cripple the human capacity for memory and imagination. Others who find Ethical Culture meaningful will tend to emphasize the future. For them the world awaits continued reformation and the present is only instrumental for tomorrow.

As important as anything in studying the history of a religious movement is the need to guard against myth and illusion. Religions are likely victims of mythologizing; once in that trap a movement is forced into the intellectually dubious process of symbolic reinterpretation and ultimately into the emotionally painful experience of demythologizing. Myths are latent in the Ethical movement despite its youth, myths focusing on the glorious golden age of its founding and its founder. Indeed, a vigorous and brilliant effort began the experiment in moral faith, but an unalloyed drama larger than life it was not. Ethical Culture is characteristic of our time and responsive to our age; its search has found failures as well as successes. It is even more pragmatic and tentative in its evolution than hindsight would lead one to believe: no grand blueprint showed the way.

PART ONE

In the Beginning

CHAPTER I

The Nineteenth-Century Setting

Few religions explicitly recognize and accept their tie to the culture in which they find themselves. Some find their meaning in a unique event, an intrusion into history from outside sources. Others see themselves as set apart from their time in a sacred enclave. Still others root themselves in revelation. By contrast, Ethical Culture claims no revelation, no mysteriously touched central figure, no sacred mystery. It was not discontinuity that marked its birth, but a natural evolution. The movement seized the key themes of its day and carried them forward to logical, psychological and social consequences.

The Ethical movement is intricately and consciously bound to the events of the world around it. Its history begins in the United States in the years following the Civil War. As in most postwar periods, the 1860s and '70s were turbulent. Energies mobilized to fight battles did not subside but found new releases in both continental conquest in the reach to the Pacific and massive urban development. Genocide bloodied the way, but the American Indian was, after all, only a "savage" and could not be allowed to stand in the way of progress. Exploi-

7

tation and economic thievery were "necessary" dictates of the expanding industrial system, a system so obviously natural and right that any means that served its ends was justified.

For the moralist, it was a time of despair. Corruption crept into the highest offices of the land, as well as into the houses of business and industry. In the burgeoning cities political machines perfected their crudest and most effective practices.

> . . . a good deal of American business and political life was taking on the morals of the gashouse. . . ."Big Jim" Fisk, an adventurer with a penchant for mistresses, opera bouffe, and gilded carriages, represented an important part of the new business community. Criticized for a particularly brazen misuse of other people's money, Big Jim was totally unperturbed. "Nothing is lost save honor," he said with a wave of his fat hand.

> Political morality slithered along. . . . so completely did [Grant] think of the Presidency as an opportunity to be exploited that he billeted an estimated forty-two relatives on the country. . . .

> The corruption of municipal and state politics was still more flagrant. Boss William Tweed's rule of New York was untypical only in the scope and daring of his grabs. . . . When Vanderbilt and another freebooter tangled for control of the Erie Railroad, hundreds of thousands of greenbacks arrived in Albany. One of Tweed's State Senators, catching the full spirit of the occasion, took $75,000 from the Vanderbilt representative and $100,000 from the other side. He preserved the morals of the new politics by voting for the higher donor.[1]

During the latter part of the nineteenth century America swelled with optimism, for she was fulfilling her destiny. Successive waves of immigrants flowed into the country to populate the growing new cities, and in the midst of their exploitation to dream the American dream of success, if not for themselves then certainly for their children. The "frontier" was won. America was shifting from a rural to an urban nation. Jefferson's "honest farmer" gave way to the political boss and the illiterate electorate who voted early and often. The industrial system forecast a wealth undreamt of in human history, but critics on the left were beginning to attack American "materialism."

The European powers were yielding their influence in the Ameri-

[1] Eric F. Goldman, *Rendezvous with Destiny,* pp. 10–11.

cas, with the exception of the British in Canada. The close of the century was to see the almost total elimination of French, Spanish, and Dutch rule in the Western Hemisphere. Granting the corruption, the immorality, the economic exploitation, the destruction of the original Americans, and the crudeness in American life, it is necessary to see the American of that time as essentially hopeful and self-confident. He had begun to recognize the need for reform, but he would advocate nothing radical.

Amid the turmoil of social, political, and economic change, a series of new and exciting intellectual concepts were to have their effect. The spiritual model of nineteenth-century America was Ralph Waldo Emerson, today, regrettably, known more by reputation than by study.

Emerson was too radical for even the increasingly liberal Unitarian pulpit. He took instead to the lecture platform, that period's equivalent of our mass media, where popular entertainment was parceled out with edification. Over the years he evolved those themes that served to bridge the transition from American imitation of European culture to New World philosophy. He spoke of things that seemed intuitively right to the American. "Self-reliance," "Individualism"— the titles of his essays read like a statement of an American credo. In a sense, he was preparing the way for our twentieth century; his words ring true today if his style does not.

Before 1850 Emerson called for a pure ethical religion, representing a basic thread in American religious life, however diverse its institutional guises. In a prophetic utterance he said:

> There will be a new church founded on moral science, at first cold and naked, a babe in a manger again, the algebra and mathematics of ethical law. The church of men to come, without shaums or psaltery or sackbut; but it will have heaven and earth for its beams and rafters; science for symbol and illustration; it will fast enough gather beauty, music, picture, and poetry.[2]

American religion, traditionally moralistic, was concerned more with action than theology and was indeed suspicious of the finely argued philosophic distinctions between one creed and another. This

---

[2] Ralph Waldo Emerson, *On Music.*

paralleled our distrust of ideology in politics and the anti-intellectualism which colors American life. Also, despite a colonial period during which religion and community were intimately interwoven, churchmen, along with schoolmen, were regarded as somewhat less than full citizens. Only by the 1950s did church rolls include more than half of the people of the United States. During the nineteenth century, membership in organized churches never passed the ten percent mark. Attempts to build a religious party in American politics have always failed.

More typical than churches and clerics were the revival meeting and the itinerant preacher. On the fringes of society, especially in the post-civil war period, many religious experiments rose and vanished with the life or conviction of their founding figures. The majority of the population was nominally Protestant, except in the largest cities, where Catholicism grew with the influx of new immigrant groups and struggled to defend itself against the vicious bias and outright violence of Know-Nothingism and nativism. The Jewish community was small and well established in the cities of the Eastern seaboard. Virulent anti-Semitism was not to appear until the end of the century and in our own time.

Emerson's call for a purely moral faith was a central, not a marginal, theme of American religion. He was also the spokesman of American transcendentalism, a philosophic movement that crossed many sectarian lines. It brought to the United States a more subtle idealism than had been present before and served to open doors that had been closed before on this continent.

By introducing and familiarizing literate Americans with transcendentalist schools of Germany, France, and England, as well as with the mystic religions of the East, American transcendentalism was preparing the way for important new developments in religious thought. . . . the transcendentalists welcomed the latest contributions to scientific and social thought with, if anything, a too glib assurance that their intuitive faith would be only further confirmed by the accumulation of natural knowledge. The theory of evolution, for instance, which presented such difficulties for orthodox theology was welcomed by transcendental Christians without regard for its ultimate consequences for the transcendental method.

A more tangible contribution of transcendentalism growing out of the same cosmopolitan awareness of contemporary European and Asiatic thought was the awakening of interest in the comparative study of religions. . . .[3]

Not uncommon for the period was a report in *The Index,* the Journal of the Free Religious Association, for December, 1875, on a lecture at the Philadelphia Concert Hall offered by Wong Chin Foo and entitled "The Great Religions of China and Japan." He advocated "universality, learning, and tolerance" and suggested that these were the criteria by which the basic moral strength of a religion must be judged.

It would not do to assume that the challenges and ideas we are discussing were popular concerns. As with most such matters, the argument was carried on by a relatively small number of intellectuals and religionists, but it colored the times. The press gave full attention to the lectures, sermons, and debates of that day's stimulating religious life. And it records that religious controversy was not masked beneath the blandness of tolerance. However, while the attacks could grow vicious, one knew that issues of importance were being fought.

Changes were occurring in orthodoxy as well, changes that were to culminate in the Social Gospel movement among Protestants and in a liberalized Unitarianism and Universalism. The great Unitarian ministers Theodore Parker and William Ellery Channing were leading the way from the congregational Christianity of colonial Unitarianism toward a liberal church that has still not completed its evolution toward an unconditioned humanism. A passage from one of Channing's sermons illustrates the direction that was being taken.

We believe in the moral perfection of God. . . . We venerate not the loftiness of God's throne, but the equity and goodness in which it is established.

Now we object to the systems of religion which prevail among us, that they are adverse in greater or lesser degree to those purifying, comforting, and honorable views of God; that they take from us our father in heaven and substitute for him a being whom we cannot love if we would and whom we ought not to love if we could.

By shocking, as it does, the fundamental principles of morality, and by exhibiting a severe and partial deity, [this religious system] tends

[3] Stow Persons, *Free Religion,* pp. 22–23.

strongly to pervert the moral faculty, to form a gloomy, forbidding, and servile religion, and to lead men to substitute censoriousness, bitterness, and persecution for a tender and impartial charity. We think too that this system which begins with degrading human nature may be expected to end in pride; for pride grows out of consciousness of high distinctions however obtained, and no distinction is too great as that which is made between the elect and the abandoned of God.

The spiritual life of man was in flux. The shift from a pastoral to an urban-industrial culture was under way and with it came changes in man's sense of himself, in his ultimate commitments, in his sense of the universe. Helping to forward this and in turn influenced by it were the evolving sciences of man. Concepts of Newtonian physics now appeared in the study of man and society. The publication of Darwin's *Origin of Species* in 1859 touched off a series of speculations. Social Darwinism, using evolution as its god and "survival of the fittest" as its motto, rationalized the worst features of economic competition and industrial exploitation. Viciousness became intellectually respectable, love and fellow-feeling a kind of unnatural sentimentality.

But other effects of Darwinism appeared as well, and one was the naturalization of man. The Copernican revolution displaced earth and man from the center of the universe; the Darwinian further altered man's self-conception. The interest in comparative religion stirred by the transcendentalists soon found disciplined attention in the work of comparative linguistics, archaeology, and anthropology. Scientific criticism stimulated by Darwin, Marx, and Freud entered the sacred precincts of the gods through the back door. Biblical scholarship sought to establish scripture, not as the literal document of Fundamentalism but as a human interpretation sacred in content but not in expression. Comparative studies began to demonstrate that the scriptures did not report unique events but had parallels in the writing of other cultures and of other times.

The secularization and naturalization of man was furthered by both the Utopian and "scientific" socialists. Whatever the criticism of Marx's economics, his message that man is a creature of social forces could not be dismissed. Man was no longer conceivable as a special creation. With Sigmund Freud the process was carried on as man's innermost being was subjected to natural causation and natural forces. Darwin, Marx, and Freud thus completed the Newtonian revolution; man and the world were naturalized and secularized. Religion now needed ways to reintroduce the sacred into a world that had little place for it.

Some were willing to give up the sacred altogether, and no impressions of nineteenth-century America would be complete without some attention to free thought and atheism. Inspired by eighteenth-century rationalism and deism, utopian communities based on secular values were tried and failed. Pamphleteering introduced radical criticism of the traditions to the public, and the leading figure of free thought, Robert Ingersoll, was a frequent public lecturer. Yet we see even here the essential psychology of messianic salvation which the Judaeo-Christian heritage had impressed on western culture:

> A vision of the future arises. . . . I see a world without a slave. Man is at last free. Nature's forces have by science been enslaved. Lightning and light, wind and wave, frost and flame, and all the secret subtle powers of the earth and air are tireless toilers for the human race.
>
> I see a world at peace, adorned with every form of art, with music's myriad voices thrilled, while lips are rich with words of love and truth; a world in which no exile sighs, no prisoner mourns; a world on which the gibbet's shadow does not fall; a world where labor reaps its full reward, where work and worth go hand in hand. . . .
>
> I see a world without the beggar's outstretched palm, the miser's heartless stony stare, the piteous wail of want, the livid lips of lies, the cruel eyes of scorn.
>
> I see a race without disease of flesh or brain—shapely and fair, married harmony of form and function, and as I look, life lengthens, joy deepens, love canopies the earth; and over all in the great dome shines the eternal star of human hope.

Thus the scene was set for Ethical Culture: an America filled with the dreams of continental conquest; demons exorcised in the blood of civil war; the mixed promise and threat of industrial society and the rapid growth of cities; religion, and philosophy marked by radical change; science coming close to human experience; eyes turning from some other world to this one to face, for better or worse, a secularized future.

CHAPTER II

Ecce Homo:
Felix Adler

Members of Ethical Culture insist that the movement was not founded by one man, but this is not justified by the record. Granting the efforts of many, one man and one man alone gave the movement its original impetus and much of its shape.

Felix Adler was born in Alzey, Germany, in 1851. His father, Samuel Adler, was a rabbi, a youngest son in a family with a long tradition in the rabbinate, and a leading figure in Reform Judaism in Europe. When invited to become rabbi of Temple Emanu-El in New York City, he brought his young family to this country and in 1857 became rabbi of the wealthiest Jewish congregation in the United States.

While Reform Judaism was not codified in this country until the Pittsburgh Platform of 1885, the introduction of modern ways of worship to the synagogue was well under way before then. To understand the environment in which young Felix grew up, it is important to understand what Jewish reform meant.

A declaration of principles [was] adopted by a group of reform rabbis at Pittsburgh in 1885. . . . The declaration began with a recognition that

14

every religion attempted to grasp "the infinite One." Judaism, however, had preserved the God-idea as the central religious truth for the human race. The Bible and the Holy Scriptures were the record of the consecration of the Jews to that idea, but they reflected the primitive conceptions of the ages in which they were written. . . . So, too, Mosaic legislation, adequate to ancient Palestine was not "adapted to the views and habits of modern civilization." Their observance in the present was "apt to obstruct rather than to further modern spiritual elevation." Only the enduring moral laws were still binding.

The modern era was hastening the "realization of Israel's great Messianic hope for the establishment of the Kingdom of truth, justice, and peace among all men." Therefore, Jews were "no longer a nation but a religious community," expecting "neither a return to Palestine, nor the restoration of a Jewish state." Instead, Israel was to labor in the world for a solution "on the basis of justice and righteousness" of the problems presented "by the contrasts and evils of the present organization of society." [1]

The presence of women alongside men during the service, more varied and contemporary music, the vernacular in the liturgy, and the discussion of contemporary social issues in the sermon were radical innovations. (Samuel Adler had already been party to many of these innovations in Europe, as his autobiographical memoir notes.) The changes were not only in reinterpretations of concept but in painful alterations of form as well. And new forms involving tangible differences were resisted more vigorously than abstract philosophic emendations.

Young Felix was regarded as a "dreamy boy," somewhat "introverted and given to fantasy." According to Horace L. Friess, Felix Adler's literary executor, "There was a story in the family that they thought he wouldn't amount to much in a professional way and that maybe they had better look around for some place for him in the jewelry business." He attended Columbia Grammar School and later Columbia College, from which he was graduated with honors in 1870. His home was filled with books, and his family gave attention to good works—the *Mitzvath* of the Jewish tradition. At his father's suggestion, he began giving talks at the Hebrew Orphanage while still a

---

[1] Oscar Handlin, "Judaism in the United States," in *The Shaping of American Religion—Religion in American Life,* James Ward Smith and A. Leland Jamison, eds., p. 137.

student and early discovered an ability for public expression and for stirring his audience.

After graduation from college he studied for the rabbinate at the University of Heidelberg. Repelled by the personal moral behavior of his fellow students and by their sexual liberalism, young Adler was unhappy—and rather stuffy too. The following letter from a fellow student at Heidelberg offers a glimpse into his student days abroad:

> . . . This was sometime during 1875 or 1876 [probably 1872], when a young man, with a diaphanous wisp on his chin called on Steinschneider. . . . He was prim and neatly dressed. . . . Twenty minutes later, the young man went away and I returned to the office. The homely face of Steinschneider was wreathed in smiles. "Du Adolphe," he said, laughter choking him, "du musst recht nett sein, denn wir haben einen amerikansichen Adler hier; er ist der Sohn eines amerikanschen Rabbiners und wird Rabbiner werden." The old wolf knew that I had an inferior respect for foreign scholars and wanted me to be very nice to the American.

> It soon turned out that the young man was Felix Adler. . . . I . . . know that Felix Adler was unmercifully twitted by the students who called him, "Der Amerikanische Adler." [Adler is the German word for eagle.] [2]

As a graduate student, Adler was influenced by neo-Kantian idealism and in particular by its critique of religion. Two Kantian concepts about religion played a major role in Adler's thought. Kant had concluded that the existence or nonexistence of the deity and immortality could not be demonstrated since contradictory conclusions could be drawn from the same data. "Practical reason," i.e., morality, could be established independently of any theological system. These two concepts—the autonomy and the centrality of ethics—became the philosophic basis for the Ethical Culture movement, adding a philosophic complement to Emerson's call for a purely ethical religion and to America's moralistic religious tradition.

While abroad Adler became aware of European social thinking on the problems of labor. In later autobiographic notes he recalled reading Friederich Albert Lange's *Die Arbeiterfrage,* which "opened for

[2] Letter from Dr. Adolphe de Castro, former American Consul in Madrid, to Gideon Chagy, then editor of *The Standard.* December 17, 1948. Ethical Culture Archive.

me a wide and a tragic prospect." Many of the guiding notions of the early days of the Ethical movement are traceable to the experiences of Adler as a graduate student—his concern with social reform, his religious and philosophic positions, his attitude on the "purity" of womanhood, his interest in the labor question and industrial society.

On his return to America, young Felix Adler was expected to succeed his father at Temple Emanu-El. As a sign of welcome Felix was to deliver the sabbath sermon at the Temple on October 11, 1873. Here was the son of the rabbi, succeeding his father in that vocation, fresh from the intellectual and cultural heartland of Europe. The congregation was made up of the most successful Jews in the nation; they were eager both to hear the intellectual news and to witness the coming of age of their collective protegé. It was an occasion of social prestige and justifiable pride for an entire community. The young man, not yet twenty-three, the vehicle of hopes and dreams, the inheritor of ancient family tradition, rose to deliver his sermon on "The Judaism of the Future."

. . . but what now? The field is cleared. The ruins are removed, but what remains? Vacancy unmeasured. . . . the best spirits of the age are turning their backs upon religion; the workmen who should rear the buildings are mistrusted, the ministers of religion have lost the confidence of the people. It is useless to indulge in self-delusion, to bury our heads in sand in order to avoid the peril that threatens us. . . . The crisis through which we are passing is of the utmost danger. On all sides we hear the end of religion predicted. . . . The question for us to answer now is not this form or that form, this reform or that reform, the question is life or death, is religion about to perish. . . ?

. . . religion not confined to church and synagogue alone shall go forth into the market place, shall sit by the judge in the tribunal, by the counselor in the hall of legislation, shall stand by the merchant in his warehouse, by the workman at his work. . . . Then shall religion in truth become a cause, not of strife but of harmony, laying its greatest stress not on the believing but in the acting out. A religion such as Judaism ever claimed to be—*not of the creed but of the deed*. . . .

. . . we discard the narrow spirit of exclusion, and loudly proclaim that Judaism was *not given to the Jews alone, but that its destiny is to embrace in one great moral state the whole family of men*. . . .[3]

[3] Ethical Culture Archive.

His words came as a shock and an insult. Embarrassment for the
father mingled with anger at the ill manners and poor grace of the
son. Certainly Temple Emanu-El was not "in ruins" and certainly
these Jews were somewhat skeptical of doing away with the identity
of Judaism to replace it with some formless "moral state" for the
"whole family of men." It was Felix Adler's first and last sermon at
Temple Emanu-El, although he probably had not intended that.
With youthful enthusiasm, which forsakes diplomacy, he tried to
share a newly discovered truth with those he presumed were ready
for it. Probably, too, the young man felt disdain for the inertia and
conservatism of the old and communicated that feeling behind polite
words and apologetic phrases.

> In an interview years later, Dr. Adler told what happened on his return to
> America. "The congregation," he said, "asked me to deliver a sermon from
> my father's pulpit." I did so and it created quite a lot of talk. Then some
> members brought up the fact that I had not mentioned God in what I
> had to say. The committee came to me and asked whether I believed in
> God. I said, "Yes, but not in your God." And such being the case, I could
> not conscientiously accept the ministry.[4]

Contributing to Felix Adler's isolation was a quarrel in the congregation; some of the members wanted a more "Americanized" rabbi
and had selected Dr. Gottheil as their choice. Felix's yeasty talk provided ammunition for their successful struggle. The "dreamy boy"
who seemed at last to have found a meaningful vocation was without
a job.

Samuel, while skeptical of the naiveté and rebelliousness of youth,
had sufficient depth of understanding to respect the integrity of his
son, a respect that continued after Felix made the final break with
Judaism and started on his new path to Ethical Culture. But what was
to become of young Felix now? A rabbi who could not in conscience
fill a pulpit, a scholar who was unprepared for the professional and
business life of the day.

Through the good offices of some of the congregation, Felix was
recommended as nonresident Professor of Hebrew and Oriental literature at the newly founded Cornell University at Ithaca. Professor

---

[4] *The New York Times,* obituary of Felix Adler, 1933.

Adler drew modern implications from these ancient studies. He traced a direct line between the intent of Pharisaic Judaism, in the sense that every man must in all ways color his life with religion rather than reserve it to a special priesthood, and the democratic ideal, in particular, the American democratic ideal. He used the past to shed light on contemporary problems, such as the labor struggle, power politics, changes in education. His professorship was a distinct success in that the young scholar could attract and hold students.

But at Cornell, Adler was also attacked as an atheist and a danger to the souls of the young. In a brilliant defense of academic freedom, the President of the University, Andrew D. White, addressed a letter to the alumni of the college:

> You have doubtless noticed that the old warfare against the Cornell University by sundry denominational newspapers . . . has been recently renewed under the pretext of [criticizing] certain utterances of Professor Felix Adler. . . .

> Dr. Adler's testimonials certainly did not appear "godless." They showed that, although of Hebrew parentage, he was a graduate of one of our most renowned Christian colleges, and has been blessed with all the safeguards against error which an institution noted for its orthodoxy could throw around him. . . .

> . . . a number of gentlemen in New York, headed by a distinguished Israelite . . . provided the funds to establish a lectureship for three years at Cornell University and Dr. Adler was called to lecture on Hebrew and Oriental literature. . . .

> In the interest of Christianity itself . . . my friends, have you thought what a tremendous charge against Christianity is involved in the assumption that any thoughtful statement of the opinions of this man is "dangerous to the Christian religion?"

> Here is a University, governed by a body of Trustees known and honored in every Christian denomination, conducted by a faculty of whom a large number are members of Christian churches, in whose chapel are preached every year over forty sermons by the most distinguished pulpit orators of various Christian denominations, which has at work in it a University Christian Association whose energy is proverbial, and it is claimed that this one young Israelite delivering a short course of lectures each

year to the small body of men interested in his line of thought and study, "endangered Christianity." . . .[5]

The grant to Cornell that had made Adler's appointment possible was reoffered after three years but declined by the University. By 1876 young Felix Adler had not yet found his career.

The German-Jewish congregation of Temple Emanu-El were the successful immigrants who had made their place in business, finance, and the professions. A vast gulf separated them from the immigration of impoverished Jewish refugees who flooded America from middle Europe in the latter decades of the nineteenth and early part of the twentieth centuries. Financially and socially the congregation of Temple Emanu-El constituted a German-Jewish establishment. Not for them the swelter of East Side slums, the sweatshops, the struggles for the dignity of labor, the experimentation with left-wing radicalism. The names that appeared on the roster of the first Ethical Society, some of whose descendents are still to be found in the New York, Philadelphia, and St. Louis Societies, included Seligman, Sutro, Price, Morgenthau, and Bamberger.

Yet these families were not self-satisfied and were alive to the social and intellectual currents of the day. They could not at first fully accept the radical uprooting suggested in Adler's Temple sermon. Although plagued by the old dilemma of how far to assimilate and how far to maintain a specifically Jewish identity, few of them sympathized with the nascent Zionism of the time. They saw Judaism as a religion among religions, modeled, one might suggest, on the denominationalism of American Protestantism. They had conscience; some less charitable observers might even speak of guilt. Certainly much of their concern for social reform grew out of noblesse oblige. Theirs was a polite reformism, a nineteenth-century "gradualism." Felix Adler was nourished in this conservative reform tradition. Highly suspicious of the call to the barricades and revolution, he was as concerned with internal change of character (a conservative emphasis) as with external social change.

Adler was a complex personality with, perhaps, as many faces as there were viewers. The words *austerity, authority, forbidding* mingle in descriptions of him with *sense of humor, enjoyment of life.* All

[5] Andrew D. White, Letter to Cornell Alumni, May 1877.

agree on his charisma; Adler evoked respect, followers, and recognition. To some he showed warmth and friendship; to many he remained a figure in the center but at a distance.

Julius Henry Cohen, an attorney and member of the Board of Trustees of the New York Society, described Adler. One of the creators of the Port of New York Authority, Cohen remained a follower of Dr. Adler all his life and gives us light on the character of both leader and follower.

Dr. Adler was bald. He had a well rounded head, a strong Roman nose—suggestive of Savonarola in profile. He wore a mustache and a scraggly beard something like an oriental's. In physical size he seemed diminutive when he came near but on the Platform he seemed twice his height. . . .

He had the gift of making one feel at home in his company. If the other fellow had any diffidence, it soon disappeared. The Doctor made him talk about himself. . . . it was in [his] house on Sixtieth Street that I came into the circle of young men whom the Doctor brought together in the late 80's to discuss political ethics. This group included Joseph M. Price, who afterwards played a great part in the movement for better government in New York City and later became President of the City Club; Arthur K. Kuhn, an international law expert; Robert D. Kohn, the architect, afterward President of the Society for Ethical Culture; Abraham L. Gutman, later one of my law partners; John Lovejoy Elliot, one of the assistant leaders of the Society; Benjamin G. Paksus and Edgar A. Hellman.

After the serious business of the evening was covered, we would adjourn to the basement of the Doctor's house. Here in his dining room, the Doctor would doff his thinking cap and the robes of a divine, and lead us into what became a student's beer and sandwich party. . . .

Up near Elmsford, the Fairview Country Club was obliged to give up its golf course . . . [and] was forced to move. . . . One day my wife and I walked over the old grounds. The pear trees were full of ripe pears and they were falling to the ground. This she thought was a great waste. She packed up a couple of bushel baskets, put them in the car, brought them home and then canned them. Later, when Doctor and Mrs. Adler came to visit us some of these canned pears were set before us. At dinner I said very seriously to the Doctor that I had a difficult ethical problem to present to him. He took on his most sober manner. I put the point that the property belonged to the City and legally the trees and fruit went along with it, at least with the title. I told him where the pears came from. "Now Doctor, the question is this: is it moral for us to eat those pears?"

Dead silence. He had started to eat the pears and he went on slowly until he had spooned the last morsel, then said, "I think it is highly immoral to eat these pears."

He was fuller of real fun, prankish, impish fun than any man I ever met. That is the way he acted when he visited us. But one day, just as we were about to finish our dinner, the front doorbell rang, the dining room had been full of joyous laughter. . . . My wife and I never saw such a change in a man as happened at that moment. As soon as our friends entered, he became again the great moral leader, taking on at once all the dignity becoming the head of the Society for Ethical Culture.

His hand was cold, barely touching yours and people did say of him as they said of the Society that they both lacked the warmth that should accompany a minister or a church. . . .[6]

Florence Klaber, daughter of Alfred Wolff, one of Adler's earliest followers, recalled Adler's frequent visits to their home. She told of a conversation between her father and Felix Adler when both were very young men in which Adler is reported to have said, "When we are together alone, you may call me Felix, but when others are present please call me Dr. Adler." Henry Neumann remembered his first visits to the Sunday lectures at Carnegie Hall around the turn of the century. He recalled Adler's small size as he entered on the Platform, and of how suddenly the man "grew" the moment he began to speak. Adler would appear on a Sunday morning in a formal Prince Albert coat, his hand tucked below his lapel. Neumann describes how Dr. Adler's bald head would grow bright red when he became angry, visible particularly as one looked down from the balcony of Carnegie Hall.

The Adler of middle age was impressive. In 1877 this description of the younger man was published:

He speaks entirely without notes and from the first sentences it is apparent that his intellect is of a keen, relentless and incisive order, and his scholarship ripe and rare. Absolute fearlessness seems to be one of his

[6] Julius Henry Cohen, *They Builded Better Than They Knew*, pp. 34–36.

leading characteristics. . . . He stood easily by the side of his desk with the air of pondering and weighing his thoughts as he gave them forth. His sentences seem to drop out of a great profound and his whole manner so singularly unstudied instead of suggesting glibness shows hardly a sign of preparation. . . . This manner—so unusual among our pulpit and platform speakers who generally come well primed with the directions "Laughter here," "Cry here," if not written down upon the manuscript, jotted down mentally—has a charm of its own.[7]

The *New York Herald* described Adler at a Sunday meeting:

. . . while the singing is in progress, a gentleman of medium height, clad in a black dress suit comes in and takes a seat on the platform. He has a high forehead, full lips, dreamy blue eyes, full beard, rather scanty brown hair, and a face expressing both intellect and spirituality. This is Professor Adler, who is modestly announced as a Lecturer of the Society. He is in reality its organizer, its Director, and you might say its priest. . . . When the music is ended he comes forward . . . places himself in front of the reading desk and begins a discourse which lasts an hour. The language is faultless, the argument compact and logical, the illustrations well chosen and the theme well developed . . . ; yet the orator has not a sheet of paper to refer to. . . .[8]

There was a certain harshness in Adler, or perhaps more accurately a rigor that brooked no compromise. John Haynes Holmes, the great liberal minister of Community Church in New York City, reported:

. . . when the Community Church had at last built a new edifice, Dr. Randall [John Herman Randall, Associate Minister of the church, 1920–1927] and I agreed . . . that we should invite Felix Adler to preach the dedicatory sermon. To emphasize the importance we attached to our invitation, we went to see him personally. . . . He was polite, if not expansive, and characteristically solemn. It took but a few moments to state our mission. . . . It took but a few moments for Dr. Adler to state his declination, and to usher us to the door. I was not satisfied, however, and paused on my way to the exit.

"Dr. Adler," I said, "won't you tell Dr. Randall and myself why you cannot be with us at these dedicatory services, which mean so much to us both and to the people of the Community Church?"

[7] *The Index,* 1877.
[8] January 11, 1880.

"That is just the reason," interrupted Dr. Adler. "I cannot afford to be identified with a church with which I am so fundamentally in disagreement as I am with yours."

"Disagreement!" exclaimed Dr. Randall. "I do not understand."

"The Community Church," said Adler patiently, "your church, has no definite attitude toward life. It cultivates no philosophy, no basic set of ideas. It is all things to all men. Which means that nobody and everybody . . . can join your church and participate in its work. This means a hodge-podge of reality, an ultimate betrayal of truth." [9]

As the founder of even a democratic movement, Adler's word had all the weight of law. His intelligence, although skilled in the abstractions of philosophic thought, always took a practical bent; he was an institutionalist as much as a theorist.

Adler sensed his importance as Ethical Leader. His Board of Trustees included men of means, prestige, and achievement; yet, when he entered a meeting of the Board everyone rose. Business was usually concluded before he arrived or was resumed after his departure. He came for about a half hour to address the Board on some subject then on his mind.

He had, apparently, a sense of destiny. His amanuensis in later years, a self-effacing man named Ernest Jacques, recorded nearly everything Adler said. Adler reserved each morning for his philosophic work, a time that was not to be invaded except, perhaps, for emergencies. He would dictate notes for future addresses and random thoughts to be followed up later. The record is, if anything, so complete as to be overwhelming. One feels that he wanted the least turn of his thinking preserved. Raise any question about Adler's ideas, and the answer will probably be found in the catalogue of his work prepared by Mr. Jacques.

We have some knowledge, too, of Adler as husband and father. He married Helen Goldmark, daughter of J. Goldmark, a successful Brooklyn chemist, on May 24, 1880. Mrs. Adler remained in the background, and yet we know of her from her work with mothers' groups and from the statements of those who knew her. She was a personage in her own right, though eclipsed, and accepting of her eclipsed, by

[9] *I Speak for Myself*, p. 259.

her brilliant and well-known husband. She bore five children—
Waldo, Eleanor, Lawrence, Margaret, and Ruth. As is often the case
where the father is eminent in public life, the family lived in the
shadow of Adler's "vocation."

During summertimes in the Adirondacks at Keene Valley, New
York, the family found some private life. They walked in the woods,
and each morning after breakfast the family gathered for a brief period of what were called "exercises." According to Ruth Adler Friess a
bit of music was played and then Dr. Adler would speak briefly to the
family about what was on his mind, something he had been reading
or some comment about nature. Then he would retire to his study at
the back of the house and dictate to his secretary. Adler enjoyed card
games and reading aloud with his wife and children. Tennis was too
strenuous for his taste, but when the family set up a croquet field
Adler joined in the fun and "was not above pushing his ball a little
when nobody was looking."

For all his concern with dignity and authoritarian attitudes toward
children and women, Adler could also express tenderness, as is revealed in a letter sent to his wife during one of his travels abroad for
the Ethical movement:

> It is all so tantalizingly beautiful and so tantalizingly unsatisfactory. We
> must hope and plan and arrange somehow that we shall take this lovely
> trip together some day before too long. But in the meantime, my own
> particular ladylove, there cannot possibly be a closer response than that
> of my thoughts to yours as they travel over the leagues of sea, annihilat-
> ing space, and defying separation. This makes me happy despite all
> grumbling, and so I will sign for tonight your discontented, yet deeply
> contented,
>
> FELIX[10]

[10] Letter from Europe, August 20, 1896. Ethical Culture Archive.

CHAPTER III

1876

The tensions of a world in transition were reflected in the lives, thoughts, and activities of the American people on the hundredth anniversary of the republic. After a century of struggle and survival, they looked toward the future with hope not untinged by doubt and fear. President Grant wrote:

> If we are to have another contest in the near future of our national existence, I predict that the dividing line will not be Mason and Dixon's but between patriotism and intelligence on one side and superstition, ambition, and ignorance on the other. . . . Let us all labor for the security of free speech, free press, pure morals, unfettered religious sentiments, and equal rights and privileges for all men, irrespective of nationality, color, or religion. Encourage free schools, and resolve that not one dollar appropriated to them shall be applied to the support of any sectarian school; resolve that neither State nor Nation shall support institutions save those where every child in the land may get a common school education, unmixed with atheistic, pagan, or sectarian teachings. Leave the matter of religion to the family altar; keep the church forever separate.[1]

[1] Letter, September 29, 1875, in *The Index,* (October 7, 1875).

In that year Adler was completing his professorship at Cornell. The echoes of his Temple sermon were now almost stilled. Yet there were some in the congregation who remembered the young man who had delivered a challenge and made a promise as yet unfulfilled. In 1927, Felix Adler recalled:

On October 11, 1873 I delivered a sermon in the Temple Emanuel in which I sketched the idea of a new type of religious organization. Among the limited number of hearers and friends there was one who would not let go the idea that I had expressed. His name was Julius Rosenbaum. He, more than any other, insisted that the plan of the new religious society should be put into operation. Whenever we met, he encouraged me in my hopes, chiefly by his unbounded faith in the truth and the need of what I had proposed. It was he who collected 100 signatures to a letter inviting me to give an address in this city in which the plan of a new organization should be stated. This address was delivered on an evening in May, 1876, and the Ethical Society established.[2]

This account, of course, abbreviates a process that took several years to complete. But the hundred signatures were collected; Standard Hall in New York City was rented; invitations were issued; and Felix Adler, now twenty-six years old, was invited to deliver a lecture expanding the theme of the Temple sermon. His address of May 15, 1876, derived from that sermon. It reflected the influence of Emerson, the Judaic emphasis on the deed and on righteousness as religion, Kantian idealism mixed with an Hebraic suspicion, if not rejection, of theology. The audience was well dressed and primarily Jewish. It was made up of those merely curious, those loyal to their rabbi, and those seeking a new faith. Samuel and the family were present.

There is a great and crying evil in modern society. It is want of purpose. It is that narrowness of vision. . . . It is the absence of those sublime emotions. . . . True, the void and hollowness of which we speak is covered over by a fair exterior. Men distill a subtle sort of intoxication from the ceaseless flow and shifting changes of affairs . . . , but there comes a time of rude awakening. A great crisis sweeps over the land. . . .

We propose to entirely exclude prayer and every form of ritual . . . freely do I own to this purpose of reconciliation and candidly do I con-

[2] Board of Trustees, New York Society, Minutes, December 5, 1927.

fess that it is my dearest object to exalt the present movement above the strife of contending sects and parties, and at once to occupy that common ground where we may all meet, believers and unbelievers, for purposes in themselves, lofty and unquestioned by any. Surely it is time that a beginning were made in this direction. For more than 3000 years, men have quarreled concerning the formulas of their faith. . . .

. . . freedom of thought is a sacred right of every individual man. Believe or disbelieve as you list—we shall at all times respect every honest conviction—but be one with us where there is nothing to divide—in action. Diversity in the creed, unanimity in the deed. This is that practical religion from which none dissents. This is that Platform broad enough to receive the worshipper and the infidel. This is that common ground where we may all grasp hands as brothers united in mankind's common cause. . . .[3]

It was a stirring address; many who heard it were now willing to accept its call to action. Clearly independent of the Temple, its message was explicitly universal. Adler made no specific reference to the first American century, but one cannot mistake his criticism of American society.

Adler's proposal for a new movement had the virtue of completing an Americanization without betraying what his listeners regarded as the core of their Jewish faith—its prophetic tradition. Its radicalism lay in the proposal to eliminate all theological considerations, to bring into one fellowship the freethinker and the theist, the agnostic and the deist, the religionist and the secularist. Its conservatism lay in the call back to the central value of an ethical humanism. In a sense, such a movement could have been suggested only in a time of uprooting. It required consensus on major "moral questions of the day." It was, we suspect, no accident that Adler's address echoed the First Amendment to the American Constitution and the Declaration of Independence, for at Cornell Adler had traced the connection between prophetic and democratic values. It must have been pleasing and tantalizing to his audience to find these democratic values embedded in the call to a new religious movement.

Though the idea of establishing a permanent religious society was

[3] Felix Adler, Address of May 15, 1876, Standard Hall, New York City. Ethical Culture Archive.

still some time off, some two months after the May meeting 128 people joined in arranging for Felix Adler to deliver a series of Sunday morning lectures to begin the following fall. On October 15, 1876, again at Standard Hall, Felix Adler inaugurated the lectures, which have remained a feature of Ethical Culture, by speaking on "the new religion of morality, whose God was the good, whose church was the Universe, whose heaven was here on earth and not in the clouds."

Gradually the decision was made to form a more permanent organization. During the winter of 1877, Joseph Seligman announced that a Society for Ethical Culture was to be organized. Seligman, a founder of the banking house of Seligman and Brothers, was President of Temple Emanu-El. He was also first chairman of the group that organized the Ethical Culture Society. His death in 1880 came as a severe blow to the fledgling movement, although his family remained active throughout Adler's lifetime and Professor Edwin R. A. Seligman, one of America's great economists, succeeded his father as President of the New York Society.

On February 21, 1877, a certificate of incorporation was filed in the State of New York, reading in part:

> The object of said Society will be the mutual improvement in religious knowledge and the furtherance of religious opinion, which shall be in part accomplished by a system of weekly lectures, in which the principles of ethics shall be developed, propagated, and advanced among adults, and in part by the establishment of a school or schools wherein a course of moral instruction shall be supplied for the young.[4]

By resolution of the Board of Trustees, Felix Adler was employed as Lecturer. The Board consisted of fifteen men, elected by the membership and charged with managing the financial and practical affairs of the Society. The Lecturer was elected by the membership and was an ex-officio member of the Board, though from the outset Adler's influence more often determined the course of the Society than democratic form would find proper. It was, in short, Dr. Adler's Society— and its members wanted it that way. The first group of trustees included Joseph Seligman as President, Albert A. Levi, Henry Friedman, Edward Lauterbach, Joseph Seidenberg, William Byfield, Max

---

[4] Article III of the Certificate of Incorporation.

Landman, Emil Salinger, Meyer Jonasson, Jacob Stettheimer Jr., Samuel V. Speyer, Samuel A. Solomons, Julius Rosenbaum, and Marcus Goldman. The generosity of Seligman helped put the new venture on its feet.

In his first anniversary address, Dr. Adler described their motivations:

> We felt a great need—religion which ought to stand for the highest truth had ceased to be true to us. We saw it at war with the highest intelligence of the day. . . . We saw that millions are annually lavished upon the mere luxuries of religion, gorgeous temples, churches, and on the elaborate apparatus of salvation. We could not but reflect that if one tithe of the sums thus set apart were judiciously expended upon the wants of the many who are famishing, distress might often be relieved, sickness averted, and crime confined within more narrow boundaries. We saw around us many who had lapsed from their ancient faith, but still preserve the outward show of conformance. . . . We beheld that the essentials of religion are neglected even while its accessories are observed with greater punctiliousness than ever.[5]

The followers of Adler were as interesting as he, men of independent reputation and achievement who were drawn together by the dynamism of the Leader and by the appeal of his ideas. Samuel Gompers, first President of the American Federation of Labor, commented:

> I have also been associated with organizations for more formal educational work. One of the first was the Ethical Culture Society. . . . As my own mind instinctively rebelled against the restraints of the orthodox, I joined this little group, afterwards known as the Ethical Culture Society. We were trying to work out ethical standards that would have meaning in the affairs of everyday life—that was what appealed to me. I failed to see how men who claimed to believe in conventional religious standards, whether Christian or Jewish, could profit through the misery of human beings.
>
> The Ethical Society . . . became a powerful good in the struggle to eliminate the tenement house cigar manufacturing system.[6]

[5] Ethical Culture Archive.
[6] *Seventy Years of Life and Labor,* Vol. I, p. 433.

Adler was to return again and again to certain basic themes of those early years. He established too the pattern of giving an anniversary address on the Sunday nearest May 15 of each year in which he reexamined the basis and motives for Ethical Culture.

Throughout this period Adler was experimenting, trying now this, now that, way of working out his philosophy. Ethical Culture had no prescribed model. Even the decision to focus its development in Societies was not made at any one moment. One vehicle for applying his philosophy was the "Union for the Higher Life," a group of men who devoted the surplus of their income to good works and who were dedicated to the purity of women and to furthering their own intellectual growth.

Henry Morgenthau recalled:

[Adler's] sincerity could not be doubted. He had voluntarily abandoned an honorable and care-free career that had been offered him by Temple Emanuel. . .

I was among Adler's earliest adherents. When he organized his United Relief work, I was one of its directors; I participated in his Cherry Street experiment in model tenements—the first in America which eventually brought about legislation to do away with the dark rooms, of which there were over 50,000 in New York City alone, and I assisted in the establishment of the first Ethical Culture School . . . and was Chairman of the Site Committee that secured the present location on Central Park West. . . .

Above all, however, I treasure the fond remembrance of having been a member of the "Union for the Higher Life"—an organization of a few of Adler's devotees. He always maintained that, as every man expected purity from his wife, it was his duty to enter the marriage state in the same condition, and the members of this "Union" pledged themselves to celibacy during bachelorhood. We met every week. . . . We read Lange's *Arbeiterfrage* and studied the labor question. We discussed the problems of business and professional men. I notice in my diary of April 24, 1882, we debated the simplicity of dress and the follies of extravagance. Then, as Dr. Adler wanted us to feel that we were doing something definitely altruistic, the members of the Union jointly adopted eight children; some of them were half-orphans, and some had parents who could not support them properly; we employed a matron and hired a flat for her. . . .[7]

[7] Henry Morgenthau, *All in a Lifetime*, pp. 95–97.

The Society rapidly drew attention to itself, not the least of the causes being the prestige and importance of its leading members. Samuel Adler often attended the Sunday lectures, apparently approving of much of what his son was saying and doing. His family made choices independently, reflecting an integrity all too rare both then and now. But storms racked the reformed Jewish community of New York. An article in the *New York Tribune*, October 12, 1878, reporting that Dr. Samuel Adler had performed a private wedding ceremony for his daughter Sarah, shocked the Jewish community because her marriage day was one of the ten penitential days when by custom if not by law Jewish marriages are not to take place. Samuel stated that nothing in Mosaic law forbade it. The headline read: "Why the Members of the Congregation did not attend the Wedding of Their Rabbi's Daughter."

Felix Adler and his movement were often the objects of critical and hostile attacks from Jewish leaders both in New York City and elsewhere. Thus, Rabbi K. Kohler, of the Sinai Congregation, protested Adler's appearance in the pulpit: "I shall not allow my temple to be disgraced by a lecture to be delivered within its walls by one who blasphemes God and Judaism."[8] Kohler referred to Adler as "The young professor, who merely by his fine oratory, combined with great arrogance, created for a while some sensation in New York."[9]

The Reverend Dr. Isaac Wise of Cincinnati, key figure in American Jewish reform and Vice-President of the Free Religious Association (of which Adler was President at the same time) said of Ethical Culture: "Nor will we deny, that being a member of any of the New York congregations, we would certainly advocate the suspension or expulsion from the congregation of any fellow member who is also a member of the Ethical Culture Society. No man can serve two masters."[10] Wise was referring to the fact that some leading members of the New York Society were also leading members of Temple Emanu-El.

A different attitude was expressed by Rabbi Felsenthal of Chicago. Writing in the *Jewish Advance*, he said:

[8] *The Index*, IX, p. 169.
[9] *Ibid.*, pp. 232–233.
[10] *The Index*, X (1878), p. 478.

If Professor Adler and the Society for Ethical Culture spurn the idea of separating definitely from the Jewish Church and if they really and honestly have the intention to remain Israelites, they may become the fathers of a great reformation within Judaism, the importance of which only a future historian of Judaism may be able to appreciate. Otherwise, they will leave but faint traces behind themselves. As Israelites, they will probably be the harbingers of a new birth of a Jewish religion emancipated from a Jewish nationality. . . .[11]

These and other attacks are perhaps best understood as a response to the manifest success which young Adler was having. *The New York Times* (April 4, 1878) reported approvingly:

The Society for Ethical Culture, which has attracted much attention and excited considerable interest of late in this community is not yet quite two years old. It will be 24 months this coming May. . . . A number of men of different nationalities, including Germans, Frenchmen, Italians, Spaniards, Englishmen and Americans founded it, having felt, as they say, the need in the city of a permanent and effective organization to support the cause of enlightenment. . . .

And *The Index* reported:

Two hundred new members have joined the New York Society for Ethical Culture the past year (1878–79) nearly doubling its membership. Standard Hall no longer accommodates the audiences, and next season the Society will occupy Chickering Hall. During the summer the Sunday meetings will be discontinued, but the philanthropic work in which the Society is engaged will go on. The secret of Dr. Adler's remarkable success is not fully explained by . . . devotion to truth and righteousness; it lies even more . . . in his faith in organization, his executive ability . . . , his controlling purpose to found institutions that shall outlast his own individual exertions. . . . Workers are no less needed than thinkers, and it is the phenomenal combination of both qualities in Dr. Adler that is giving him great success where so many others have failed, a success not likely to be ephemeral.[12]

The regular Sunday morning meeting was the core of the developing Society, mobilizing new followers, encouraging those already

11 *Ibid.,* p. 85.
12 *Ibid.,* p. 241.

committed, suggesting new efforts, and most important of all providing a context and meaning for the work to be done. Adler's addresses combined the philosophic and the practical. His early lectures were devoted to moral problems. He spoke on comparative religion, the latest religious scholarship, the newer developments in religious liberalism. A major interest in education appeared repeatedly. And he continued his attack on orthodoxy and dogmatism. In 1877 he said:

> Our great want is culture, the harmonious development of all our faculties. This cannot be supplied by the 350 or more colleges in the country because they are built by the Church, and, each sect having its own, the result is ludicrous impotency. Besides, the sectarian spirit [within] the colleges has science within its grasp, and stifles its liberty which is [its] life. The right of free utterance is curtailed . . . ; investigations when not in accord with Church creeds are suppressed. Natural science, even, is taught with bias, and our future lawyers, doctors, and statesmen are sent forth with no knowledge, or with a distorted knowledge of the great conflicts waging in the scientific world. That great good has been done by the church in lessons of pure morality we admit; sincerely and emphatically yes. But for their dogmatic teachings, they have been evil, and the source of evil.[13]

Of course, Adler and his Society were attacked as atheistic. The fine distinction between a nontheistic position and a denial of the deity was certainly a mystery to most people. Ethical Culture was accused of taking away the security of faith and with it the sanctions for a moral life. Apparently Adler felt this criticism deeply. In April, 1879 he said:

> Is there . . . no certainty? Have we no firm convictions concerning the Highest, which will prove our safeguard in the perilous struggles of life. There is, indeed, such a safeguard, and earnestly and with my whole soul I have sought to point out how it may be secured. . . .
>
> The people want a confession of faith, I am told. Hear then mine—a simple one. I believe in the supreme excellence of righteousness; I believe that the law of righteousness will triumph in the universe over all evil; I believe that in the law of righteousness is the sanctification of hu-

13 Reported in *The Index,* VIII, p. 61.

man life; and I believe that in furthering and fulfilling that law I also am hallowed in the service of the unknown God.[14]

The dreamy boy had become a man; the renegade rabbi, a prophet; the vague stirrings of feeling for new directions, a movement. Much was new in the work Adler undertook, and much was traditional. A sense of continuity was clear. The synthesis was woven of many strands—American and immigrant; Kantian, Emersonian, and Hebraic; industrial complexity and the simplicity of moral righteousness. The mood is reflected more accurately in the reminiscence of an older Adler than in the antagonisms and stresses of a fledgling movement:

> The separation was not violent. . . . It was all a gradual smooth transition. . . . I have never felt the bitterness often characteristic of the radical, nor his vengeful impulse to retaliate upon those who would impose the yoke of dogma upon his soul. I had never worn the yoke, I had never been in bondage. I had been gently guided and consequently, the wine did not turn to vinegar, the love into hate. The truth is, I was hardly aware of the change that had taken place until it was fairly consummated. One day I awoke and found that I had traveled into a new country. The landscape was different and looking casually into a mental mirror as it were, I perceived that I too had become different. I was sure also that I had gained, not lost; that into my new spiritual home I had taken with me not indeed the images of my Gods, like Aeneas fleeing from Troy, but something for which those images had stood and which in other ways would remain for me a permanent possession.[15]

[14] Felix Adler, Address on *Atheism*, April 6, 1879. Ethical Culture Archive.
[15] Felix Adler, *An Ethical Philosophy of Life*, p. 14.

CHAPTER IV

Deed and Creed

Cities have been the locus of most advances in culture and civilization. Here are found the experiments; the interplay of people of many backgrounds; the libraries, universities, and laboratories. But, for a people of rural values and used to village life in Europe and America, the city was strange and bewildering. The extended clan of rural culture gave way to the small isolated family. The resources of support, advice, and tradition broke down. The problem of the city, then as now, was to make sense of human life within it.

New York was the model of the new city. For most immigrants it was the first and often the only point of contact with America. Here they came to live, work, and die; to raise their children; to dream the American dream—and, for some, to be devoured by an indifferent industrial system.

Voluntary organized charity began in New York City in the late eighteenth and early nineteenth centuries, and was organized along sectarian, ethnic, and national lines. There was a Society for the Prevention of Pauperism, German societies for the Encouragement of

Emigration from Germany, the Assistance of Needy Emigrants, and the Dissemination of Useful Knowledge among Countrymen; the Irish Emigrant Society; The Society for the Relief of Distressed Debtors; The Ladies Society for the Relief of Poor Widows with Small Children. Often these charitable efforts served to reduce even more the dignity and self-respect of those who needed help.

Every city in the nation witnessed increasing degradation and poverty, unhealthy living conditions, poor housing. Jane Addams found these in Chicago, other reformers in St. Louis and Boston. Moreover, the nation was simply unready to deal with a problem that, as yet, was noticed only by a few on the frontier of social criticism.

Adler had called for a movement of "deed, not creed," which some have interpreted as a kind of crude activism. One must read the phrase in a Kantian key: deed without creed is meaningless; creed without deed is empty. More accurately, deed before creed; theory and philosophic principle were to be the consequences of experience. In the beginning was not the word, but the act.

Ethical Culture began in the cities. Since many of its first members were Jews the movement was not uncomfortable in an urban environment. For generations prejudice had forced them to live in cities and to play city roles in finance, small household manufacture, and the like. Excluded by an alien environment, Jews had developed habits of social welfare among themselves; the record of Judaism in self-help and mutual responsibility through the generations is brilliant. Adler and Ethical Culture in effect proposed to universalize this experience. Thus they created a magnificent pioneering record of social service and set a pattern for the movement.

Among the first efforts of the new Society for Ethical Culture was its District Nursing Department, founded in 1877 and the forerunner of today's Visiting Nurse Service. Poor people crowded into city slums saw doctors only when death was near. The antiseptic clinics of today were almost nonexistent; simple health practices were little known. Tuberculosis in particular was a major killer and attacked the poor especially hard. The tubercular cough was an ordinary sound of slum life. Making their way into the crowded railroad flats were a handful of brave women trained in the new profession of nursing and organized and paid by the Ethical Society. One report read:

To Dr. Richard Wiener
From E. O. Cowles, Visiting Physician,
New York Dispensary

> A longer trial of the system of District Nursing not only does not allow me to retract anything I have formerly said in its favor but verifies all that has been claimed for it and very much more. . . . It is impossible to estimate the good she [Mrs. Dilts, one of the first visiting nurses] has done. . . .[1]

Florentine Scholle Sutro, a member of the Board of Trustees of the New York Society and one of its major benefactors, described her experience of District Nursing:

> The first District Nursing was started under the auspices of the Ethical Society. Miss Dennison was the first nurse. . . . She was the forerunner of the District Nurse who has become so popular and necessary since. . . . Some of us who were in Dr. Adler's class . . . visited the families. . . . When I was about sixteen I had the case of a young man dying of tuberculosis. . . . Mother went with me because I was too young to go into the slums alone. One day we met some Sisters there. Mother . . . boasted to the Sisters that the creed of the Ethical Society was to help others not for any future reward, but simply because we thought it was right to do right. . . . I am afraid the Sisters were startled by mother's belligerent attitude—in any case, they never showed up at the young man's house again. We asked the patient on our next visit whether he had heard from the Sisters since and he hadn't and he did not care because whenever they came they spoke to him of death and offered to send the priest to give him the last rites. He said he preferred our visits because we brought food to nourish his body while the Sisters were primarily interested in saving his soul.[2]

The ethics class to which Mrs. Sutro referred was organized by Adler for the children of the members of the Ethical Society. Adler was not content that their learning be only academic, and he recalled accompanying his mother on her charitable errands when he was a child. His efforts to put ideas to work were supported tangibly in many ways. Not unusual in character, though unusual in amount, was

---

[1] *District Nursing Reports*, 1881, p. 10. Ethical Culture Archive.
[2] *My First Seventy Years*, pp. 28–29.

a report in *The Index* in 1870. "Dr. Felix Adler was recently the recipient of the handsome sum of $10,000, the gift of a wealthy patron of his Society to be used at his discretion for purpose of benevolence." [3]

A nonsectarian effort at social service was rare at that time. District Nursing was one of the first instances of organized philanthropy that sought neither theological loyalty nor ethnic identification. While Mrs. Sutro's mother may have tried to proselytize the Sisters—who must have been utterly puzzled by her—there was no attempt to "convert" the people helped by Ethical Culture. No doubt there was unexpressed hope that the good work would have consequences for the growth of Ethical Culture, but "the religion of duty" as preached by Adler would find such a thought unworthy and morally suspect. The good deed was its own justification; any other motive jeopardized its value.

The work of Ethical Culture was described in a contemporary article:

> The name of the Society for the promotion of Ethical Culture is about as repulsive as can be conceived; but under the direction of Felix Adler it is doing some actual mission work that quite surpasses anything that was done by Mr. Frothingham's society, whose place it seemed to fill. It has a kindergarten for little children of the poor in this city, an industrial school for the larger children, a committee of supplies for the needy and two or three trained nurses who have each a district in which they visit the sick poor under the direction of the hospital physicians. . . . It seems strange to hear that these nurses are directed to leave religious comfort to religious teachers. The sick cared for are almost wholly Catholics. . . . a poor German father on 17th street whose sick child was at the point of death went to the priest only a half-block away and begged him to come and baptize the child. The priest refused rudely, giving the father a bottle of holy water and telling him to baptize him themselves. "That is because we are poor," said the parents with tears. Perhaps one of these days those parents will get attached to the Society for the promotion of Ethical Culture which nursed their baby in its sickness and the Church will be wondering why it cannot retain the immigrant Catholics.[4]

[3] *The Index*, X (1870), p. 485.
[4] *The Index*, XI (1880), p. 157.

The successful experiment with district nursing established a pattern for Ethical Culture. There was no call for the overthrow of ailing American society. The members of Ethical Culture were not revolutionaries. Their lives were detached from the actual misery of the poor. Adler and other reformers of the day did not give up their own comfortable lives to share the lot of the slum dweller, but they gave up complacency to criticize and to try to ameliorate what they saw as unjust.

These early efforts at social service also set a pattern of response to social need. A project for meeting that need would be devised and implemented, and thereafter move toward independence and ultimate lack of identification with Ethical Culture. Perhaps the austerity of Adler's ethic was a disservice to the movement he sought to build, for it guaranteed that much of the wealth, energy, and competence that rallied to Ethical Culture would be put at the disposal of causes outside of the movement itself.

The people who needed health services also required decent housing and good neighborhoods. Thus began the Ethical movement's continuing interest in bricks and mortar.

> Led by his own commitment into the civic market place, Adler worked zealously for social reform. His efforts prompted the tenement house investigations of the early 1880's and the enactment of the first anti-sweating legislation. His lectures inspired the founding of a company headed by Joseph W. Drexel and Oswald Ottendorfer, dedicated to replacing rickety tenements with exemplary ones. By 1887, the Tenement House Building Company had erected on Cherry Street six model buildings costing $155,000 and housing Russian Jews engaged in the making of shirts, ties, and cigars. As civic reform projects multiplied, Adler responded to the call. . . .[5]

Felix Adler was appointed to the New York State Tenement House Commission in 1882. The "professor" was learning the ways of the practical world and was becoming an influential figure in the day-to-day affairs of both city and state. Where he went, the Ethical Society went with him, and parallel to the private responsibility to build houses and employ nurses was the attempt to develop public respon-

[5] Moses Rischin, *The Promised City*, p. 202.

sibility as well. He entered political life, but, like most reformers, with basically nonpartisan politics. It was an exception to find Adler a delegate from New York to the Independent Republican Convention in Chicago in 1880. In 1885 he supported Henry George as candidate for Mayor of New York City. Nor was he unwilling to preach politics from the Ethical Platform. It became a tradition on the Sunday before an election day for Adler to explain his view of the forthcoming election and sometimes his own voting intentions. He was one of the founders of the City Club and for many years secretary of the Citizen's Union. He served as a member of the "Committee of Fifteen," a group of influential citizens who sought to reform the corrupt political life of the city.

Adler tried to separate his work as a citizen from his actions as representative of Ethical Culture. Actually, the distinction existed more in his own conscience than in the public's mind. He drew along with him to public work the members of his Society, and the Ethical Platform echoed with calls for new work and criticism of existing conditions.

Adler's leadership was not simply a matter of form. It was intrinsic in the man, recognizable, undeniable, and irresistible—though there were of course those who could not abide his austerity and authority. But no one could deny Adler's preeminence nor the fact that he was Ethical Culture. Jacob Riis described Adler's work on the Tenement House Commission:

The Commission . . . met at Police Headquarters and I . . . heard every word of the testimony which was more than some of the Commissioners did. . . . One man the landlords . . . never caught off his guard. His clear incisive questions, that went through all subterfuges to the root of things, were sometimes like flashes of lightning on a dark night discovering the landscape far and near. He was Dr. Felix Adler, whom I met there for the first time. . . . Adler was born a Jew. Often when I think of the position the Christian Church took, or rather did not take, on a matter so nearly concerning it as the murder of the home in a tenement population of a million souls . . . I am reminded of a talk we had once in Dr. Adler's study. I was going to Boston to speak to a body of clergymen. . . . He had shortly before received an invitation to address the same body on "The Personality of Christ," but had it in his mind not to go.

"What will you tell them?" I asked.

The Doctor smiled a thoughtful little smile as he said: "I shall tell them that the personality of Christ is too sacred a subject for me to discuss at an after-dinner meeting in a swell hotel."

Does that help you to understand that among the strongest of moral forces in Christian New York was and is Adler, the Jew or heretic, take it whichever way you please? [6]

In his own way, Adler was interested in the problems of labor for he saw the economics of exploitation as one more element in the moral corruption of the city. He believed that the indignities suffered by the workingman were as great as his economic want, that lasting destruction of personality was a consequence of regarding the worker not as a human being but as a "hand." And he came to understand that this destruction was transmitted from father to son, mother to daughter, a social legacy as binding in its way as the inheritance of genetic material. He was not given to picket lines and union organizing; he was suspicious of Marxism; and he believed not in the glorification of the working class but in its transformation. The Ethical movement thus came to emphasize education as a tool of change and to reject the uses of power as a means of reform. Naively, perhaps, it sought to challenge the conscience of the rich as it undertook projects of reform.

A shaping experience for the young Adler was the attempt by a group of printers to organize a cooperative printshop. Raising a small amount of money during a time of severe unemployment, the shop was launched in 1877. Its history was brief and stormy, for as soon as the opportunities for commercial employment improved, the cooperators began to quarrel among themselves and the shop closed. This "selfishness," as Adler perceived it, led him to conclude that he had better start with the young, that cooperation needed to be learned.

The Ethical Society had started a free kindergarten for the children of the poor in January, 1878. It was the first of its kind east of the Mississippi, an earlier one having been founded in St. Louis following the lead of the German educator, Froebel. The kindergarten kept children off the streets while their parents were at work, cleaned and

---

[6] *The Making of an American,* pp. 160–161.

clothed them, and fed them at least one good meal each day. Within the year other such ventures were started in San Francisco and Denver on the model initiated by Adler, and he was invited to come to Denver in June of 1878 to speak about his kindergarten and its meaning.

The work of the kindergarten extended naturally into more formal education, and this, together with the example of the printers' cooperative led in 1878 to the founding of the Workingman's School. Augustus Paine, Secretary pro-tem of the New York Society, revealed the thinking that prompted its establishment:

A free Kindergarten for the poor having been successfully established, . . . it is now proposed to erect on this basis a model school for the education of working men and working women. An endowment of $10,-000 has already started the undertaking. . . . A peculiar feature of the model school is to be the introduction of industrial education even in the lower classes and the progressive continuance of it up to the highest. It is designed to give a special fitness to those who will be artists later on. . . . This the public schools are not doing. . . . The chief importance of industrial education is as part of a liberal education. Our hope is to educate through the hands, the brain. Our aim is that the graduates of the school shall not only be *working* men and *working* women, but working *men* and working *women*.[7]

Alfred Wolff, who helped Adler develop the school, reported on the occasion of its twenty-fifth anniversary in 1903 the difficulty they first had in securing pupils. He and Adler "invaded the gas house district around 42nd Street" distributing leaflets announcing the opening and trying to induce parents to enroll their children. They were greeted with suspicion—were they trying to kidnap the children or was this some new scheme for recruiting child labor? Gradually they secured an enrollment. The people in the neighborhood called it the "soup school," referring to the lunches served each day. V. T. Thayer, who became Director of the Ethical Culture Schools in 1928, described some of the motives for initiating the Workingman's School.

The reaction against the nature of public education, stereotyped, formal and strictly academic . . . led him [Adler] to be interested in educa-

7 Ethical Culture Archive.

tional reform. The Workingman's School included an elementary school
with distinctive features: progressive, foreign-type academic studies, a
concern with the education of the hand. . . . So that the school was
one of the first educational institutions in the country to introduce hand
work, art work, weaving, shop work, etc. Of course, it is obvious that Adler and others were influenced by the advanced work in education going
on in Europe by Pestalozzi etc. . . . and there were experiments in industrial education prior to Adler in this country . . . but this was one of
the outstanding efforts to introduce the [teaching of academic subjects]
through the varied types of activities. . . . [It] served as a demonstration of what education might be so that the school from the beginning
had its eye on the contribution [it] might make to education in general
and public education in particular. . . .[8]

The "deeds" found expression for Ethical Culture in social service,
in housing, in politics, in education. The new Society for Ethical Culture took shape, and its interests crystalized around concerns that
were to characterize it to this day. But if progress was steady, the way
was not smooth. A speech by Alfred Wolff in 1903 suggests certain of
the rough waters and tells more than perhaps intended about how
clearly Ethical Culture was the extension of one man in those founding days:

> . . . But I must warn you against taking literally what Professor Adler
> has said in praise of the trustees. . . . He has over-praised us. . . . He
> has made liberal use of his poetic licence. . . . It is true that during
> these 25 years our financial troubles have been serious . . . they would
> sometimes have driven an ordinary businessman to desperation. But Pro-
> fessor Adler soon taught us that this was not an ordinary business venture;
> and he induced us to substitute for ordinary business methods the very
> extraordinary and unbusinesslike principles of faith and hope. And we
> have thrived. . . . When we cried aloud that our treasury was dry and
> that we were athirst in the wilderness, he simply smote the rock with his
> rod and the waters gushed forth. When financially we were on the point
> of starvation, he lifted up his hand in prayer and there was always a
> faithful band of enthusiasts . . . ready and eager to hold up their hands
> for our salvation. These, I say, were old fashioned and unbusinesslike
> methods, but they were always successful.[9]

[8] From an interview with V. T. Thayer, 1964.
[9] *The Ethical Record,* February 1903.

CHAPTER V

The New York Society for Ethical Culture

The first decade of Ethical Culture saw the establishment of four Societies: New York, Philadelphia, Chicago, and St. Louis. New York's, the largest and strongest, was characterized by three lines of development: the Ethical Platform, the work in social service, the development of an educational program for children. Except for a guiding idea and vigorous leadership, there was little institutional cement holding the three together; they could have existed as discrete responses to the needs of the day. The Ethical Platform served to edify and inspire the members and to air social criticism. The curious came to listen but with little intention of affiliating with the strangely called Society for Ethical Culture. One doubts that, save for those acceptable to the founding group, a hearty welcome would have been extended. In those first years applicants for membership needed the sponsorship of a member.

While the by-laws are silent on the matter, it is evident from the record that, by and large, this was a masculine society. The women stayed home to cook the Sunday dinner; the men returning after the meeting would report to their wives the latest utterance of Dr. Adler.

His addresses were usually so well organized that reporting was not difficult. The Sunday Meeting was a social occasion, too. Here one greeted old friends, came to see and be seen, came to be entertained. The sober compulsive church-going of modern American religiosity was noticeably absent. There was, of course, a good deal of formality and the dress coat and high hat were a common sight on Sunday morning.

Following the address, Dr. Adler would report on the work of the Society, for he and his followers meant to translate the words of Sunday into the deeds of the rest of the week and they managed for a long time to do so. The appeal to the conscience of the wealthy and successful seemed to work rather well for this group. Emotionally and intellectually the founders of the first society were translating theory —the centrality and independence of ethics as a basis of faith—into substance. They saw practical experience as essential, not peripheral, to religious commitment. Gradually, the evolved an educational philosophy, testing it in the kindergarten, in the Workingman's School, in the ethics classes conducted by Dr. Adler.

Though he was at one time a colleague of John Dewey's at Columbia, Adler had a life-long suspicion of "progressive education." Yet no observer of the educational experiments of the Ethical Culture movement can fail to see them as ventures in pedagogical progressivism. The introduction of manual arts to the curriculum, the use of drama and music, the opportunities for direct experience, the evaluation of those experiences, the attention to the individual child—all mark a progressive philosophy of education, whatever Adler's intellectual rationale may have been. His pedagogy had an ethical (and often a moralistic) coloration too. He saw the work of reform as educational in itself, as a way not only of changing society but of changing the reformers. The Kantian insistence on "good will" led Adler to an abiding concern with motivation and the growth of character. One Adler motto reads, "In the attempt to change others, we must inevitably change ourselves."

Gradually, and primarily after 1883, attention turned inward to the form and character of the Society itself. One can sense a growing awareness on Adler's part (and on the part of his membership) of the need to establish an institution which would serve to carry on the existing work, give it consistent focus, and act as a basis for new ventures. Adler came to believe in the necessity of an institutional foundation for good works. Resistance to institutional religion was, of course, to be expected from those who had seen such institutions lose their reason for being in the drive for buildings, bureaucracies, wealth, and prestige. The prophetic style of Adler and his followers made them particularly unsuited to the paraphernalia and discipline of organization. But they overcame this—and began to structure an Ethical Culture Society.

Thus the records of the New York Society reveal increasing attention, from 1883 onward, to the normal problems of institution—questions of finance and budget, of legal right and recognition, of personnel and propaganda. Concern, too, for the various functional aspects of religious institutions began to appear, i.e., with marrying and burying, with the uses of music, with what are traditionally called ceremonial and pastoral duties. One of the forces motivating the effort to lead these people out of the temple and church had been the desire to discover a "consecrating influence in their own lives and the lives of their children" consistent with their intelligence. Thus we find the beginnings, too, of the religious education of the children.

In part because of the habitual Jewish resistance to proselytizing, in part because of a belief that truth will be its own best messenger, there was little attention to what we would call public relations. Ethical Culture seemed to make it difficult for people to discover it or, having discovered it, to find their way into its ranks. In some circles the impression still exists of a rather select group, admission to which is difficult. We suspect that this was, in a measure, true in those early days, a reminder of which is the fact that in most present-day societies, people are elected to membership. Nevertheless, Adler and others did want the point of view and ideas of Ethical Culture to reach as wide a group as possible. In the Trustees' Minutes we find repeated comments through the years calling on the Society to engage in active propaganda. One of the first to this effect dates from 1884:

> Dr. Adler addressed the Society and spoke of the necessity of establishing a "literary bureau" or Commission on Publications to attend to the publication of a Handbook of Religious Instruction of Children. He urged the importance of active propaganda on behalf of the Society and its princi-

ples. He also referred to numerous inquiries coming from all parts of the country.[1]

A year later, with the success of the Workingman's School already evident, Adler spoke to his Board of the need to organize a school for the children of members. Alfred Wolff offered a resolution establishing a committee to "expedite the project," and it was unanimously passed.[2] Whatever "expedite" may have meant, it was not until ten years later that the Ethical Culture School was established by changing the name of the Workingman's School and liberalizing its admission policies. Already evident in the record too was that inevitable sign of institution—the appointment of committees.

The ceremonial needs of people persist even when they have broken with traditions. Human beings need to mark the epic moments of their lives in some special way not only for themselves but publicly as well. Though free spirits may cavil at barbaric customs and resist what they regard as irrational practices, most of us—free or otherwise—want the gestures of community sanction at times of birth, marriage, death. For the young Ethical Culture movement, this called for breaking new ground. Traditional rites could not be used; neither could significant occurrences go unmarked. Ethical Culture evolved approaches to ceremony that seem cold to some people, but that are highly personalized, without prescribed form, and without theological reference. The ties of life, the obligations of human beings to each other, the sacredness of personality, and the quality of human dignity became the symbols of Ethical Culture ceremonials. Adler wrote:

> It is upon those we love that we must anchor ourselves spiritually in the last moments. The sense of interconnectedness with them stands out vividly by way of contrast at the very moment when our mortal connection with them is about to be dissolved. And the intertwining of our life with theirs, the living in the life that is in them, is but a part of our living in the infinite manifold of the spiritual life. The thought of this, as apprehended not in terms of knowledge but in *immediate experience* begets the peace that passeth understanding. And it is upon the bosom of that peace that we can pass safely out of the realm of time and space.[3]

[1] New York Society, Board of Trustees, Minutes, May 12, 1884.
[2] New York Society, Board of Trustees, Minutes, May 11, 1885.
[3] *An Ethical Philosophy of Life,* p. 361.

In April of 1885, the President of the Society discussed with the Board the organization of a cemetery company, and such a company was formed to own and operate the Mt. Pleasant Cemetery in Westchester County, New York.

The performance of marriage raised yet another difficulty for Ethical Culture. Since marriage is both a sacred and secular rite in Western practice, the state asserts interest in the marriage contract. The question whether or not the Ethical Society and its Leader could legally perform the marriage ceremony had to be faced, somewhat complicated by the fact that Ethical Culture had not organized as a church and did not therefore automatically come under existing domestic relations law in New York State. In October of 1886, a committee was appointed to draft a bill empowering the "lecturer" of the Society to give a certificate of marriage "with the same force and effect as that of a Minister or Priest." Again in December of 1887, this time on Adler's initiation, the Board appointed another committee to look into the matter. Finally in February of 1888 a bill authorizing the "Leader" of the New York Society to solemnize marriages passed the lower house of the state legislature and was sent to the Senate. On April 2, 1888,

> It was reported that the Bill authorizing a Leader of the Society to solemnize marriages has become a Law, the secretary was instructed to write suitable letters to Senators Cantor and Langbein and Assemblyman Crosby thanking them for their aid in passing the Bill.[4]

The question of ceremonial raised implicitly the question of whether the Leader of the Society was a cleric like a priest, rabbi, or minister. That the Leader of the Society did indeed function as a clergyman on some occasions was undisputed. But that he had no special rights or sacramental quality in virtue of his office was equally evident. Leadership was a consequence of personality, not the title of an institutional functionary. The Leader was scholar as well as priest; reformer and prophet at least as often as preacher; teacher and counselor rather than keeper of a sacred altar.

The problem of the nature of Leadership troubled Adler. He sought to describe the "vocation" of Ethical Leadership as new and

[4] New York Society, Board of Trustees, Minutes, April 2, 1888.

unique (not unlike Chief Justice Warren's call a few years ago for "ethical counselors"). Yet when confronted by the fact that some of his members did not see Ethical Culture as a church, he occasionally expressed disappointment.

> Dr. Adler said that only once in the history of the Society had he been called upon to assist in the celebration of the birth of a child. The Ethical Society should gradually undertake all the functions of a Church.[5]

The nature of the Sunday Meeting reflected this ambiguity. The content of the Sunday address, from Adler's point of view, had to include both immediate practicalities of the day and basic, perennial spiritual concerns. It was to be "the flame burning on the altar," not merely another lecture. Yet often, the material was didactic, and the fear of ritualism often gave a prosaic quality to the meeting. No special poetry or music was included in the structure of the meeting. Emotions were touched only when the address, which was central to the meeting, could stir and involve its hearers. Often, though, the audience remained unmoved, certainly when the speaker was less inspired than Felix Adler. Repeated attempts were made to meet the problem, though not with permanent success. In 1889 Frank Damrosch was engaged to provide music for the New York Society.[6] From time to time a choir was organized, but the congregation would not sing. Emerson's prophecy "it will fast enough gather beauty, music, picture, and poetry" was unfulfilled.

Ethical Culture seemed to have a predeliction for cumbersome and strange-sounding titles. Certainly the name of the movement was clumsy. Not the least of the unfortunate names which attached to Ethical Culture was "Leader," the title of its spokesmen and professional workers, although this was not a poor description of Felix Adler's role as founder and guide of the first Society and the movement. The choice of a title was accidental and the designation did not come into general use until some ten or eleven years after the founding of Ethical Culture. In May of 1887 the Board of Trustees passed a resolution making the official title of the lecturer, Leader of the Society

[5] New York Society, Board of Trustees, Minutes, January, 1900.
[6] New York Society, Board of Trustees, Minutes, October 7, 1889.

for Ethical Culture; this was ratified at a general meeting of the membership on May 9, 1887. Adler described what happened:

> And now but one word as to the name of Leader. . . . This designation originally came into use without my knowledge or consent and at first I was considerably taken aback by it. It was adopted at the time when a special law was enacted by the Legislature of this State authorizing me to perform the marriage ceremony. At that time some title was needed to distinguish the head of the Ethical Society from a mere platform lecturer. . . . Leadership implies a claim upon the loyalty of others, and how, I said to myself, can anyone be presumptuous enough to set himself up as Leader and regard himself as worthy of others' loyalty. But after a time it seemed to me that the position indicated by this designation need not be a false one. Because in a certain sense, we are in turn, each of us leaders, each of us followers in the direction in which we have had special training and special experience, in which to some extent we are experts, we are leaders. . . .[7]

Adler describes here how the role of the members grew with the institution. The Morgenthaus, Seligmans, and Sutros, later the Kohns and Wolffs and others, would be identified as ethical leaders. The Fraternity of Ethical Leaders, which Adler organized toward the end of the first decade, included not only professional workers of the movement but others who had, as it were, a natural claim to leadership, whether in the law or the arts, in scholarship or in business. Again the difference between church and movement was illustrated; while churches do indeed have leading laymen, a sharp distinction is made between the sacred office of cleric and the secular role of communicant. Such a distinction was not made in Ethical Culture, though efforts to "professionalize" the Leadership have tended in that direction.

Slowly, and occasionally painfully, an Ethical Culture Society proper was worked out. No one model was followed. If the Sunday meeting was reminiscent of the pulpit-centered service of Protestantism, the scholarly pursuits of the Leader were far more characteristic of Judaism. If the ethics classes were like Sunday schools, the practical works which its students undertook were more reminiscent of organized Jewish benevolence. If the form of the ceremonials at birth,

[7] *The Ethical Record*, Vol. VII, No. 4 (June, 1901), p. 233.

marriage, or death seemed to echo tradition, the content was modern and humanistic. There was little self-consciousness in borrowing from the past, no apology for the eclectic structure of the society. It was an instrument for an idea and had, in itself, no other reason for being. Therefore its shape and texture were alterable to meet the needs of each goal. Adler and his followers sought to keep alive the concept of a fellowship of people seeking a common ground, a base for meeting the ethical challenges of the time within which to find the inspiration, support, and clarification needed to meet those challenges, and most important of all, a matrix for their own ethical transformation. They organized an Ethical Society to "save themselves alive."

CHAPTER VI

The Religious Neighborhood

Ethical Culture was one expression of the small but vigorous liberal religious community developing in this country. Adler and his Society felt themselves to be part of this community, responding to Emerson's call for a purely ethical faith. Ethical Culture was also interpreted as a movement out of Judaism paralleling the similar movement of Free Religion out of Christianity. There were mixed reactions among the liberals, in part appreciative, in part competitive. *The Index* of the Free Religious Association often reflected approval of Ethical Culture.

Last Sunday we had the great pleasure of meeting the Society of Ethical Culture in New York City. . . . [It] meets every Sunday at Standard Hall . . . , which seats about 600 and is usually so well filled that numbers are unable to obtain seats. . . . To us there is the profoundest meaning in the experiment here tried; for the originators of this movement are Jews who have come out from Judaism upon the broad ground of humanitarian religion. . . .[1]

[1] *The Index,* IX (1878), 145.

Other liberals were not so sure. Some regarded Ethical Culture as redundant, as an echo of the best in reform Judaism or in liberal Unitarianism. Thus, Rabbi S. H. Sonnenschein of Temple Israel in St. Louis spoke on "The Attitude of Judaism Towards the Ethical Culture Society" in 1887. Responding to a letter from a member of his congregation who expressed support for the newly founded St. Louis Society, Rabbi Sonnenschein attacked Adler and his movement. He insisted that Adler's attempt to dispense with the God idea was bound to fail, for "a religious movement without the God idea is sheer nonsense." To find religion which places deed before creed, one need look no further than Judaism itself. And, he concluded:

> For whatever is ethically true in the philosophy and faith of any new religious movement is not new to us. We, at least the best and noblest among us, knew and practiced it centuries ago. And whatever is new in all their best efforts and enterprise to supersede Judaism is not true, is false in its inception, seditious and sophisticated in its application, barren as well as short-lived in its consequence.[2]

One had the impression that the Rabbi felt threatened by this new movement. His uncritical defense of Judaism was more apology than argument. No doubt he felt keenly the loss of some of his leading congregants to the Society in St. Louis. Then, too, he experienced the drift away from the Temple of many who, while not willing to exchange affiliations, nevertheless found no meaningful allegiance in religious Judaism, even when reformed.

The Leaders of Ethical Culture delivered repeated attacks on dogmatism and on existing religious institutions, including the more liberal of them. Thus Burns Weston of Philadelphia spoke on "Why Christianity Does Not Satisfy Us" and William Salter on "Why Unitarianism Does Not Satisfy Us." They seemed to be following Adler's unspoken thesis of "Why Judaism Does Not Satisfy Us." Salter's address was characteristic of the critiques of "nonsatisfaction." Orthodox Unitarianism, he insisted, had driven its best men from the pulpit, followed a conservative course, and given no concrete expression to its ethical commitments. Finding a more liberal spirit in the nascent midwestern Unitarianism, he hoped it would sever its ties from tradi-

2 Ethical Culture Archive.

tion and become a purely ethical movement. Salter criticized Unitarianism's dependence upon traditional Christianity:

> . . . the only reason why Unitarianism cannot become the religion of the future is that . . . it was not willing to take its stand on that high ground, but must seek to keep its standing in the Christian Church and cling to its small, half-believed remnant of the Christian Creed. . . .

Ethical Culture, he continued, was radically different:

> For think not . . . that in making morality the basis of our Society, we have in mind only what is left of the old religions, after we have divested them of their dogmas; that we propose to feed the souls of men with a few kindly feelings or good habits, adding perhaps for the sake of novelty a philanthropy or two; no, morals are nothing save as they are vastly more than this, and philanthropies are nothing save as they are incidents of a thought that takes not this or that but all good in its grasp. What we want is a sight of principles, to aim not at the better but at the best, to fear not to make the rule of a perfect life the rule of every day, to bring the glory and sanctity of heaven here on earth. . . .[3]

Such an attack did not go unanswered. John W. Chadwick, minister of the Second Unitarian Church in Brooklyn, responded in 1885, "Ethical Culture, Why It Does Not Satisfy Us." Chadwick apologized for his "polemical" title but felt provoked by similar tactics in Ethical Culture. He generously credited the movement for its good work but subtly cast doubt upon Adler's role in a movement that pretended to be "republican" and that criticized the churches as monarchical. ". . . Generally, the Christian ministers are few who are, so literally as he [Adler], monarchs of all they survey, whose will is law to their people to such a degree as his to those who are associated with him in his work. . . ." Chadwick suggested that the "non-creedal" posture of Ethical Culture was actually "negative dogmatism."

> Seeing that these things are so, I do not see that there is any valid reason why we should exchange our own position for that of Ethical Culture. . . . Ours is indeed the larger freedom for it neither says "thou shalt"

---

[3] "Why Unitarianism Does Not Satisfy Us," May 20, 1883. Ethical Culture Archive.

nor "thou shalt not believe." If we say God, we only say what Ethical Culture is obliged to think and feel; if we may not dogmatize concerning the immortal life we may hope for it with a grand and purifying hope. Debarred from all petition, whether for material or spiritual things, we may still lift a reverent heart to the Ideal and to the Infinite Reality which is, of all ideals, the source and end. . . .

Chadwick wanted the right to believe in a deity, in immortality, in prayer, and he felt that by excluding these beliefs Ethical Culture needlessly narrowed religious freedom. Adler's attempts to shift the ground of religion from theology to ethics was lost on Chadwick; but then it apparently was blurred in Salter's address too. The dangers in playing the "theological game" were clearly illustrated by this exchange.

While the liberal debate was going on which was to result in a freer Unitarianism and in an established Ethical Culture movement, the Social Gospel movement was developing within Protestantism; the Pittsburgh Platform was adopted by Reform Jews; and laissez-faire capitalism had roused secular reformers. It is difficult to assess the general public's attitude toward these developments. One suspects that insofar as they were aware of them they were suspicious. The press, which from time to time found the efforts of Ethical Culture praiseworthy, could be harsh in its criticism. The issue of the *New York Herald* following Adler's first address to the new Society commented editorially:

He [Adler] is wantonly disturbing the public peace. When he is prepared to affirm something the public may have an interest in hearing him. His negations are simply silly and indecent. A professor who has nothing more important to teach is in a very bad way.[4]

His Sunday addresses were reported on at length for many years and occasionally provoked negative editorial comment. Under the headline "A Communistic Sermon," the New York *Evening Post* said:

Professor Adler . . . delivered a communistic discourse yesterday. . . . He formally rejected "that form of social organization" [and] described his plan as "cooperation"; . . . He is in favor of a graduated tax upon

4 1876.

incomes. . . . Of course a tax of 100% is simply confiscation. Mr. Adler at least deserved credit for courage in not flinching from this conclusion. . . .

Now there may be a technical and refined distinction between "cooperation" of this sort and communism, but certainly there is no difference in spirit. Cooperation implies [a] voluntary proceeding, but there is nothing of this sort in the confiscation which Mr. Adler proposes in the form of a tax. . . . Who is to judge how much money a man can "use for human purposes"? Not the man himself, of course. Is the question to be determined by Mr. Adler, or by the Society for Ethical Culture, or by society at large? How is "humane" use to be precisely defined? Ethical Culture such as this might well provoke a smile, if it was not in sober harmony with some of the most vicious of contemporaneous notions.

Between Mr. Adler's "cooperation" and communism there is very little to choose.[5]

A symptom of public misunderstanding appeared in the confusion as to whether or not Ethical Culture was a religious movement. The subjects of Adler's lectures gave some support to this confusion, for what was "religious" in a discussion of the income tax? The fact that many of Ethical Culture's leading members were identified with traditional religious institutions also confounded those trying to understand Ethical Culture. Adler himself seemed, at times, ambivalent about the nature of his movement; but in later life he put it clearly:

Now the daring thought that we had in beginning the Ethical Movement was to unite in one group . . . those who had this religious feeling and those who simply cared for moral betterment. That has given a somewhat flickering meaning to the word "religion" as we have used it. . . .

The Ethical Movement is religious to those who are religiously minded, . . . and it is simply ethical to those who are not so minded. . . .[6]

If the founder, himself, saw multiple interpretations of Ethical Culture, we may be sure that others were far less sure of what the movement was all about. This raised difficult problems both internally and with the community at large. Illustrative is the following:

[5] *The Evening Post,* New York City, February 9, 1880.
[6] Horace L. Friess, ed., *Our Part in This World,* pp. 66, 68.

The secretary reports that the [New York] *Herald* had refused to publish the notices of our Sunday Lectures under the Religious Notices. The secretary was instructed to communicate with the publishers of the *Herald* and protest such action. [The protest was successful; the lectures were placed among religious notices as of March 3, 1884.] [7]

Ethical Culture's nearest neighbor during these founding years was the Free Religious Association. It was certainly closer than either Reform Judaism, which held to many traditional forms and concepts, or Unitarianism, which centered on the figure of Jesus. The Free Religious Association had been founded in 1867 by Francis Ellingwood Abbot, who had resigned his Unitarian pulpit, by O. B. Frothingham, who had developed an independent religious society, and by other religious liberals. It drew together liberal Unitarians and Universalists, progressive Quakers, some representatives of progressive Judaism, and many transcendentalists. With headquarters in Boston, it included in its membership leading figures of American reform and philosophy, and counted among its members Emerson, Lucretia Mott, Wendell Phillips, and Julia Ward Howe.

Its goal was to "liberate religion from bondage to every kind of ecclesiastical authority" and to express the religious conscience in "moral and humane deeds." The individual was free to follow his own conscience in matters of belief. "Absolute freedom of thought and expression" was guaranteed to the membership. Growing out of an impatience with Unitarianism's failure to reform itself more rapidly, the Free Religious Association was a major influence in ultimately liberalizing Unitarianism. It helped to create the Western Unitarian Conference, which was basically humanistic in its philosophy and which by and large was quite independent of traditional Bostonian Unitarianism.

The Free Religious Association's most successful venture was the publication of *The Index*, a paper which appeared weekly for some twenty years. Addresses were reprinted, ideas exchanged, news of organization circulated. It was a useful liberal forum and, in a sense, has never been replaced. Frothingham served as President of the Association for many years. When he relinquished the office Felix Adler

[7] New York Society, Board of Trustees, Minutes, February 4 and March 3, 1884.

was elected to the presidency in 1878. Reformation was Adler's platform. Many of his proposals were familiar: a system of education including moral and ethical training for the young; a school for the science of religion to train free religious leaders; the endowment of chairs in the science of religion at existing universities. He wanted to see the establishment of local societies of free religion and called on the Association to take an immediate and practical interest in the problems of "poverty, industrialism, and property."

The members of the Association did not unite on this platform—or any other. When Anna Garlin Spencer proposed in 1881 that "local correspondents be appointed in each state to gather information on legal restrictions upon religious liberty, religious influences in public education, and the possibilities of forming local Free Religious Societies," the latter recommendation was referred to the Executive Committee after extensive and angry debate, and quietly allowed to die. Organization seemed to some of the members a first step toward developing a new clericalism and ecclesiasticism. Adler was not happy with this resistance; in 1882 he resigned the presidency in protest.

Felix Adler had proposed his plan of action in 1879 and had waited for three years while the Association debated the merits of home rule and the potential dangers of sectarianism. . . . Adler's patience was exhausted by 1882 and at the Annual Meeting of that year he resigned. . . . Although he remained heartily in favor of the principles of the Free Religious Platform, he was disgusted with the scrupulousness of the Association's policy. . . . Adler's personal creed of agnosticism placed supreme emphasis on benevolent action, and he measured all religious professions against that standard. It was time for the free religionists to stop talking and act. "What has Boston done for the honor of our principles?" demanded Adler. "What great charitable Movement has found its source here among those who maintain the principle of freedom in religion? What living thing for the good of mankind, for the perfecting of morality among yourselves and others emanated within the last twenty years from the Free Religious circles of this city? I say to you, friends . . . these annual meetings will not answer." [8]

Adler's resignation in 1882 marked, we believe, the final step in the decision to build an Ethical Culture movement. If the Free Religious

[8] Stow Persons, *Free Religion*, p. 96.

Association had turned in the directions Adler thought necessary, an independent Ethical Culture movement might well have died in the first years of its birth or been assimilated into some other, larger venture.

During the ten years following the Temple sermon, Adler had worked actively to discover his vocation. On a personal level he had found the rabbinate and the academy unsuited to his ideas, interests, and temperament. He had initiated ventures in education and social service, and learned that these needed a base, a central core, in order to have support and meaning. He had concluded from the failure of the printers' cooperative that long-range methods of change were required. Although founding the Union for the Higher Life, he believed that a more open, if not as committed, group of people was necessary too if the practical implications of an ethical faith were to have any chance of successful support. With the failure, from Adler's point of view, of the Free Religious Association, the road was clear. A separate permanent movement had to be established if his ideas were to have the freedom and scope which both he and his followers felt they needed and deserved. While one may date the founding of Ethical Culture with the lecture in May of 1876, the decision to build permanently and more widely was related chronologically and emotionally to the 1882 meeting in Boston of the Free Religious Association. From this time onward Adler engaged actively in searching for and training colleagues to work with him, sought to found other Societies and to unite them in a parent body. While Adler remained in touch with university life, with education, and with reform, he now made his central vocational commitment the Leadership of his own movement.

CHAPTER VII

Spreading the News— Chicago, Philadelphia, and St. Louis

No man, no matter how skilled and brilliant, could hope to build a movement alone. In his address to the Free Religious Association Adler had called for the searching out and training of "free religious leaders" and the developing of regional and local societies for free religion. With his resignation from the Association, Adler now began to apply this program to his own movement.

The *Chicago Times* under the headline "An Ethical Society," in September, 1882, reported:

Last April, shortly after the lectures of Professor Felix Adler in this city, a number of gentlemen held a private meeting for the purpose of forming a Society of Ethical Culture. Among those present were Judge Henry Booth, George C. Miln, Julius Rosenthal, Otis S. Favor, Max Eberhardt, Levy Mayer, Judge C. B. Waite, Max Morgenthau, Albert Schultz, Max Stern, Messrs. O'Dell, Brown and Hutchens. . . . Mr. Miln was sent to New York . . . for the purpose of seeing Professor Adler and Robert G. Ingersoll. . . . Owing to the lateness of the season, the movers in the matter afterward concluded to defer definite action until the present time. A meeting attended by several liberal gentlemen was held last Thursday evening. . . . It was decided to ask Professor Adler and Mr. William Salter to deliver lectures in this city at an early date. In reply . . . the gentlemen informed the members that they would be able to deliver lectures there on Sunday, October 1. . . .[1]

On October 5, 1882, at Chicago's Grand Pacific Hotel, Adler once again explained the principles and organization of his movement, and on October 9 the group of organizers formally constituted themselves the Chicago Ethical Society. The first Board of Trustees named Judge Booth as President, F. S. Holz as Vice-President, A. B. Hosmer as Secretary, and Otis Favor as Treasurer. Other members of the Board were I. K. Boyesen, Levy Mayer, Max Morgenthau, H. W. Palmer, Ernst Preussing, Albert Schultz, I. N. Stills, Robert Tilley, and Frank B. Tobey. The statement of organization declared:

> We, the undersigned, convinced that the time has come for a larger and higher statement of religious truth than the dominant theologies offer, and believing that the stress of religious teaching should be laid in the duty of moral improvement . . . and that religion should guide and inspire us in the sublime path of moral progress, and having before our eyes the example of the Society for Ethical Culture in New York City . . . do hereby constitute ourselves . . . the Society for Ethical Culture of Chicago. . . .[2]

By June of 1883 membership had risen to seventy-two, including "ladies."

Adler's six lectures in Chicago had apparently aroused sufficient interest. He was careful to insure that the founding group consisted of men of influence and wealth. Nor would he encourage a society to start without a full-time worker. William MacIntyre Salter, who became leader of the newly founded Chicago Society, had been working with Adler for about a year prior to 1883 in New York. This pattern of apprenticeship persists; the school for training free religious leaders which Adler had envisioned was never established.

Salter was born in Burlington, Iowa, in 1853 and came of a devout Congregational Christian family. Educated at Knox College, Illinois, he discovered, as did so many young people of his day, the work of

[1] *Chicago Times, An Ethical Society,* September 27, 1882.
[2] Ethical Culture Archive.

Channing and Emerson. His thoughts turned to the ministry and in 1871 he entered Yale Divinity School, but found that orthodox Christianity was not for him. He transferred to Harvard Divinity School in 1873, hoping that he could find a place for himself in Unitarianism. A combination of ill health and strong conscience prevented him from taking a pulpit after graduation in 1876. For two years he withdrew to Colorado, where he worked as a sheep herder while regaining his strength. Toward the end of this period he began to think again of returning to work related in some way to religion. While traveling to Boston in 1879 he met Felix Adler, learned about his movement, and in 1881 joined Adler in New York.

Thomas Davidson, whose Breadwinner's College in New York City was a kind of Socratic Academy in the New World and whose most illustrious pupil was Morris Raphael Cohen, spoke of Salter as having "the heart of a Christian Saint and the head of the Humanitarian Positivists trying to work themselves into harmony." [3] At the time of Salter's death in 1931, John Elliott penned the following note to Felix Adler,

The thought of Mr. Salter has been constantly in my mind these past few days. There was something in his relationship to you which differed from any of the rest of us. It was, I believe, because he was the first to follow in the way that you had marked out. In a certain way I always thought of him as the first-born of those who have attempted to face life from the point of view of the truths and the position that you have given. I always looked to him and distinctly had the feeling for him as an older brother, more than for any other of those who have attempted leadership in the Ethical Movement. In some ways, too, he was better able to realize the truths and the life that you have indicated. His going has, strangely enough, made me feel the sense of fraternity more than ever before. . . .[4]

Of a philosophic turn of mind, Salter produced, among other things, an excellent book on Nietzsche in 1917. Salter chose a stormy and difficult career. The Chicago Society, following the New York model, began relief works—district nursing, and the like. Salter's lec-

[3] *The Ethical Record,* III (1890), p. 230.
[4] July 21, 1931.

tures at the Chicago Opera House, beginning with a series on the
"Basis of the Ethical Movement," focused on issues of social ethics.
The Chicago Society seemed on its way to a flourishing future, when
in 1886 a bomb was thrown in Haymarket Square—and with it a
monkey wrench into the growth and development of the Society.
Hysteria about anarchists shook the city; fear, suspicion, and violence
gripped the population. A policeman was killed and eight men were
found guilty of murder, though to this day no one knows what really
happened. Salter, together with Henry D. Lloyd, a Unitarian minister, secured signatures of many prominent Chicago citizens on a petition to the Governor asking clemency and insisting that the trial had
been grossly unfair and unjust. Henry David described the situation:

> Another liberal on whom the Haymarket Affair was to have a marked
> effect . . . was Dr. William M. Salter. . . . Salter worked tirelessly to
> save the men. Many years later he wrote that it was an error to combat
> anarchistic propaganda with force and that he was certain that the Chi-
> cago anarchists urged the use of force only to repel force. . . . Salter ex-
> perienced a disturbing inner struggle from the clash of his Ethical Culture
> ideas, his desire to see justice done, his predisposition to side with the
> underdog, and his conviction that the men as anarchists threatened the
> existence of the State and society. . . . On October 23, 1887, in the grand
> Opera House in Chicago, Salter lectured before the Ethical Culture Soci-
> ety on "What Shall be Done With the Anarchists?" After summarizing the
> evidence, he concluded that although the bomb-thrower was unknown,
> Lingg, Fischer, and Engel were guilty as accessories; that Fielden's vio-
> lent harangue was responsible for the appearance of the police; and
> that if the police had not arrived the bomb would not have been thrown.
> The evidence against Spies, Schwab, Fielden, and Parsons, he felt, "is
> not such as to convince any fair minded unprejudiced man beyond rea-
> sonable doubt." This assertion however, he immediately qualified, "I do
> not say because the four I have mentioned are not guilty they are there-
> fore guiltless of any connection whatever with the Haymarket crime.
> They are simply not guilty of the crime with which they are charged.
> They were not accessories to the murder of Degen. . . . If not guilty of
> the crime with which they are charged, of what are they guilty? . . .
> They are guilty of sedition, of stirring up insurrection. They were all
> members of a conspiracy against the State." [5]

5 *The Haymarket Affair*, pp. 398–99.

Reasoned analysis did not impress many Chicagoans who concluded that any good word for the anarchists was treason. The Chicago Society, along with Salter, became identified in the public mind with anarchism and lost many of its influential supporters. Attendance at the Sunday meetings dropped drastically, and Mr. Salter was deeply concerned (and was even standing at the back of the room each Sunday to count the audience). He feared that he had done irreparable harm to the cause of Ethical Culture in Chicago, yet knew that he could not have done other than speak out against injustice.

The work of building the Society went on nevertheless. In 1888 the Chicago Society reported 162 members and by 1891 it had grown to 208. In 1888 Joseph W. Errant spoke to the Chicago Society on "Justice for the Friendless and the Poor," calling attention to the lack of adequate legal services for those who could not afford private attorney's fees. From this address came the motivation to organize the Bureau of Justice known today as the Legal Aid Society. In the Third Annual Report of the Legal Aid Society in January, 1908, appreciation is expressed to Frank B. Tobey "for many years President of the Bureau of Justice and its successor, the Legal Aid Society." Tobey, a founder of the Chicago Society, had been its President from 1898 to 1908 and its honorary president until 1913.

In May, 1886, the Chicago Society arranged a series of monthly conferences at Hull House Coffee Shop. In addition to Mr. Salter and various members of the Society, speakers at these meetings included Felix Adler, Jane Addams, John Dewey, and Clarence Darrow. The Society and Salter were integral to the small group that was to do so much to change the city and to bring to the American scene reform in education and in the newly created field of organized social work.

In 1888, too, and for some years thereafter, the Chicago Society organized Economic Conferences between business- and working-men, the first of these a series of seven meetings on,

"The Aims of the Knights of Labor," *by George A. Schilling*

"Banking and the Society System," *by Lyman J. Gage*

"The Labor Question from the Standpoint of the Socialist," *by Thomas J. Morgan*

"Is the Board of Trade Hostile to the Interests of the Community?"
by Charles L. Hutchinson

"A View from the Labor Sanctum," *by Joseph R. Buchanan*

"Socialism as a Remedy," *by Franklin MacVeagh*

"An American Trade Unionist's View of the Social Question," *by A. C. Cameron*

The Chicago Tribune commented extensively on the series and even offered some words of praise.[6]

But the social climate in Chicago was not conducive to reform. Salter, for all his gentleness, repeatedly led the Society into areas destined to stir resistance and to retard its appeal to men of position. Chicago, still a frontier city in many ways, was not New York; and Salter was far more radical in his social criticism than Adler ever was. In December of 1891, speaking on "Freedom of Thought and of Speech," Salter returned once again to the question of anarchy:

> . . . as a matter of principle, I would say that people have a perfect right to be anarchists . . . , to meet as anarchists . . . , to teach and preach anarchy—have a right, not only morally, but let us be thankful, under the Constitution and the laws. What anarchists have not a right to do is to incite to violence, to stir up those passions that would lead to murder and arson; to do this they have no more a moral than a constitutional right.
>
> I asked one of Chicago's prominent businessmen at the time of the anarchists' trial if he had considered whether the evidence was sufficient to justify the execution of the men. He said he did not care about the evidence; they ought to be hung. . . .
>
> There were many businessmen in Chicago who even looked askance at our innocent Economic Conferences. They did not want discussion and a stirring up of things; they thought their brother businessmen who lent a helping hand were cranky.[7]

The Chicago Society could not come out from under the cloud. Hence in 1892, Mr. Salter left to become Leader of the Philadelphia Ethical Society. This decision was not easily made. In all probability

---

[6] *The Ethical Record,* I (1888), p. 60.

[7] December 6, 1891.

the leading figures of the Chicago Society asked for the move reluctantly. We may also surmise that Dr. Adler gave tacit if not explicit approval since we know that no move was made without his agreement. Coming to Chicago to replace Salter was M. M. Mangasarian who had been apprenticed in New York for about three years. A tall, handsome man with magnificent mustaches, he was a brilliant speaker and organizer. During his brief tenure in Chicago he helped the Society grow, participated in the Parliament of Religions during the Columbian Exposition of 1893, and helped organize the World Congress of Religions. But Mangasarian revealed a growing anti-Catholic bias, and his Sunday lectures came increasingly to consist of diatribes against the church. Since Ethical Culture's work was in more affirmative directions, it was made clear to Mangasarian that he was not suited for Ethical Leadership and ought to resign. This he did in 1896, but took with him about half of the then flourishing Chicago Society to organize an independent fellowship. Salter then resumed Leadership in Chicago, but he returned to a Society split on the Catholic issue and even weaker than when he had left it. He stayed until 1907. The Society continued along its rocky road uncertain of its survival.

The problems in Chicago were some years in the future when Adler turned to Philadelphia for his third venture in Ethical Culture. In 1885 Adler installed S. Burns Weston as Leader. Recalling the start of the Philadelphia Society, Mr. Weston wrote:

> Coming to Philadelphia in the spring of 1885 to address the first public meeting that was held for the purpose of organizing an Ethical Society . . . I took as my topic, "The Need of an Ethical Religion." A Society was soon organized. . . . For the first five years I held the position of Lecturer of the Society and afterward, for now close to thirty years, that of Director. In the interim between these two periods Mr. William M. Salter was Lecturer of the Society for five years.[8]

Proximate to New York, Philadelphia seemed a natural place for the extension of the movement, and Weston particularly suited to the en-

---

[8] "A Confession of Faith," in *Essays on the Ethical Movement,* Horace Bridges, ed.

vironment of that city. Weston was a "gentleman," born in Maine and "surrounded and influenced by the mildest type of New England Puritanism." When he was thirteen years old he went to the Preparatory School for Antioch College and graduated from Antioch eight years later in 1876. That fall he enrolled at the Harvard Divinity School, while there coming under the influence of the Free Religious movement and learning from newspaper accounts (probably *The Index*) of the work of young Felix Adler in New York City. After graduation from Harvard in 1879 he occupied a Unitarian pulpit in Leicester, Massachusetts, for three years, though without accepting formal ordination. His resistance to orthodox Unitarianism was marked and public, so much so that he was forced out of the pulpit by the Council of the National Unitarian Conference. Coming to New York, he met with Felix Adler in the spring of 1881 and then left for two years abroad on Adler's advice. Adler used his own pattern of education to mold men for the new career of Ethical Leadership. For many years a doctorate from a German University was an unofficial prerequisite for work in the movement. On his return from Europe, Weston enrolled at Columbia University for advanced studies in political and social science, at the same time working with Adler in the New York Society.

By 1885 Adler felt that Weston was ready to try his wings and the decision to go to Philadelphia was made. The pattern of deeds was repeated. In 1888 Weston initiated the Neighborhood Guild with himself as headworker, a settlement house that still exists as Southwark Neighborhood House. Welfare services were organized: "Family Guild: open every day and evening of the week, free library, reading room, art collection, exhibition, social intercourse; expenses for the year, $2000 plus." [9]

The Philadelphia Society started a school modeled on the Workingman's School in New York but after several years was forced to discontinue it for lack of funds. The school was directed by Stephen F. Weston, who reported in 1888:

> Besides the usual branches of common school education, the course also includes modelling, free-hand mechanical drawing, sewing, and workshop instruction. The methods of instruction pursued in all branches are those applied in Manual Training Schools and the New York Working-

[9] *The Ethical Record*, Vol. I, p. 154.

man's School. The system of marks and rewards is not adopted and there is no sectarian teaching.[10]

Burns Weston was a poor speaker and, unlike most of us, soon recognized his inability. He developed a pattern at the Philadelphia Society of making its Platform a free forum for some of the leading figures of the city and the nation. Among its guests were William James, who became a member of the Philadelphia Society. Weston was in every respect the image of the gentleman reformer. An indication of his standing in the city of Philadelphia was his founding of the Contemporary Club:

> The Contemporary Club now for eighteen years has ranked high among Clubs of its kind. . . . Its aim from the first has been to make its membership representative of the higher phases of thought and activity in the many sided life of our city and it has consequently been non-partisan in politics, non-sectarian in religion and non-sectional in lines of social fellowship. The Club has been so successful . . . that membership has been valued by the best citizens and its limit of 200 has been constantly pressed by a long waiting list. . . .

> In the month of October, 1886, three persons, George M. Gould, Horace Traubel, and S. Burns Weston met and agreed that steps should be taken to bring together once a month the more thoughtful and active representatives of different professions and occupations to listen to and discuss papers on important questions of the day, to hear occasional presentations of the results of scholarly research on subjects of contemporary interest, to afford opportunity for a free interchange of ideas and social intercourse. . . .

> The first formal meeting to carry out this idea was held Wednesday evening, November 3, 1886 at the Ethical Society room. . . .

> . . . the first literary meeting held after the Club received its name was entertained by a distinguished member, Walt Whitman, who read from his own poems. . . .[11]

Traubel and the followers of Whitman remained with the Philadelphia Society until the turn of the century, when the Society refused to

[10] *Ibid.,* p. 110.
[11] "The Contemporary Club: A Brief Sketch of its Origin and History, 1886–1904." Ethical Culture Archive.

follow some of the naturalistic implications of Whitman's thought, including his plea for "free love."

Salter's brief tenure in Philadelphia made no significant change in the course of the Society which grew steadily throughout those early years. During Salter's leadership, Weston devoted full time as head-worker of the Neighborhood Guild, resuming his work with the Society when Salter returned to Chicago.

Perhaps the most significant contribution of the Philadelphia Society was establishing an informal publishing house for Ethical Culture. Propaganda leaflets, books, pamphlets came in an increasing flow out of Philadelphia, with Weston acting as editor, copy boy, chief factotum. Among the publications was the *International Journal of Ethics*, which was transferred to the University of Chicago in 1914 and is still continued under the title *Ethics*.

The fourth Society was founded in St. Louis. An abortive attempt was made to establish a Society in St. Louis as early as 1883, and the minutes of the New York Society for that year report: "Dr. Adler reporting—some of the best and strongest men have already signed up [in St. Louis] but *no Leader*." It was not until 1886 that a Leader was found and Adler felt justified in permitting the Ethical Society of St. Louis to be organized. In April of that year at the St. Louis law offices of Charles Nagle, Sr., later President of the Society and Secretary of Commerce of the United States, a group of men came together to found the Society. Burns Weston was there with his brother-in-law Walter Sheldon. Sheldon was asked to deliver three lectures on "The Possibilities of a New Religious Movement in America." In November the Society was formally organized and he became its leader. Adler, naturally, came to deliver the inaugural address. Classes for children were organized, philanthropic work begun, and a program of adult education initiated. For the first time, the unabashed use of "Sunday School" was made in describing the education of children. The membership included the "best and strongest men" in the city and was primarily drawn from the older German freethinkers' movement.

Sheldon was like Weston a New Englander, born in Vermont and, until his senior year at Princeton, a devout member of an evangelical Christian Church. Graduated from Princeton in 1880, he spent a year traveling in the Middle East. While he had contemplated entering the ministry, studies during his senior year in college gave the final blow to his beliefs, and he planned instead to teach literature or philosophy. To prepare for teaching he went to the University of Berlin and there met Burns Weston in the fall of 1881. Weston told him of Felix Adler and Ethical Culture, and Sheldon developed an interest in working for a movement that sought to be religious without theology; he thus returned with Weston to New York in 1883 to meet Adler. He was invited to participate in the work of the New York Society while continuing his studies at Columbia University.

Sheldon continued his personal interest in literature and philosophy, lecturing regularly on these subjects from the platform and teaching them in the courses organized by the Society. As its first institutionalist, however, he made his mark on Ethical Culture. It was no accident that St. Louis organized a Sunday school within six months of its founding, for Sheldon believed in the importance of training the generations not only in the general field of ethics but specifically for Ethical Culture. In an address entitled, "What is an Ethical Society," he said:

> It is plain every day observation that children do not carry into practice the teaching of the Sunday School. . . . We wonder vaguely after so much religious teaching that children are so little influenced by it. . . . The teaching is begun at the wrong end. The first question put to the child is "Who made you?" When it ought to be "Whom do you love?" "To whom should you be faithful?" "What ought you most to care for?" Fidelity in human relations should be the starting point in religious education of the young.[12]

Sheldon devoted most of his energy to educational pursuits. For him none of the storms of Chicago, nor even gentler efforts at organized reform and social criticism. Typically, Sheldon addressed himself one Sunday in 1889 to the topic "Count Tolstoi from an Ethical Standpoint," saying: "The essential features of the right system of ethics would be that it should be able to alter our habits and change us from creatures of habit into creatures of principle." The focus on inner change was the predominant note sounded throughout Sheldon's leadership—change oneself and reform will take care of itself.

[12] *The Ethical Record,* II (1889), 168.

To this end Sheldon devoted himself to the preparation of curriculum materials. He edited a series of Bible stories adapted for an Ethical Sunday school and produced "responsive exercises for the young." His Platform sought not so much to stir his listeners into organizing for action as to force them back into self-examination and contemplation. It is ironic that the one Leader who had not been trained for the ministry should take this direction. Salter and Weston, each in his own way, had experienced the failings of the clerical profession, and their careers were marked by an almost willful rejection of all reminders of it. Adler had created his own pathway, borrowing from clerical practice, but often departing in his own directions. Sheldon, however, embarked on an attempt to create an ethical ministry.

But it is to Stanton Coit, like Sheldon without ministerial background, that we must turn to see an Ethical Leader who consciously sought to be a churchman in an Ethical Culture pulpit. Stanton Coit, born in 1857 in Ohio and raised in an Episcopalian household, came under the influence of Emerson's thought at the early age of fifteen. Impressed by Emerson's call for a church of "pure ethics . . . formulated and concreted into a cultus . . ." Coit recalled:

> One day in 1881, to a college friend at Amherst, I was expounding this idea when he exclaimed: "But you ought to hear Felix Adler, the radical! He is *doing* the very thing of which *you* are *dreaming!*" Soon I went to New York to hear the man who was putting my creed into deed. After hearing him once, I realized that what my friend had said was true, and on the following Monday at nine o'clock, all uninvited, I called at Professor Adler's house and announced: "I have decided to be an Ethical Lecturer." . . . I devoted many years to social service in the poorer neighborhoods of New York and London and to the cause of moral instruction for children. But from the first I have felt that the supreme need of our age is to "concrete" Pure Ethics into a cultus, a fraternity with Assemblings and holy days, with song and book, with brick and stone. . . .[13]

Adler arranged for Coit to go abroad to the University of Berlin for graduate study. Returning to this country, he followed the footsteps of Sheldon and Salter with further work at Columbia University and apprenticeship under Adler in New York. During his stay in New

[13] *The Fiftieth Anniversary of the Ethical Movement,* pp. 193–194.

York, and in consequence of what he had seen at Toynbee Hall (a university settlement house) in England, Coit established the first settlement house in this country. Antedating Jane Addams's work by some two years, he founded the Neighborhood Guild in New York City in 1886, today known as the University Settlement. We now take settlement houses for granted, yet a revolutionary spirit and ideology motivated the early settlement house movement. The workers in the settlement houses, usually young radical students, took up residence and shared the life of the people they served. They aimed to establish a base of organization among the people in order to effect social change and to bring power to bear upon the political and economic leadership of the community. Rejecting the doctrine of violent revolution, they nevertheless worked for radical reformation of society. Coit made this clear in his book, *Neighborhood Guilds:*

> If this first step, the organization of the masses mentally and morally, were taken, the second step, the enlightenment of the people in social principles, could easily be made, and then the realization of a just state would not be remote nor would it be brought in with violence. Now such a general organization of the life of the people . . . the Neighborhood Guild would presume to assign to itself. . . . As to special measures, I shall simply assume that whatever be the final and widest sweeping reform, whether the wage system is simply to be modified or is to be superseded by a better method of production and distribution, still the immediate line of advance will be through the organization of all laborers, women as well as men, into trade unions, through a reduction of the hours of work, through Friendly Societies, through greater domestic conveniences and healthier surroundings, better education in general, and through increased recreation and higher amusements. With these specific schemes of reform, Neighborhood Guild is already alive.[14]

Many university students were attracted to the work of building settlement houses. Within five years of the founding of the first one others had been initiated, the most famous of which was Jane Addams's Hull House in Chicago. Her experience had been similar to Coit's in England though there is no record that she and Coit knew of each other's initiatory efforts. The newly formed American University Extension Movement (forerunner of the National Federation of Set-

[14] Pp. 4–6.

tlements) sought to bring the various separate ventures into touch
with each other. Weston had established a similar project in Philadelphia; somewhat later, Chicago did the same with its Henry Booth
House. In New York both Madison House and Hudson Guild were
inspired by Coit's pioneering work. A close parallel in our own day to
the mood and dedication of the early settlement house pioneers is
best observed among the young college students who participated in
the civil-rights revolution in the early 1960s.

Coit was also a careful and competent scholar, translating Nicholai
Hartmann's three-volume *Ethik* into English for the Library of Philosophy. He taught in the Workingman's School and took over some
of the ethics classes which Adler had organized for children of members of the Society. In 1887 news came that South Place Chapel in
London wanted Coit to serve as its minister. Coit was agreeable to the
invitation on condition that South Place join the Ethical movement.

Founded by an American in 1793, South Place became Unitarian in
1802 and then independent in 1816. In that year it changed its bond
of membership from theological to ethical grounds and thus in a sense
predated Adler's more complex venture by about fifty years. From
1863 until 1884 its minister was Moncure Daniel Conway. Conway,
born in 1832 in Virginia, was graduated from the Harvard Divinity
School in 1854 and in 1856 assumed the pulpit of All Souls Unitarian
Church in Washington, D. C. He was a liberal greatly influenced by
Emerson and free religion. He was, too, a vigorous abolitionist, so
much so that he was forced out of the Washington pulpit for his views
and became minister of the First Congregational Church in Cincinnati. During the Civil War he lectured in England on the cause of
union and abolition, influencing British labor against working on
southern cotton. A man whose interests were literary, religious, and
political, he led the South Place Chapel in directions that made the
transition from independent church to Ethical Society almost imper-
ceptible.

Coit went to England and Ethical Culture thus moved beyond the
American continent, foreshadowing the next decade of its history.
With South Place as a base, Coit developed the British Ethical Union,
which attracted to its ranks leading figures in philosophy and ethical
thought. Among its early followers were the British thinkers Muirhead, Bosanquet, and Sidgewick; more recently under the umbrella

of the British Humanist Association it has attracted men like Julian Huxley, Boyd Orr, and Bertrand Russell. Relationships, too, were developed with the Fabian Society, forerunner of the British Labour Movement. The British movement under Coit's leadership also worked for church reform. Away from Adler and New York, Coit began to experiment with various forms and rituals he found attractive, seeking to give these an ethical content. He wrote an extensive commentary on the *Book of Common Prayer*, eliminating all theological references. His Ethical Church had an altar dedicated to man, the lecturer wore a clerical robe; music and responsive readings were included in the Sunday meeting. Coit developed an ethical creed for use in the service of the Ethical Church:

We believe: in the ideal of truth, beauty, and righteousness; it is the principle of life. The benign and mighty father of man's spirit, the God of Reason, Joy and Love. . . . Its service is perfect freedom, with promise of the lordship of Man over the forces of Nature, and over the wayward impulses of his own heart.

We believe in those who have sacrificed for truth, beauty, and righteousness; and we look to them as saviours of the world from error, ugliness, and sin.

We believe: in man's effort to establish the ideal on earth; it will draw all nations into everlasting brotherhood of creative work.

Ceremonies and ceremonial were part of Coit's interpretation of Ethical religion. The most elaborate of these was his two-volume *Social Worship*, including orders of service, appropriate readings, music, suggested ceremonials at times of death, marriage, and the naming and confirmation of children. Believing in the need for a continuing ministry in the Ethical Church, Coit organized the International Foundation for Moral and Religious Leadership, one consequence of which was the recruiting and training of a number of men who came to the United States during the first part of the twentieth century to become Leaders of American Ethical Societies. These men included Percival Chubb, Horace Bridges, Henry Golding, J. Hutton Hynd, Edwin Collier, and George O'Dell. The shape of the British movement was in part a consequence of its environment, but as important was Coit's almost literal interpretation of Emerson's thought.

Such a development could not have occurred in the American movement. Elaboration of form was foreign to it; a church-like character
would have alienated those of Jewish background, and the explicitly
ceremonial practices of the "cult" would have driven away those who
sought to escape clericalism. Adler was deeply troubled by Coit's
efforts in these directions and at times felt that he had been betrayed.

True, Adler had from time to time called for the development of
"genuine symbols." He was nevertheless concerned to unite the secularist with the religionist, the moral reformer with the person who had
"cosmic awareness." To Adler and to most of the American movement, Coit's Ethical religion was alien; Americans recorded the dis-
comfort they felt when they visited the Ethical Church in London.
Nevertheless, Coit continued throughout his life acting in the belief
that symbol and ceremony were essential if Ethical religion was ever
to develop a permanent hold on people.

> Coit believed in the use of symbols. . . . He engaged outstanding ar-
> tists to fashion the symbols which adorned his Church. . . . He was
> well aware that symbols had been used and abused by the religions, but
> he claimed that a rational religion should find a place for symbols and
> the cultus. On the right hand side of the handsomely carved pulpit of the
> Ethical Church stands a statue of Christ by Thorwaldsen. On the base of
> the statue are written the words of Emerson, "Attach thyself not to the
> Christian symbol but to the moral sentiment which carries innumerable
> Christianities, Humanities, and Divinities in its bosom." The words sug-
> gest the high purpose behind Coit's use of symbolic form. The moral sen-
> timent is all, as in his use of the statue of the Buddha and of Kwan Yin,
> the mythical goddess of mercy who refuses to enter heaven while one
> sinner remains outside. . . .[15]

Each of the four men who joined the Leadership was individual,
yet they shared characteristics which set them apart from Adler himself. None of them was of German-Jewish background; all had felt the
influence of free religion and Emerson. They brought to the movement, begun out of Jewish and German influences, native American
and liberal Christian concerns and ideas. For the most part Adler and
his followers welcomed all who seriously wanted to build beyond

[15] J. Hutton Hynd, *The Task of Rational Religion,* p. 15.

church and synagogue. Their coming and the spread of Ethical Culture westward and across the Atlantic began to diffuse the unified philosophy and program that had centered on Adler and New York. While the founder continued his focal role, never again could the movement recapture the singleness of purpose and voice which it enjoyed in its first six years.

The figure of Adler did not loom larger than human; his words were not carved in stone; his life did not climb to a climactic event. While his personality pervaded the movement and his colleagues shared his philosophic attitude (all were philosophic idealists and transcendentalists), Adler was the first among equals, not a transformed symbolic image. Each of the Leaders and each of the Societies took a somewhat different pathway within a common pattern. The movement developed richness and complexity from the many springs that fed it, from the strong, diverse personalities who joined its work.

CHAPTER VIII

The End
of the Beginning

The heroic years were now drawing to a close. They had been adventurous and fruitful. The outlines of the new movement had emerged. Societies existed in four major cities with professional workers serving each of them. A pattern of Leadership was established and recruits from the ranks of free religion seemed readily available. Adler, whose future had seemed so dubious in 1873, was now embarked upon a growing venture on the religious frontier. At least in liberal circles, the Societies for Ethical Culture were acknowledged, albeit sometimes uncomfortably, as leaders of reform. Schools, settlement houses, and philanthropy represented extensions of the philosophy of deed before creed. Audiences filled the halls in New York, Philadelphia, St. Louis, and Chicago. It was indeed a golden age for the movement. Everything tried had the appeal of novelty, every success was a "first."

The tenth anniversary represented the high-water mark of this period when membership in New York neared six hundred, in the movement nationally, more than 1200. On the occasion of that anniversary in 1886, the First Convention of the Ethical Societies met in New

York. Naturally, Adler was elected President of the Convention and later President of the Union which was formed. The following year, in St. Louis, it was agreed that a Fraternity of Ethical "Lecturers" and a Convention of Delegates "shall govern this Union of Ethical Societies." The inevitable committees were appointed: on publications, on schools, on the formation of "auxiliary" Societies, on a College for the Training of Ethical Teachers, and on drafting a constitution for the Union. Men predominated, but some women were admitted to the councils of the movement. At the Sunday meeting on May 16, 1886, Dr. Frances Emily White of Philadelphia was the first woman to speak from an Ethical platform. She shared it with all of the Ethical lecturers and William J. Potter, editor of *The Index*.

The Committee on Schools, chaired by Alfred Wolff, reported:

1. That a School for each Society in which the children of members may enjoy the advantages of a rational education, similar in spirit to that sought to be given in the Workingman's School in New York City, is a necessity in order to successfully achieve the highest aim of the Society for Ethical Culture—the education of moral men and women.

2. That the highest moral culture cannot be obtained without an adequate basis of intellectual culture.

3. That such schools will result in a desirable spirit of fellowship and association which cannot be equally secured in any other way.

4. That in view of these and other like reasons, the institution of such schools be encouraged and made a vital part of the Societies' work.[1]

It was agreed that membership in the Union might be encouraged in places where insufficient numbers existed to establish a Society. A "missionary" group was to be formed to arouse sympathy and support for the movement. Provision was made for admitting new Societies into the Union: Ten or more persons might apply for membership "provided that some representative of the Union shall have visited them at *their* expense and be satisfied of their fitness to form a Branch Society." Such Societies were required to meet at least once every two weeks regularly for at least seven months in each year and to have a

[1] Report of the First Convention of Ethical Societies, 1886. Ethical Culture Archive.

budget, one quarter of which was to be devoted to some philanthropic enterprise. The paraphernalia of institution were beginning to surround the pioneers.

The delegates must have felt satisfaction in the accomplishments of the first decade. They sensed that the road ahead, promising as it might be, was long and difficult and that the romance of the founding had now to give way to hard, often tedious, work. The movement, which self-consciously had set itself the task of responding to the tensions and problems of an urban and industrial society, now found itself forced to pay attention to its own growth and survival. The initial ambivalences, which had blocked a clear decision to build an independent movement in the first half of the decade, were replaced by the decision to proceed nationally and soon internationally. Within thirty years America was to become deeply involved with the rest of the world, and the movement was to find the challenge of building Ethical Culture more difficult when its arena became multinational.

But this was in the future as the delegates met in 1886. They had succeeded in founding a purely Ethical religion, unencumbered by pastoral and medieval loyalties. They had managed, most of them, to find an independent position between the rationalist's hostility to all tradition and the twistings and turnings of orthodox apologetic seeking to modernize itself. Adler's common ground existed, for a time at least, alone on the American scene:

> . . . Most Unitarians were not willing to follow the extreme course of Parker and Emerson but continued to locate themselves, albeit uneasily, within the Biblical and Christian perimeter. The logical conclusions of the more radical position were drawn by the Free Religious Association, Ethical Culture, and other numerically minor secessions from the Christian camp.[2]

They had welded Emerson's ethical faith, Adler's religion of deed, and America's religion of democracy.

---

[2] A. Leland Jamison, "Religions in the Christian Perimeter," in *The Shaping of American Religion: Religion in American Life*, Smith and Jamison, eds., p. 183.

PART TWO

Years of Hope
and Fulfillment

CHAPTER IX

Ethical
Culture
Abroad

Adler and his followers had established a new faith for the transplanted and Americanized immigrants. Could this religion with its New World flavor be carried beyond the national boundary? Was there a message here for all men?

An article in the *Ethical Record* said:

According to Immanuel Kant, there is an invisible church, made up of earnest thinking people who regard the true service of God to consist not in creeds and religious ceremonies, but rather in disposition towards an upright life. If these persons unite with the exclusive purpose of working against evil in the world and strengthening the cause of good, if they thus hold up a standard of virtue as the basis of union for all who love the good, then they constitute an "Ethical Society." [1]

Stanton Coit was leading the Ethical Church in London, but England was different from the continent, and besides, the Ethical

---

[1] Gizycki, "Ethical Societies and The Church," *The Ethical Record*, Vol. II, No. 1 (1889), p. 47.

Church had for some fifty years been under the leadership of Americans. Certainly the moral disarray that Ethical Culture sought to counter was not unique to America. Europe was beginning the prolonged crisis that would lead to world war and revolution as industrialism, Marxism, and nationalism became driving historical forces. Japan, seeking power, began its climb into the modern world with a war on Russia. Racism and anti-Semitism, soon to infect most of the "civilized" world, revealed their virulence in the Dreyfus affair.

But certain voices were raised to oppose these excesses, voices that cried out for moral and humanistic rights. A young Indian lawyer named Ghandi living in South Africa was formulating the philosophy that was to free his country. Fabian Socialism in Britain and Marxism on the continent grew out of a sense of injustice. Many of the isms and organizations that dotted the world landscape were social idealism clothed in socio-political costume. The motives for reform from each of these sources reflected a heightened awareness of social need. Why should Ethical Culture not serve as a world answer to that need?

Moncure Conway, lecturing in London, said hopefully:

> Among all the outburnt craters, I see but one peak from whence the sacred fire is now ascending. The Movement which in strength, freedom, and influence may now be regarded as succeeding to that of Channing, Parker and Emerson, is the one in New York which undertakes to found a religion purely on the basis of morality.[2]

The International Congress of Philosophy, at its Paris meeting in the summer of 1900, called on Ethical Culture to become a genuine international philosophy and for Ethical societies to spread throughout the world.[3] Dr. F. W. Foerster of the newly formed International Ethical Union reported in 1898,

> The apparently unpunished success of an era of ruthless governmental policy of coercion on the one hand, and the apparent powerlessness of idealistic efforts at a unification of the fatherland on the other hand, have stifled in all levels of society, irrespective of political lines—but

2 *Ibid.*
3 *The Ethical Record*, October, 1900, p. 17.

particularly in the circles of academic idealism—the faith in the historical power of a moral ideal, and have allowed to take root in its place the conviction that all great social changes are brought about only through a pact with the devil, and that humanity advances, not by means of the gradual growth of fidelity, sympathy, and insight, but by means of so-called great decisive acts.[4]

Much of human history has been characterized by fear of the stranger. If the Greeks saw all others as barbarians, their view was not unique. The great international movements—Roman Catholicism and Marxism—found stumbling blocks in national and tribal loyalties. The scientific community discovered that scientists were torn by the same tensions that beset the rest of us. Yet the struggle to develop awareness of a common human destiny began to gather force. The organization of an International Ethical Movement was part of an evolving international spirit.

Dismayed by moral degeneration and moved by a growing sense of world community, Ethical Culture sought to maintain an appreciation of the affirmative contributions of cultural and national differences. In 1893 Dr. Friedrich Jodl wrote:

> Ethical Culture can no more be limited in its activities by political boundaries than by the differences between economic and social classes. . . . Ethical Culture is fundamentally international, not because it disparages nationalities or regards them as ethically valueless, but because it believes that the highest development of a national life is impossible except under an ethical organization of the whole of humanity.[5]

Little insistence was put on a single pattern of organization. Perhaps those developing the international movement were making a virtue of necessity, but their appreciation of difference was more than expediency. Implicit in Adler's conception of the uniqueness of personality was the uniqueness of culture as well. One more universal church was not the goal, but the sharing by self-determining individuals and groups of a common bond of loyalty. "*E pluribus unum*,"

---

[4] Report of the International Ethical Secretariat, cited in Rudolph Penzig "Ethical Culture in Germany after the War," in *Essays in Honor of Felix Adler*, Horace Bridges, ed. (1926), p. 371.

[5] *Ibid.*, p. 369.

motto of pluralism in the American experiment, was the unspoken ambition of Ethical Culture's international efforts. In a "foreign letter" to the *Ethical Record* on the "Outward Form of European Societies," we read:

1. No paid and permanent lecturers.

2. No Sunday services; the traditions of going to church and of being connected with some religious body have not grown here into a kind of social obligation as it has in the Anglo-Saxon countries. Our free-thinkers, and many religious people, too, show no need for these things.[6]

Thus, Ethical Culture, beginning its international adventure, responded to three essential themes: the need for moral reconstruction, the evolution of internationalism, and the effort to work out a dynamic relationship between cultural differences and continuity of concerns.

Stanton Coit had been directing the Ethical movement toward a national Ethical church, and by 1889 some 600 people were attending Sunday meeting regularly at South Place. At the universities an academic fellowship program was instituted, helping to fill the pulpit and lecture platforms of the various English Societies.

The Ethical movement in England developed close ties, too, with the British Socialist party. In 1890 the London Progressive Association reported that it had "made a new departure" and altered its subtitle to A Society for Ethical Culture. And in 1898, a speaker for the socialist Labour Party stated:

Even if tomorrow we were given the most perfect social organization and constitution, our social questions would by no means be solved if these institutions were not permeated and supported by a far higher understanding of the duties of a citizen and of a human being. The Ethical Movement must become the religion of the Labour Movement.[7]

The relationship to Fabianism was not greeted with uniform approval on either side of the Atlantic. The *Ethical Record* for April,

---

[6] *The Ethical Record*, 1889, p. 4.
[7] Quoted by Penzig, in Bridges' *Essays*, p. 374.

1902, reported that "the Ethical Movement in London has got into trouble." Accused of being socialist it lost some of its major supporters, among whom was Herbert Spencer, who withdrew in protest. A comment in the United States on the association of the Ethical and Labour movements questioned whether this tie might not make the Ethical movement "superfluous."

Coit, on a periodic visit to the United States, addressed the Board of Trustees of the New York Society in February 1912,

> Dr. Stanton Coit was then invited to make a few remarks. He touched, in a humorous vein, on the difference between the Ethical Movement in America and that in England. In regard to the material comforts, it was his opinion that the American Societies were far more advanced than the English. The Movement in England was making greater strides inside the churches than outside, however. . . . He spoke of the four services held each week at the London Society, of the new Gregorian chant and of the periods of "social silence." [8]

(We can imagine Adler's reaction to Gregorian chant *new or old* at an Ethical Culture meeting.)

With Wilhelm Foerster, the famed astronomer, as its first President, an Ethical Society was established in Germany in 1892. In its first year, 1100 members joined, most of them in Berlin, and a weekly newspaper was launched. A key figure here for many years was Rudolph Penzig, who, because of his rejection of the church and criticism of German nationalism, had been unable to get a teaching post. Hearing of the organization of an Ethical movement in Germany he returned home from Switzerland to become its traveling lecturer and editor.

The German movement saw its tasks as the reconciliation between classes in society and the opposing of "Prussianism" in the arts and education. Challenging the religious establishment as well, it attracted many free-thinkers who had rejected all religious forms. Unlike its British and American counterparts, the movement was not organized in congregations but rather engaged in propaganda and social criticism. The following is an example:

[8] New York Board of Trustees Minutes, February 5, 1912.

Editor Naumann, a Christian minister, . . . is quoted in the Socialist paper, *Die Hilfe,* "Religion has to do with the inner life, it must not disturb politics by sentiment, nor interfere with the iron necessities of national growth."

. . . The disbelief in the ethical teaching of Christ is almost greater within the church than outside it. . . . no Christian paper in Germany opposed Pastor Naumann's attitude. They left it to *Vorwärts,* the organ of German Social Democracy, and to *Ethische Kultur* to arouse the nation to self-criticism, and to a defence if the most elementary ethical demands of civilization.[9]

In the last decade of the nineteenth century Ethical Societies appeared in many different places. Professor Friedrich Jodl organized an Ethical Society in Vienna in 1894. In 1902 Wilhelm Boerner, who was to work with the Vienna Society for nearly fifty years, joined it after reading Jodl's lecture on the nature and task of an Ethical Society. In Lausanne and Zurich, Jean Wagner organized the Ligue pour l'Action Morale. Wagner, while studying with Coit in London, had done his doctoral thesis on the Ethical Church. In Switzerland, Sunday lectures were given, moral instruction of children was undertaken, and a "People's Institute" organized for workingmen.

A letter to the *Ethical Record* in 1899 reported on a "remarkable resurgence of ethical ideas" throughout France. A monthly newspaper was published, a university extension movement was founded by M. DuHemme, secretary of the Union pour l'Action Morale, and centers of ethical teaching were begun in that country. A People's Institute for the moral, intellectual, and social needs of workingmen was planned. And the French cited as a reason for their Ethical Society the "moral bankruptcy" of the church as shown in its attitude on the Dreyfus case.

Interest in Ethical Culture was not confined to Europe. A society was established in Tokyo, which gave monthly lectures and issued propaganda and which attracted a small but strong following at Tokyo University. Organized in 1898, the group devoted most of its attention to contemporary ethical problems aided, no doubt, by the humanistic elements in Buddhism and Confucianism.

A pamphlet called *Buddhism in the West* commented:

[9] "Foreign Letter," *The Ethical Record,* October, 1900, pp. 15–17 passim.

. . . The second circumstance favourable to Buddhism's having become popular in the West was the Movement for Ethical Culture. . . . This new movement had some points of contact with Buddhism. . . . Though Buddhist ethics is more individual and Ethical Culture more social, the formation of character was important for both, and both did not entirely agree with crass materialistic science, and both had to fight against a common enemy: the orthodox Christianity of that day. . . .[10]

The Aukland Ethical Society of New Zealand was founded in 1906. Wherever Ethical Culture took root, it drew to its ranks leading intellectuals, reformers, social critics. Adler's work was translated into many languages and served as a philosophic bond among distinctive national organizations. International travel—especially between the United States, England, and Europe—fostered numerous important, though informal, relationships. The influence of the various national movements within their own boundaries has yet to be assessed. We know, for example, of the philosophic importance of the movement in England, influencing views as different as Sidgewick's utilitarianism and Bosanquet's idealism. In France, the struggle against clericalism, especially in the schools, was aided by the Ligue pour l'Action Morale. After the First World War the Viennese Society worked to combat the growing wave of suicides (the *Lebensmüde Stelle*) by providing counsel and support to men and women in despair. But national movements require a detailed examination, which must be left to some future historian. Ethical Culture evolved in many places and at a rapid pace; a remarkable variety of organization and activity was undertaken in the name of an "ethical" idea and ideal.

Adler and his American followers could proudly boast that their movement was universal and, if not particularly large or well organized, at least relevant to cultures quite different from the bustling raw and young America. Encouraged by the apparent readiness in many parts of the world to respond, the European, British, and American groups called for an international organization. In 1893, at Eisenach, Germany, the International Ethical Union was founded.

Primarily the international organization facilitated communication among existing groups. However, at the Zurich meeting in 1896, an

---

[10] Ven. Nyanasatta Thero, "Introduction to Buddhism in Europe," *Buddhism in the West*, Series No. 16, Buddha Rasmi, Ceylon, 1956.

attempt was made to develop a common statement of aims, a world-wide ethical platform. *The Zurich Declaration* began: "The prime aim of the Ethical Societies is to be of advantage to their own members. The better moral life is not a gift which we are merely to confer upon others; it is rather a difficult prize which we are to try with unwearying and unceasing effort to secure for ourselves."

The conference, including representatives from the United States, England, Germany, Austria, Italy, and Switzerland, called for more associations of like-minded people and for moral education of both children and adults. The Declaration spoke of the need for moral reform, for attention to social issues, for the desirability of peace, and for intellectual "armor to serve in the social struggle." One section was devoted to the rights of women and to the support of monogamous marriage. Another opposed chauvinism and militarism. The Declaration reveals the compromises made to achieve consensus. Conflict over both pacifism and nationalism was accepted as inevitable, but "within the limits prescribed by morality . . . and with a constant eye to the final establishment of social peace." Support for "the masses" was considered a duty in efforts to "obtain a more humane existence," but ". . . an evil hardly less serious is to be found in the moral need which exists among the wealthy who are often deeply imperiled in their moral integrity by the discords in which the defects of the present industrial system involve them." (One can hear the Marxists snorting at that.) Recognizing the judicious balancing of interests in the Declaration, one can feel the weight of Adler's report to the New York Society: "The great proportion of university professors connected with the societies [abroad] is characteristic of the foreign movement and is at once a source of strength and of weakness as they are cut off from the people."

While affirmative about the conference and hopeful of building an international movement, Adler was not sanguine about the immediate prospects. He feared that the ideological whirlpool might engulf the newly born federation; also, he questioned the ethical validity of a purely academic movement. In a sense Adler was more Americanized than he realized, for much of his hesitation about the Zurich meetings reflected a New World impatience. Adler's prophetic roots never failed him; in the considered debates and polite conventions of the conference, he sought a commitment to righteousness. In giving voice to his criticism, he restated in a fresh way the intent of the American movement:

What I found lacking in the foreign Ethical Societies was the spiritual element. . . . This side was neglected [at Zurich]; the drift was in the external direction as if the ethical society should exist for the benefit of others . . . an ethical society exists primarily for the moral benefit of its own members. By this test I distinguish the real members from the quasi-members. The real member of an ethical society feels that he has not yet finished his moral education. . . .

. . . we recognize that we must grapple with the social and political questions of the day, but nevertheless, our moral growth is still the principal aim. We must emphasize that the changes must not be merely external but must be effected in ourselves.

We are to regenerate society primarily by regenerating the one individual member of society for whom we are responsible.[11]

Debate of the Zurich Declaration in the American movement was long. Not until 1900 did the New York Society decide against taking official action on the Zurich program.

In 1896 the international movement appointed Dr. Wilhelm Foerster, son of the first president of the German society, international secretary, and in 1906 Gustav Spiller was named to succeed him. Spiller had served with Stanton Coit in England. He was a printer by trade and after the First World War devoted his life to the League of Nations.

Ethical Culture, as a transnational phenomenon, sought to make moral sense of day-to-day issues. Efforts were made to clarify the difference between an ethical and an unethical patriotism, between legitimate and illegitimate conflict. The movement's criticism of Germany's militarism and jingoism contributed to building an opposition, if not a check, to the destructive forces shaping that country. Adler's wish for uplifting personal life also found expression. For example, the regularly published "foreign letter" to the *Ethical Record* reported:

---

[11] Felix Adler, "The Recent Congress of American and European Ethical Societies at Zurich," *Ethical Addresses* (Third Series, 1897), 139–47 passim.

. . . the fact is that in the University of Vienna a fourth of the students suffer from sexual diseases. . . . Hence the members of the Ethical Societies have sought . . . by founding . . . small groups to promote purer thoughts and deeds in sexual relations.[12]

The meetings and publications on moral education and on race echoed resoundingly the ethical note Adler had sounded in his earlier years.

In 1908 representatives of some twenty nations convened in London to study the problems of moral education. The International Union of Ethical Societies was credited with the idea for the convention. Among the subjects that came under discussion were moral training in school and home, values of coeducation, moral values in the curriculum, and juvenile literature. Meeting at the University of London under the presidency of Sir Michael Sadler of Manchester (described in a contemporary journal as "perhaps today the strongest personality in the field of British pedagogy"), the 1,200 participants addressed themselves to the philosophic and practical problems that by the middle of the century would touch the lives of most of the world's children. Public compulsory education for all was a recent development. The conflict between religiously sponsored private schooling and secular public education was widespread and was recognized in that congress as one of the great issues of modern times, but "In all the eight sessions the debates were conducted by Roman Catholics, Anglicans, Unitarians, Jews, Rationalists, and others with mutual courtesy." A report in 1909 said:

. . . Nor could they have heard from that platform the declarations or real convictions so fearlessly and so temperately expressed but for the fact that the leaders of debate had for the last two years been working privately together on the Moral Instruction Inquiry, and learnt, in their common search for truth, to respect one another's convictions.[13]

In 1912 a second congress was convened at The Hague, which drew delegates from Argentina, China, Egypt, Haiti, the Dutch Indies, Japan, and India, as well as from Europe, the USA, and the British

[12] April, 1902, p. 161.
[13] *Moral Instruction League Quarterly,* January 1, 1909, p. 2.

Isles. Adler gave a major address on "A Course of Ethical Development Extending Through Life," in which he explored the parallels between ethical evolution for the individual and for the human race. Percival Chubb, with prophetic insight, said:

> . . . never, I suppose, in the history of the race has it been so important to provide for the profitable use of leisure as it is today. And this for two reasons, first the demoralizing thraldom of work and second, the ethical bankruptcy of work—by which I mean the failure of work to subserve the larger ends of character development.[14]

Congresses on moral education were interrupted by the First World War, but resumed in 1922 at Geneva, in 1926 in Rome, in 1930 at Paris, and finally in 1934 at Cracow. As the world drew closer to cataclysm, helplessness mixed with hope in the discussions. The origins of the congresses were perceptible in 1934 although by then Hitlerism rode the wave of the future, and the connections between Ethical Culture and the moral education movement were attenuated. The proceedings of the final congress stated, ". . . we insist that no section or course of education shall escape the control of the moral ideal." In the shadows, the delegates murmured: "We appeal to the folk of all languages and colours. . . . It is not formulae that count, it is the spirit and hope and faith of youth that count, it is our reverence for youth that counts."

A second venture for the International Ethical Union, under Spiller's supervision, was the International Races Congress held in London during the summer of 1911. An Empire convocation for the coronation of George V had just concluded, assuring the presence of Asians and Africans. The organizers rejected political solutions alone, reasoning that a new age had come to man and for that new age old attitudes had to give way. The papers of the congress represented advanced social and scientific thought, but the most important thing about that London meeting was that it happened at all. For the first time in modern history equal and reasonable dialogue was exchanged between peoples who had traditionally regarded each other as subject and master, as backward and civilized, as conquered and conqueror.

[14] Percival Chubb, *Proceedings of the Second Moral Education Congress* (1912), p. 46.

The synthesis of scientific thought, of the problems of power, and of moral judgment was important and original. Franz Boaz, the world-famous American anthropologist, in a paper called "Race and Culture" reported on his researches which challenged the idea of inferior and superior races. W. E. B. DuBois presented a radical black critique of racism. The New York Society recorded that Adler

> . . . spoke at some length about the Races Congress. . . . it was hoped [it] would be the forerunner of an important movement toward the amelioration of the conditions of what had been called "the subject races." He spoke of the very valuable utterances of scientific men (ethnologists) at the Congress who took ground against the pretext of essential inferiority in these races and the similar attitude, taken by 3 or 4 important British proconsuls. . . . Dr. Adler said that the credit for the hard work done in getting the Congress together was due to Dr. Spiller, Secretary of the International Ethical Union. . . .[15]

The attitude of the American movement was not always affirmative. Although gratified by acceptance abroad, the Americans were often suspicious of turns that Ethical Culture took when not under their watchful eye. Appeals from the International Ethical Union for financial support were granted, though not always willingly. Issues that exercised the enlightened European community did not always receive a favorable hearing in the United States. For example, when Dr. Foerster sought American support for endorsement by the International Ethical Union of Emile Zola in the Dreyfus affair, the American societies hedged by responding that they were "not justified in taking action in this matter."

Meanwhile Adler was gaining increasing personal recognition. In 1908 President Roosevelt appointed him Theodore Roosevelt Professor at the University of Berlin upon nomination by the Board of Trustees of Columbia University. At Berlin Adler delivered a series of lectures on "The Foundation of Friendly Relations Between Germany and America" with the theme of "mutual elicitation of excellence between individuals and nations." His daughter, Ruth, recalled something of the experience:

[15] New York Board of Trustees Minutes, October 2, 1911.

. . . [he] had a directive from Theodore Roosevelt . . . asking him to consider especially better relations between Germany and the United States. . . . He had become known as a very interesting lecturer so there was a big crowd in the big University Aule. . . . At that time the Exchange Professor was an important person. . . . He was presented at the court [of Kaiser Wilhelm II]. . . . I was at a boarding school which I didn't like. I was used to the Ethical Culture School. . . . the very oppressive atmosphere of the school in Berlin was hard on me. . . . The whole set-up was very unsympathetic to anybody who was democratic minded. Berlin was full of [the] military. The atmosphere was very Prussian, officers going around on the streets, and pedestrians who were in their way more or less pushed out. . . . [Yet] I think intellectually he [father] found it stimulating. . . .[16]

From his comments to the New York Board and from addresses delivered on his return, Adler apparently had not found the Berlin environment congenial. However Germanic his background and education, he was American. In his first major address to the Society after his return, "Foreign Experiences and Loyalty to American Ideals," he said: "The American who goes abroad, especially the American scholar, has not employed his time to best advantage unless he comes back a more intense, a more convinced, a more fervid American than when he set out."

At Cornell Adler had drawn a line between Hebrew prophets and American ideals. Now Adler believed that America, despite its manifest imperfections, was the model for the reconstruction of ethical ideals. His belief in the preeminence of America and the American movement contributed to his own ambivalence toward the international Union. In the 1890s Coit had begged Adler to spend several months each year in England and on the continent, but Adler held back. Despite the efforts of Spiller, the International Ethical Union remained only a channel of communication. Buffeted repeatedly by wars, the Depression, and fascism, Ethical Culture did not survive in the international community.

[16] From an interview with Ruth Friess, 1964.

CHAPTER X

All Education Is Religious

In *Aims of Education,* Alfred North Whitehead says:

We can be content with no less than the old summary of the educational ideal. . . . The essence of education is that it be religious. Pray, what is religious education? A religious education is an education which inculcates duty and reverence. Duty arises from our potential control over the course of events. Where attainable knowledge could have changed the outcome, ignorance has the guilt of vice. And the foundation of reverence is this perception, that the present holds within itself the complete sum of existence, backwards and forwards, the whole amplitude of time which is eternity.

Ethical Culture would add that the essence of religion is that it is educational. The behavioral sciences were postulating the malleability of man. This led naturally to a pedagogy of personality, formulated variously as personal growth, maturation, self-fulfillment, or self-realization. Ethical Culture, interpreting its role as "character formation," gave an ethical turn to what otherwise was essentially psychological.

This concept in part led to the creation of the Workingman's School and the organization of moral education classes for children of the members. However, while the connection between religion and education was affirmed, it was not the only motivation at the start. A philanthropic intent was central too. The "ethics classes" in seeking a "consecrating influence" asserted a traditional philosophy reminiscent of "religious education," although without its theological component. These were the starting points, but Ethical Culture's experiment in education evolved toward a unique contribution.

Ethical Culture did not yield its moralism, while remaining alert to currents of educational reform. This contrasted sharply with the more open pragmatic and psychological viewpoint of progressivism. Ethical Culture sought to be modern in method without giving up the classic, humanist tradition. Moralism, modernism, and classicism produced a dynamic educational philosophy. And the aim continued to be the "always becoming" of the religious man.

The curriculum of the Ethical Culture schools included the favorite progressive pastime of learning by doing. Side-by-side with projects were an ethics program and a program of social service. The results of recent scholarship in anthropology were explored; activity programs introduced crafts, drama, and dance. Latin and Old Testament study vied with an examination of labor problems. The new and the old, the abstract and the plastic, were woven together by a coordinating moral ideal.

Education was focused on maturing an "ethical" personality, as an instrument for an ideal, not an existent culture. This transcendent impulse, manifested in training for reform and social criticism, lay at the heart of the connection between religion and education. Education was a kind of "continuous revelation"; experience and learning were its sacred text. Teaching became a "priestly" vocation. Thus Adler referred to the Ethical Leader as the first "learner" in an Ethical Culture Society. Whitehead said that duty and reverence were the meeting place of religion and education; Ethical Culture sought to reconstruct both in exposure to contemporary experience. The attempt to "ethicize" all the relationships of life was a new solution to the conflict between the sacred and the secular. Education, not grace, was the bridge between them. Character formulation was a naturalization of the old dream of salvation. Ethical Culture pedagogy was not pure pedagogy at all. It used educational symbols and methods to vitalize moral religion, giving concreteness to that ideal with contemporary, relevant, growing, and changing methods that was to culminate in the Fieldston Plan of 1926.

When the Workingman's School was no more than ten years old, it had more than fulfilled the hopes of its founders. Its operations even gave promise of meeting the objective that Adler and the movement had set: a method of ameliorating the personal and social consequences of the industrial revolution. In an article on "The Influence of Manual Training on Character," Adler said: "Let there be no machine work. Let the pupils turn out complete articles for only thus can the full intellectual and moral benefits of manual training be reaped." [1] Eminently realistic, Adler preached a middle way between the "alienating" system and the "liberating" technology.

He was aware, too, that ethics required decisions. Commenting on scientific scepticism, he asserted that suspended judgment was an unpermitted luxury in politics, economics, and ethics. Ethical education had to teach the lessons of action and the inevitable distinctions between the pure and the applied.

> . . . [But] we must *act* in the meantime. The principle, I think, that should guide us in such questions is not the absolute, the scientific rule . . . but having obtained what light we can, having made up our minds as carefully as we know how with the help of precedent, analogy, experience, we should venture boldly forth upon the sea of action—action in these cases is the great correction of error. By trying our theories we test their validity—action itself teaches us how we ought to act.[2]

Transformation of the individual's ethics was a process of risk and commitment.

In 1888 a group of young mothers joined together to form a class under the awesome name of The Society for the Study of Child Nature. Florentine Scholle Sutro recalled,

> After a year of hard work, our efforts were recognized by Professor G. Stanley Hall of Clark University who arranged for a syllabus for us to

[1] *The Ethical Record*, 1889, p. 119.
[2] *The Ethical Record*, 1888, pp. 10–11.

work on through the summer, which was then used as the first study of children by the pupils of the University.[3]

The mothers' group was one of many efforts at formal adult education. The decade of experience with the Ethical platform and other methods of teaching showed their strength as goads to thought and action—and their weakness in lack of continuity and discipline. A more ambitious theme was sounded in Adler's proposal for an ethical college. First described in 1888, the project was a major item at the Annual Convention of the American Ethical Union in Philadelphia in 1889. Adler prepared impressive support for the proposed School of Philosophy and Applied Ethics. The Convention heard support for the college from leading figures in the Academy, religion, and public life. Messages came from Josiah Royce, Thomas Davidson, William James, Moncure Conway, the Reverend Edward Everett Hale, the Reverend Jenkin Lloyd Jones, Judge George C. Barrett, and a host of others.

O. B. Frothingham said, "I know of but one divinity school [Cambridge] where full intellectual liberty is allowed and none where a system of applied ethics was adopted." [4] Anna Garlin Spencer spoke for women:

> She wants knowledge . . . ; she wants to know what habits breed and stimulate the vice she abhors. . . . The woman who, hearing always "the sad music of humanity" seeks with a world wide love and sympathy to succor the poor and wretched and befriend the forsaken, must have something beside love and sympathy or she will blunder where she most would help. . . .[5]

Francis Ellingwood Abbot explained the "need for reconstitution of philosophy and ethics on the basis of scientific method" and called for a "genuine philosophic [re]construction." [6] Impressed by what they had heard and ready as ever to follow Adler's lead, the Convention adopted a resolution proposing to start a "School of Philosophy

---

[3] *My First Seventy Years*, p. 48.
[4] *The Ethical Record*, II (1889), p. 40.
[5] *Ibid.*, p. 38.
[6] *Ibid.*

and Applied Ethics." Its primary goal was the "training of educators and practical workers in these important provinces of learning and life. . . ."

Bringing the school to birth proved impossible. However, a Summer School of Ethics at Plymouth, Massachusetts, was begun and conducted each summer from 1891 to 1895. Participating in its program were such leading American intellectuals as William James, Josiah Royce, and Henry Carter Adams; Bernard Bosanquet, visiting this country from England, visited Plymouth too. Tuition was about $20 per week, and Adler took a leading part both as Director and as teacher. The Plymouth school offered one of the first courses in labor relations ever given in the United States. In 1894 Samuel Gompers spoke of the members of Ethical Societies as "first among religious and professional groups that supplied the best and most persistent advocate of the cause of labor." But even the summer school proved too much for the small movement to carry with its limited membership. A prior commitment was the Workingman's School, where pressure had been building for the admission of children who were not from deprived families. Complaints were heard against making wealth a disqualification for admission. Then too, as educational philosophy matured the disadvantages of a "class" school were realized. On grounds of equity and pedagogy, therefore, the School had to change.

As early as 1890 a Committee on Education of the Society in New York reported that the teachers unanimously recommended admitting paying pupils to the schools. In the same resolution the teachers insisted that the number of such pupils be limited to no more than fifty percent of the total enrollment. Adler, reflecting on the problem, wrote,

> While the object of this institution is educational and the methods pursued applicable to children of all classes, it is a special aim of the school to aid by educational means in the solution of what is called the "labor question." [7]

[7] Wm. Howe Tollman and Wm. I. Hull, eds., in *Handbook of Sociological References for New York* (New York, 1894).

It was not until 1895, however, that the Workingman's School formally became The Ethical Culture School and not until 1899 that the School was transferred from the United Relief Works, a separate corporation of the Society, to the Society itself. Consistently, in accord with its earliest motivations, the Society safeguarded the scholarship ratio. When the transfer was finally completed, for example, free tuition for one hundred children was guaranteed in perpetuity. The changes were more than formal and economic. The shift in the student body, while easy to accomplish in principle and justify in philosophy, had effects on the lives of the pupils and their teachers. Florence Anspacher, one of the first "pay pupils" remembered,

. . . I was sensitive about inviting my friends from school to my home, particularly those who didn't live the way we did. . . . When the weather was bad, mother would send a carriage for me. Oh, how I hated that. . . . And I had one friend. One day she became faint. I told my teacher . . . and she said the child had better go home. I asked if I could take her home. She lived near the school (54th Street) and [she] protested frantically. She did not want me to go home with her. . . . When we got to her home (she lived on the ground floor and her mother or father may have been the janitors in the tenement house), her mother . . . invited me in for cookies and milk. This child did not come back to school for several days. When she did, I ran up to her and said I was glad she was back. She was very distant, turned her back and walked away. After that she never was friendly with me again. . . . It wasn't until a long time after that I realized that it was [because] . . . she was apparently ashamed of her environment. I was terribly unhappy about it because she was one of my best friends in school. . . . Ideally it [admission of pay pupils] was a good thing, but I am not sure it was *really* a good thing because I had no school friends at all.[8]

With pay pupils often coming from among member families of the Ethical Society and with the transfer of the School to the Society a new problem arose—was it to become a parochial school? Drawing lines between parochial education and education guided by a philosophy of ethical reform was difficult. The evolving educational philosophy based on a vision of life and society hardly simplified the prob-

[8] Interview with Florence Anspacher, 1964, related to Scholle and Sutro families by marriage, and among the oldest member families of the New York Society.

lem. While it was relatively easy to establish legal and institutional distinctions, it was more difficult to understand how Ethical Culture sought to differentiate a sectarian institution from one guided by a "liberating" philosophy. From time to time the question arose of seeking state aid for the schools. But, despite the temptations (scholarships were costly and deficits perennial), the Board of Trustees agreed that this was neither legally possible nor morally desirable. With respect to more subtle issues, the basic posture adopted was for both School and Society to lean over backwards in efforts to insulate the School from the slightest suspicion of sectarianism.

In 1898 a normal school formalized the teacher training which had been part of the Ethical Culture School from the beginning. Using the classroom as a base, a two-year program was established. Sidonie Gruenberg, member of the Society and a noted educator, recalled the training course in kindergarten education:

> It was a place that was seething with ideas and very thorough training. When I finished at the Normal School and went to Teachers College [Columbia] it seemed an anti-climax after the work I had gotten in education and psychology. They [the normal school] were so far ahead of anything that was being done at Columbia that it seemed as if I wasn't taking a graduate course. . . .[9]

Each few years brought some innovation in education. The New York Board in 1898 appointed a special committee to give attention to "the intellectual advancement of the Ethical Movement." This group was instructed to review all plans for educational, literary, and scientific work to be undertaken by the Society, to take the initiative in proposing plans, as required, and to report regularly to the Trustees on progress. At that same meeting and as part of the same discussion, Adler spoke of the newly founded *International Journal of Ethics,* which was to bring to a literate public the best ethical insights of thinkers around the world.

Ethical motive and pedagogical idea had found institutional expression for Ethical Culture. With the Ethical Culture School functioning, a normal school organized, and a student body more integrated, the older motive of philanthropy and the solution to the

---

[9] Interview with Sidonie Gruenberg, 1964.

"social question" needed revision. Building upon some twenty years of experience, as the new century dawned, Adler addressed himself to the prophetic element in education. Its purpose is,

> to train reformers. . . . By "reformers" are meant persons who believe that their salvation consists in reacting beneficiently upon their environment. This ideal of beneficient activity, beneficient transformation of faulty environment, is the ideal of the Society and the School. This then is what is meant by character building.[10]

Reform was the bridge between the classes (a "common ground" of effort) even as it was the continuous transformation of the secular into the sacred.

The educational program which evolved out of an ethical philosophy and which in turn helped that philosophy emerge also brought with it practical demands. For many years, the School had rented facilities. Now, its base secured and its goals more rounded, was a good time to move in the direction of a permanent home. This became particularly necessary with the development of newer, more complex techniques in education. Appreciation of the School was widespread and its unique contribution to education in this country recognized. Thus, the American Secular Union, dedicated to the complete separation of church and state, saw in the Ethical Culture School attempts to teach the "purest principles of morality without inculcating religious doctrines." Dr. Abram S. Hewitt, Director of Cooper Union and reform Mayor of New York City (1886), said on hearing of the School's plans,

> I am glad to learn that your Ethical Schools . . . intend to erect a suitable building . . . [which] . . . will properly stand as a monument to the good work . . . already done and the great improvement which you have accomplished by your example in the modern system of public education. Your undertaking is the parent of the Kindergarten system in this city. . . . You were also the first to introduce manual training as a regular part of the system of the education of the young. . . . The greatest feature, however, of your system of education has not received from the public the recognition which it deserves. You propose to accompany mental development with ethical training. In former times religious in-

10 *The Ethical Record*, 1901, p. 107.

struction was relied upon for the development of the moral character of
the young. Under our system of public instruction religious training is
rigidly excluded from the public schools and no adequate system of ethical training has been submitted. . . . in time the system of public education will be modified in accordance with the results which you have
already worked out and are still improving as a part of general education. . . .[11]

In 1904 at Number 33 Central Park West in New York City a home
for the School was opened with suitable ceremony.

Meanwhile, The Society for the Study of Child Nature had continued its work. In 1904 a second child study group was organized in
downtown New York City. Sidonie Gruenberg described its program:

> It [the first group] met regularly once a week for ten years. . . . There
> was no child development literature. They had to develop [by] reading
> fundamental things and trying to see how they could apply them to
> practical experience day by day. It was a creative job. . . . They were
> all middle class wealthy women who had brownstone houses and cooks
> and nurses. . . . [Then] Chapter II started and the women were all
> former teachers, an entirely different kind of woman. We met at Mrs.
> Pilpel's house. . . . [When] she became ill, suddenly I was the leader
> of this study group. . . .
>
> There were a lot of things we did that Dr. Adler didn't believe in at all.
> We were very much influenced by psychoanalysis. . . . We started to
> have sex education classes. . . . I had many occasions to talk to him
> about different speakers. . . . And he said, you know I don't like any of
> these . . . , but he never said don't have them. . . .
>
> So much originated there [in the Society]. It was such fertile soil. But
> there wasn't much tending of the garden . . . you see we didn't feel
> that we were being appreciated. . . . We weren't part of anything and
> then we were so busy growing . . . until we literally [found] it was too
> small a place and just had to go. But I always regretted the fact that
> there wasn't some inter-relationship. . . .[12]

[11] Letter to Felix Adler from Abram S. Hewitt, February 14, 1901. Ethical
Culture Archive.

[12] Interview with Sidonie Gruenberg, 1964.

Adler was not happy with this project in adult education. Much as he was concerned with relevance and change in education, he resisted certain trends despite their immediacy. Ruth Pilpel Brickner, daughter of Mr. and Mrs. Emanuel Pilpel, who had been among the founding families, and a graduate of the School, told about Adler's diffidence. As a practicing psychiatrist, she was particularly competent to make the following observations:

. . . he [Adler] was opposed to the kind of scrutiny of the intimate, private life which psychiatry and especially psychoanalysis was promulgating. . . . My mother was one of the members [of the group studying child nature]. . . . this group of women began to go roaring ahead and of course uncovered Freud. . . . Among other things, they got interested in A. A. Brill, who was the first translator of Freud into English, and my mother and Dr. Brill got to be friends. . . . [They] got to the point of intensive exploration, which offended Dr. Adler. . . . he felt that there was something inviolate about the core of the human spirit which should not be probed. . . . The more I have worked in this area, the more I feel that there is something to be said for his point of view.[13]

The mothers' program was developing a life of its own. Increasingly they moved outside the orbit of Ethical Culture, at least as conceived by Adler and his closest advisors. Organizing itself as The Child Study Association, by 1915 it had severed its official ties to Ethical Culture and become independent.

Adult and professional education remained a concern for the movement. In 1905 the Board approved a plan for developing a night school—but nothing came of this. Meanwhile, harking back to the Ethical College and the Plymouth School, the annual conference of Ethical Leaders at Glenmore in upstate New York, 1907, once again discussed a summer project. What was needed, they said, was a program to consider "in a large and informal way the problems which confront the ethical leader and teacher. We desire criticism and suggestion of those who are not officially identified with the Ethical Movement. . . ."

The next year a Summer School of Ethics was organized at Madison, Wisconsin. In the fall of 1908 John Elliott was able to report,

13 Interview with Dr. Ruth Pilpel Brickner, 1964.

. . . the rooms were filled to overflowing and the people [were] standing both in the rooms and hallways. . . . The people reached were
earnest people—young college professors, high school principals, etc.
. . . The University showed its good will at the close of the session by
making advances in the way of offers to credit the students who had
taken work and inducements to the School to return to Madison next
year. . . .[14]

The summer school at Madison continued for four years under the
directorship of Anna Garlin Spencer, who was now an Associate
Leader in New York. It was, in the main, self-supporting and worked
in close cooperation with the University of Wisconsin. On its faculty
were Jane Addams and several of the younger men who had come to
the Ethical Leadership: Henry Neumann, David Muzzey, and John
Elliott. The major theme was moral instruction—the attempt to help
teachers, social workers, and ministers educate for moral growth.
There were difficulties too. Poor publicity adversely affected attendance during the fourth and last year of the program. Plans for a
School of Religion at Madison promised a competition in the area.
There were occasional attacks on the school as "unChristian."

Adler was not closely involved in the Madison venture. During its
first year, he had been abroad as Roosevelt Exchange Professor in
Germany. And the International Conferences demanded his attention. Coupled with these distractions, Adler felt that the summer
school at Madison was too popular in its appeal. The pure and austere
discipline of ethics might find itself compromised in the market place.
The late Dr. Henry Neumann reflected,

> Dr. Adler was not any too enthusiastic. . . . We finally persuaded him to
> come out during one of the sessions. . . . He gave one address . . . it
> wasn't well received at all. . . . his manner seemed very cold. . . . He
> didn't like Wisconsin. . . . He feared [that] Ethical Culture as he saw it
> would be contaminated. . . . So the Summer School of Ethics wasn't
> continued even though it had some good results. . . . Not that he [Ad-
> ler] would merely say, "no." But after a while people would give up try-
> ing to warm him up because when he was chilled you had to be careful
> that you didn't start sneezing. . . .[15]

14 Board of Trustees, Minutes, New York, October 5, 1908.
15 Interview with Dr. Henry Neumann, 1962.

Again the motivation for the continuous investigation and teaching of ethics to adults could not find permanent expression.

But if failure marked the application of ethical pedagogy to adult education, the school for the young flourished. A philosophy of community found expression in the school with the formation in 1909 of a student council in the high school and, in 1910, of a teacher's council. Adler had taught well the lesson of social ethics.

His colleagues played their part in this evolution. Percival Chubb, reporting to the Second Congress on Moral Education in 1912, spoke of the "festivals" which had developed in the School. Highly critical of what he called "fad-ridden and overcrowded" curricula he sought to find correctives for education's tendency to verbal abstraction and compartmentalization. Building on the idea of the school as community, he pointed out that the citizens needed communal celebration, i.e., that meaningful community included an expressive aesthetic dimension. Through festivals and other free dramatic forms, the arts, history, and the sciences could be brought together, as it were, naturally. The creativity of the person as citizen, the recognition of beauty as a valid element of community were part of the experiment in education that was the Ethical Culture School.

In a different way, yet building on the same principle of community, John Elliott spoke to the same International Congress on Moral Education of the need for student government as, "the most effective kind of moral training [which] makes the pupil feel a sense of his own responsibility for thinking out right ways of acting for himself and for his own group." Student government, moreover, was a natural outcome of the ethics classes and insurance against their becoming empty exercises. Elliott continued, "All who are to receive a genuine impulse from the ethics lessons must in some way, I think, become active, both the individuals as individuals and the group as a whole. . . ."

Student self-government was not conceived as a panacea, nor were there any illusions about its inherent problems. At the January, 1913 meeting, the New York Board of Trustees discussed discipline in the schools. The principal, Mr. Lewis, reported, "The policy is to throw the responsibility for maintaining the proper order upon the pupils themselves. . . . The object is pedagogical—to cultivate self-control. We cannot cultivate self-control by forcing control on individuals when they are able to control themselves." Mr. Lewis admitted that this did not lead to a perfectly ordered school; there were frequent cases of disorder, boisterous talking, and laughter in the corridors. But, there was none of the "traditional antagonism between pupil and teacher," and when issues were put before the students they "tended to respond constructively."

The application of community to the schools, the continuing effort with adult education, and a better defined philosophy of education were contributions of this period in the movement. However, Adler's limitations were beginning to pose problems. His pure idealism, which had led to the conscientious break with the synagogue, his prophetic passion, which had stirred thousands of people, and his skill in organization, which had carried the Ethical Society from one lecture platform to world organization, were not matched by sensitivity to trends of the times. Evidenced by his attitudes at Madison and toward the Child Study Association, Adler's suspicion of psychology (at least in its "analytic" manifestations) and of popularity was a source of tension as his movement entered the twentieth century.

By then Adler was nearing his fiftieth birthday. His ideas had been shaped by an earlier day, and a rapidly changing world had moved too fast. For all that this was a period of fulfillment of an earlier promise, it was, too, a time of emerging difficulties.

CHAPTER XI

John Lovejoy Elliott

Emerson's moral religion may have had heaven and earth for its beams and rafters, but it had flesh and blood human beings for its pillars. Adler, Coit, Salter, Weston, Sheldon—each stamped his personality on the society he was creating. The men and women who joined them did so for the sake of an idea, but also in response to the particular way that each of these men embodied that idea in institution. Ethical Culture was not revealed in the desert, or in words engraved in stone, or by the voice and thunder from the mountain top. The symbol for this urban industrial movement became an identifiable face, voice, and personality in the shapeless, anonymous crowd. In a sense, biography replaced theodicy.

No one more clearly illustrated this than John Lovejoy Elliott, whom the New York Board of Trustees voted in 1894 to employ "for one year at a salary of $700 as an assistant to Professor Adler." Elliott was born in 1868 at Princeton, Illinois, and raised in the Midwest. His parents, Elizabeth and Isaac, were neither wealthy nor poor. He walked to and from the one-room schoolhouse where he was educated, rode horseback, and was nourished by the out-of-doors life of the farm frontier. In a letter written near the end of his life, Elliott recalled that childhood nostalgically:

> . . . anything that reminds me of the farm where I grew up is pleasant. One of my brothers said that I was probably the most ignorant boy about work that ever left a farm, and while this is possibly true, I have very pleasant memories if not about work, at least about neglecting it. In the first place, I can't remember the time when I didn't have a horse or a pony that used to take me far and wide into the woods, off to a house of a distant neighbor where I would spend the night with a best friend; and then there were the sunrises and the sunsets and the stars and the storms. . . . The farm animals had real personalities and I still claim that I knew how to be a wet nurse to a calf as well as anybody. . . .[1]

But the family was not ordinary. Elizabeth Elliott was the step-daughter of Owen Lovejoy, congressman, abolitionist, friend of Lincoln, and the niece of Elijah Lovejoy, crusader and editor. Isaac Elliott had served with Robert Ingersoll in the Civil War. The ideas of Paine and Voltaire were familiar to the Elliott household. The family were not churchgoers; indeed, a "close association with the anti-slavery movement and with civil war had caused the nation . . . largely to take the place of the church." [2]

John was the oldest of four boys, who in their younger days waged the inevitable conflict; later, Elliott's younger brothers, Walter and Roger, were to join him in his work at the Hudson Guild. Elizabeth Elliott, a remarkable woman, did more than the schoolhouse to educate her sons, especially her eldest. Her influence continued and her concerns became his: an idolization of Lincoln and outrage at injustice.

In 1888 John Elliott enrolled at Cornell University, where he became a very popular student and was elected senior class president. He remained an ardent alumnus. During his first two years there, Elliott expressed doubts about his career, writing that he was "deeply perplexed about the future." But in 1889 Felix Adler addressed the student body as guest lecturer about his work in Ethical Culture. Adler made a plea for workers in his movement: "There is a new profession, one that endeavors to teach people how to live. . . ."

[1] Letter to Mavis Chubb Gallie, December 26, 1940. Ethical Culture Archive.
[2] Elliott, *Fiftieth Anniversary Volume*, p. 95.

This struck a responsive chord in the young man. A year later, when Stanton Coit visited Cornell, Elliott made known his interest in the "new profession." Letters between New York and Ithaca were exchanged; Adler gave his approval, and Elliott was sent off to Germany to study for his doctorate. Elliott's letters from Halle to his family in Illinois, 1892–1894, are a mixture of homesickness and discovery. Adler had arranged introductions for Elliott to people in German society and in its intellectual community. Adler no doubt wanted young Elliott to develop greater sophistication than had been possible in his Midwestern and undergraduate experience. With good humor, Elliott half complained: ". . . the formal visits, the ball room conversation and manners generally are enough to bring my bold heart in sorrow to the grave. I never have seen much of fashionable society but I pray the Lord to keep me from experiencing any more of it."[3] Nevertheless, he enjoyed this new world and greeted it with an irrepressible humor that was characteristically his. In another letter he reported:

> The Kaiser's birthday was a great occasion, celebrated with cannon, flags and fireworks. In the evening young Germany had patriotism instilled into him by being allowed to parade the streets with a lantern and sing, "Heil Wilhelm, Heil!" Personally, I don't think much of the Kaiser. He never has taken any interest in my affairs and I don't know why I should in his.[4]

The tall, handsome young American met many young ladies, but he reassured his family, "I'll tell you when my heart is in danger, but so far it has never even been exposed."

Student societies were major enterprises in German university education. Dueling and dueling scars were as much a mark of the student there as fraternity pins and hazing were in the United States. Elliott never took it seriously:

> The president of the political economy society . . . was challenged to a duel but did not turn up to fight it. . . . A letter was written . . . asking that he resign his presidency. I signed it. . . . Well, the Herr Presi-

[3] Letter to his family, February 5, 1893.
[4] Letter to his family, January 29, 1893.

dent seemed to have gotten his courage back for what did he do but challenge the whole eight of us who signed the letter to mortal combat with sabers. . . . And the way that my seven co-writers have ceased to talk about honor is something remarkable. When the friend of Herr President came to ask me to give "satisfaction" I explained to him that I did not sign on account of the duel part but because Herr P. had not behaved . . . like a decent man. He then told me that I would be put under the ban by his society, and I told him I'd be glad to go under the ban if it would make them feel better. . . . He said that I could not associate with the aforesaid society and I told him that was a heavy blow but as I never had and did not care to associate with them I'd try to stand it. . . . You can form no conception of the feelings of this gentleman till you know what solemn awful occasions the challenging of a mortal foe are. Your loving son may come home with his erudite head chopped off. I have been going around all this week with a broad grin on my face. The other fellows don't know what they will do, but don't enjoy the situation as much as I do. . . . Did you ever hear of such asininity? [5]

Elliott was also studying hard. His German was rapidly becoming passable. His doctoral thesis, completed in 1894, was "Prisons as Reformatories." Preparation for the new profession neared completion and Elliott had developed into a witty, urbane man, though never losing the directness learned as a youngster. His interests had broadened. Toward the end of his European experience he wrote:

. . . and the music here in Germany, oh the music! You know I was always fond of it, but never could get enough till now. One hears such glorious music for such small prices compared to ours in America. But there is one country in the world for a poor man and that is America. There are a lot of things that we have not but we have a freedom in society and in politics that is worth it all. [6]

Returning for a brief visit to Illinois, he came to New York City to take up his work as assistant to Dr. Adler. The contrast between the two was striking: Adler was short, Elliott was tall; Adler had a wispy beard and balding head; Elliott, a full mustache and head of hair. Coming of German-Jewish background, Adler spoke in a high-pitched voice; Elliott, with American parents and grandparents, had a big

[5] Letter to his family, May 6, 1893.
[6] Letter from Berlin to his Aunt Jennie in Chicago, April 10, 1894.

voice and the purest of Midwestern accents. The scholar Adler looked to the idea, whereas Elliott, never quite comfortable with his Ph.D., found pragmatic responses. Both men had a sense of humor, but Elliott's was earthy and his relationships with people informal and open. Anger caused Adler to freeze and withdraw, but Elliott to raise his voice and pound the table. Both men insisted on a certain formality. Characteristically, remembrances of Elliott are expressed by anecdotes, usually humorous ones, while people who recall Adler seldom speak intimately. Henry Neumann, for example, recalled that Elliott's jackets "always had holes" in them because he was careless with his ever-present pipe. Jerome Nathanson, one of the young men whom Elliott most influenced, said:

> He was simple in his dress to the point of your having to tell him to go and get his shoes shined once in a while. . . . He liked beauty. He liked to look at beautiful women. . . . He loved music, art, . . . people. There was a kind of unpredictability about him. He was a man who surprisingly loved to engage in . . . backstairs gossip. When I was having dinner with him, not too long before his last illness, he suddenly looked at me with a smile and said, "Well boy, I finally got a good one on you." . . . And I said, "What is it?" I never found out . . . and I will die without ever knowing what it was. Now it wasn't real malice, but it wasn't gentleness. . . . I remember in a seminar one time, during the Hitler period, he was saying something and I said, "For all your talk about being this and that and the other philosophically, you're sounding like a complete absolutist." And he pounded the arm of his chair and said, "I'm no absolutist but some things are absolutely right and some are absolutely wrong." [7]

Elliott, though many recall him with a warmth and reverence that is near idolatry, could be cruel and his judgment of others very harsh. Many an amateur psychologist has speculated about his bachelorhood and about his lifelong devotion to his mother. Frieda Altschul, a member of the New York Society, reported: "One of our associates . . . said that the only time she ever saw Dr. Elliott in a temper, and it was a terrible temper, was when she asked him why he never married. She said he was just beside himself. . . ." [8]

[7] Interview, 1964.
[8] Interview, 1964.

Abstract matters annoyed Elliott and he kept his attention on the concrete, particularly problems of human relationships. Elliott carried on a lifelong love affair with human beings, mostly troubled ones —criminals, the poor, the degraded, the exploited. His doctoral research on prisons was indicative. In 1894 he spoke of "the colored question" and commented that the country seemed to be going back on a stand it had taken thirty years earlier.

Elliott was at his best when he was with people informally and at his worst when he spoke from the Ethical Platform. Unable to copy the image of his teacher-scholar-prophet, Elliott achieved his greatness as the prototype of the social worker. Sidonie Gruenberg recalled, "You know we all idolized Dr. Elliott. He was so beautiful. . . . He was very jolly and friendly. And he always used to tease me because I must have been such a sentimental teen-ager and I felt that he was just wonderful."

Teen-agers and children—these friends tell much about the man. Janet Robbins, daughter of Mark McClosky, who was one of Elliott's "boys," remembered how "Dr. Elliott picked you up and hugged you as a little girl. We used to sit on his knee and he used to take out his pivot tooth and show it to us." Algernon Black said:

> A number of people who knew him said they never knew anyone who loved children more or enjoyed seeing children happy. When at the movies . . . he was looking at the children's faces reflected from the light on the screen. And he loved it when they laughed at the comedies. They howled, they clapped their hands. When there were good western adventures, you could hear the silence. He loved their eyes just sort of popping open watching these things happen on the screen. Or when he took children to the zoo—which he often did—he was really watching them more than the animals, . . . and he loved to get children who came into his room to "holler." He loved to "holler" himself, just to make a big noise.[9]

Characteristic of Elliott was how he helped young men growing up in the slums of New York's West Side. When they went to prison, as many did, he visited them and kept in touch with their families. He sought pardons for them; found jobs for them, or, when he could not,

[9] Interview, 1964.

found ways of providing money for them, usually out of his own pocket. If he did not marry, he never lacked for family. Perhaps his closest father-son relationship was with Mark McClosky, a West Side boy who later worked at the Hudson Guild and in time became a major public figure in federal and state government. McClosky referred to Elliott as "my beloved teacher." Elliott was a frequent visitor in the McClosky home and Janet McClosky Robbins recalled him as ". . . . the handsomest man in the world. . . . He used to stand in the doorway and anyone that knew him would recognize his chuckle and the way he had of throwing his hands up in the air in greeting." Edna Lemle described Elliott as "a man with the body and attitude of a prizefighter and the soul of a saint." [10]

Elliott and Adler not only bridged the gulf of their differences but worked together harmoniously to build the Ethical movement and its keystone, the New York Society. Perhaps the very contrast between them contributed to their successful relationship since neither could be a threat to the other. Perhaps Adler took particular satisfaction in seeing his movement validated by its appeal to a "typical" American like Elliott. Their difference in age (they were separated by a generation) eliminated doubt about authority and seniority.

Adler expressed confidence in his new associate, reporting to his Board in 1899 that he considered that "Dr. Elliott has the affairs of the Sunday School and of the many departments of the Society quite thoroughly in hand and he is a growing man." Elliott commented during this same period: "I feel very proud as Felix thinks I am working too hard. It makes me grin because I am not, but am quite willing that he should think so." The two conferred regularly—but not always amicably:

Felix and I have a walk and a talk every Monday at five, and it is a bright spot in the week. One thing, however, disturbs me very much. I am still living in this brainless and purposeless world of attending to little things with the sense of being driven from morning till night. . . .[11]

As Elliott developed a career of his own, he ceased to pay strict attention to the "many departments of the Society," which was a source

10 Interview, 1963.
11 John Elliott, Memory Book, 1900.

of tension between the two men. Thus Elliott wrote, "Temporarily, I am on very good terms with Dr. Adler—almost chummy in fact—but probably his dyspepsia will get out of order and then I will hate him for a while." Yet Elliott's respect for Adler never wavered. Jerome Nathanson recalled, ". . . next to [Elliott's] mother on the pedestal was Felix Adler. He revered Adler . . . [as] the most important influence on his life next to his mother without question. And I've been trying to think if I ever heard him say anything unkind about Adler and I can never remember anything." As V. T. Thayer saw it, "John Elliott . . . exemplified in his actual relationships with people what Felix Adler was preaching as a prophet."

When Elliott was elected Senior Leader upon Adler's death, he was hesitant at moving into Adler's office at the New York meeting house. Grace Gosselin Lindquist described the situation:

> The whole room [Adler's study at the New York Society] had a stiff feeling. . . . Dr. Elliott said to me, "You know, I have never felt that this room was mine. It always seems to me . . . Felix Adler's room." . . . One afternoon . . . I called Mr. Kohn, who was then the Chairman of the Board, and asked if it would be all right if I had Dr. Adler's desk moved. . . . Mr. Kohn said, "I think that's fine." So I got the desk out of there and began to shove the furniture and got some plants in the window and a bowl of fresh flowers, and turned up all the lights, and left Dr. Elliott with his Morris Chair and his own table. When he came back in the afternoon he was so grateful. He said, "You know, for the first time I feel as if that room is really mine." [12]

Elliott was not content merely to tend to details, and he could not be just an assistant. He did not acquiesce to Adler (though he saved disagreements for private discussion) but formulated his own thoughts. Elliott sought ways of making his own mark in the name of Ethical Culture. Thus began the association of John Elliott and the Chelsea district on New York's West Side, a social but a personal story as well.

New York's West Side in 1895 was a noisy, crowded, dirty slum; the streets were scenes of violence; every block from West 14th to West 34th Street was dotted with bars; lumber and freight yards, ships and

[12] Interview, 1964.

docks, were bustling with activity. And the vocal pattern was an Irish brogue. If there is truth in the old saw about the attraction of opposites, Elliott's romance with Chelsea was its demonstration. Fresh from his European experience with a brand new Ph.D. (the people in the neighborhood never fully understood the Dr. in Dr. Elliott's title) and committed to his "new vocation," Elliott at twenty-six started his life work among the people of one of New York's worst neighborhoods.

People in the slums were rightly suspicious of uptown "do-gooders." They'd been betrayed too often. The law, the landlord, the boss, the politician, the social worker were the enemy. Violence and alcohol were good medicine for the pain of living. No one chose to live in places like Chelsea; poverty is never romantic to the poor.

Elliott moved into a rented room in Chelsea, which was in itself a puzzlement and a break in the usual pattern of uptown benevolence. He seemed to want nothing for himself, nor was he saving souls or converting the heathen. He was just there, and curiosity led people to him. At first it was the young, more adventurous perhaps, certainly more than willing to test any intruder. One of the Chelsea gangs, the Hurly Burlies, found Elliott first. Seventy years later, the *Chelsea-Clinton News* wrote:

> Chelsea's crap-shooting teen-agers moved into a room Elliott rented, and no sooner were the doors opened than other boys began to come, by the hundred, to drink, break the furniture, break each others' heads. . . . Within two years the clubs had proliferated so fast that new quarters were found in a loft over a mattress factory. . . .[13]

By 1897 more than 200 people were involved with Elliott in the clubs, gymnasium, library, and employment bureaus known collectively as the Hudson Guild. Since the young were involved, their parents became interested, too. For support Elliott turned to the New York Society and its Young Men's Union, urging the importance of "bringing the men and women of the educated class in direct contact with the poor and uneducated classes of the City." [14] The response was good and the Guild continued to grow.

---

[13] *Chelsea-Clinton News*, 1965.
[14] Board of Trustees, Minutes, May 10, 1897.

When Elliott brought gangs into the clubs, he did not impose irrelevant rules of conduct. Nor did he seek to import middle-class
standards into the neighborhood. Instead, he identified himself with
the people of Chelsea and their problems. His efforts didn't tame the
wilder impulses of the young people. In 1900 Elliott wrote:

I had a very enjoyable and quiet Sunday, but woe is me, when I got back
on Monday morning the whole neighborhood was up in arms. Our small
boys had been playing ball on the street during Sunday, and the doctor
up the street, the policeman on the corner and the old lady next door
were all quarreling for pieces of my scalp.

When I want to go out I have to watch and see if the coast is clear, and
then . . . make a dash for a trolley car. Last night a policeman came
. . . and delivered himself of an oration, his theme being, "The Scum of
the Earth."

I really do not blame these people very much as we are a noisy lot, but
nevertheless, they will have to stand it.[15]

Elliott's guiding idea was helping people to help themselves. While
never developed as a philosophical alternative to Adler's transcendental idealism, that outlook informed his lifelong experiment with
"neighborliness." And certainly he evaluated his experience as he pro-
gressed. It was a satisfying way of looking at life, perhaps too home-
spun and simple to be intellectually respectable, yet it accomplished
for Elliott what religious ideas are intended to accomplish. Mrs.
Lindquist remarked:

Dr. Elliott was one of the few relaxed people I think I knew. He had a
great passion for getting things done. . . . But he was never sharp and
shrill about it . . . as I came to know him better, I think he was a man
at peace with the world. . . . He was never satisfied with what he himself could do but he believed in the ultimate goodness of everybody.[16]

As the neighborhood grew, so too did the Guild. By 1899 there
were 250 members, six clubs for adolescents, a kindergarten, a
mothers' club, and a variety of classes. A self-governing Guild council,

---

[15] Elliott: Memory Book.
[16] Interview, 1964.

the first neighborhood council in the country, was formed. An innovation was the presence of women as voting members. Everything was grist for the mill—fighting landlords, preventing eviction, checking truancy, nursing sickness, finding jobs. H. Daniel Carpenter, now headworker of the Hudson Guild and a member of the Board of Trustees of the New York Society, said:

> . . . Back in 1907, someone made a survey in the block and there was not one bath tub in [it]. The city had been establishing public baths. . . . As the story goes, they invited the President of the Board of Aldermen to come and eat with them and they packed the gym with mothers, and as he arrived they chanted "we want a bath, we want baths." And, they got the baths.[17]

In 1904 the Guild formed its own court to deal with internal discipline. A flat was rented in 1901 to house five workers who moved into Chelsea to help Elliott. Relationships were developed with other settlement houses in the city, many of which had been started by members of the Ethical Society.

The Guild also founded a number of related agencies. In 1912 a proposed print shop received a small grant from the Printing Trades Union which was matched by New York printshop owners and a School for Printers' Apprentices was started. An employment bureau for unskilled women, now a part of the New York State Employment Service, was developed. There were free outdoor movies in the summertime and a co-op store. In 1915, on the twentieth anniversary of the Guild's founding, the neighborhood presented a bronze bust of Lincoln to the Guild in honor of Elliott. Proudly, they reported they had raised the money themselves without any help from uptown.

A year later a model tenement was built by the Guild. Janet Robbins commented,

> 441 West 28th Street was the first one of the limited dividend houses built through the interests of both Hudson Guild and the Ethical Society through Al James. . . . It had indoor plumbing, a bathroom in each apartment. . . .

17 Interview, 1964.

A number of the staff of Hudson Guild lived there, and it made it seem like a family. Dr. Elliott kept an apartment there. . . . I can remember his library—a room that was a kitchen in other apartments—a large family kitchen . . . with leather chairs.[18]

In 1917, in the shadow of war, the Guild was given a 500-acre farm in northern New Jersey. Produce from the farm was sold at the co-op store, and the acreage was developed for use by the families of the Guild. In cooperation with the Child Study Federation, 200 Chelsea children were enrolled in the first all-day summer play school in the city. The romance of 1895 was by now a well-established and successful marriage. If, as with most marriages, there were occasional problems, including paying the bills, Elliott insisted with sublime confidence that problems would be solved, money would be found, and work would go on.

Elliott gave more and more of himself to the work in Chelsea, where he derived his greatest satisfaction. Yet he continued to carry much of the burden of the New York Society and the Ethical Culture Schools. He taught in the Ethics classes, visited the Sunday school, spoke from the Platform, officiated at marriages and burials. Through his work both at the Guild and at the Ethical Culture Society he became a leading figure in social reform. He signed the petition to found NAACP in 1909, was a co-founder of the American Civil Liberties Union, and chairman of the National Federation of Settlements. Visiting cities across the country to meet with Ethical Societies, he kept in touch with the rapidly expanding field of social work.

Elliott was appreciated by the members of the Ethical Society, who regularly supported the Guild. Participation in its work was one of the exciting privileges, especially for the younger and newer adherents of Ethical Culture in the city. On the other hand, few Guild people found their way to Ethical Culture.

Elliott, ever mindful that he was working out the dimension of his "new vocation," wrote:

Although these occupations are varied and may seem disconnected, they have a common source and a single purpose—the attempt to perceive "the uncommon good in the common man" and to give that good new

18 Interview, 1964.

ways of expression. . . . To have seen a spiritual ideal, a pure religion, taking body and form, acting upon individual men and women and moving in the life of communities has given me perhaps the deepest ground of hope in the present and conviction and faith for the future. . . . The churches celebrate the holy communion as their most sacred symbol of the relation of God with man. The Ethical Religion bases itself on another kind of holy communion, that of man with man, and endeavors to express this sense of the ultimate sacredness of daily living and in the work of the world.[19]

For Adler, the nature of man was to be sought in an infinite ideal universe of which this world was but an imperfect indicator. Human nature as a social and psychological phenomenon was not, for Adler, the subject of uncritical appreciation. He rejected as naive and false a belief in the natural goodness of man. Adler distinguished the transcendent worth from the empirical value of every human being, and empirical determination might well show that many human beings were of little value. Elliott's "uncommon goodness in the common man" was, for Adler, a highly sentimental notion. In this Adler was the more astute psychologist; Elliott, the more effective social worker. While Elliott never gave up entirely Adler's transcendent faith, his work and life challenged Adler's austere and rarified aristocratic view of an Ethical Culture. Elliott's religion of democracy was personal and never fully realized as a reformation of the founder's pure moral religion. Elliott's lack of philosophic interest, his pragmatic and highly personal approach to problems, served to diffuse Adler's sharply defined and sophisticated position. Yet Elliott's sensitivity to the problems of urban man and his highly effective solutions were necessary to remove the movement from its nineteenth-century mold. The tension between these two different yet essentially related perspectives held "uptown" and "downtown" apart for Elliott. Elliott juggled the two in a sometimes precarious balance, and Ethical Culture inherited an uncompleted transition.

[19] *Fiftieth Anniversary Volume*, 1926, pp. 98–99.

CHAPTER XII

The City Wilderness: The Social Worker's Response

Islands of ethnicity grew in every American city by the turn of the century. Although America dreamt of itself as the melting pot, the reality was the hyphenated American. Each neighborhood had its characteristic accent, language, stores, churches and synagogues—and the neighborhood house, or settlement, became a bridge between past and future. Together with the public school it provided a means for passing new citizens into the American mainstream. If early Ethical Culture represented a way for the "successful" immigrant to Americanize himself, as the elder Morganthau had suggested, the settlement house and related agencies helped the "deprived" immigrant accomplish the same ends.

Coit had introduced the settlement house to America from the example of Toynbee Hall in London. Ethical Culture experimented with similar ventures in Philadelphia, Chicago, and St. Louis; Jane Addams founded Hull House in Chicago in 1888; in New York, Lillian Wald did the same on the lower East Side. Social work theory was beginning, led by innovators like Robert Woods in Boston. By the turn of the century, fifteen years after Coit's pioneering venture with the University Settlement, settlement houses were well established. Every major city had its neighborhood projects, some privately sponsored, some initiated by churches and temples—all the work of a handful of dedicated, inspired individuals. In many ways it was a family affair. Settlement house workers across the country were unified by their desire to create a constructive alternative to the callousness of lassez-faire individualism. These early workers all knew each other's dilemmas and frustrations—and experienced occasional petty jealousies:

> Lillian Wald is raising a great campaign for money. . . . Of course, this makes us all bitterly jealous; even Dr. Adler rages when she claims to have started all the things that he himself started. Well, on Thursday, I had a little row with Dr. Adler and made him quite mad because I wouldn't write a letter to Lillian Wald telling her that she wasn't as smart as the papers said she was. I declined to write the letter because I thought if anybody wanted to write it, Dr. Adler should do it himself.[1]

New York City was the scene of the most elaborate development for the settlement house. The city's location as doorway to immigration, its large Jewish population for whom the settlement house was a natural extension of the secular thrust of much of Jewish culture, and its growing population made likely this new kind of social reform. Ethical Culture, interested from the outset and deeply committed under Elliott's leadership, maintained close and continuing ties. *The Ethical Record* regularly devoted a section to the "social settlements." In 1900 *The Record* reported on Maxwell House near the Brooklyn Navy Yard—"negroes in the area are not coming in"; the development of a summer house at Green Farms, Connecticut, by the Friendly Aid Settlement; East Side House; the University Settlement complaining of the "distressing moral atmosphere of the district due to incompetent and corrupt political administration and lack of a paid worker"; the Alfred Coming Clark Neighborhood House; Hartley House; Greenpoint Settlement under the direction of the Pratt Institute Neighborhood Association; Whittier House in Jersey City; the College Settlement on Rivington Street on New York's lower East Side; Hull House in Chicago. Included were descriptions of the strug-

---

[1] John Elliott, Memory Book, 1916.

gling labor movement, efforts at adult education, job placement, probation work, legal aid, kindergartens, schools for children of working mothers, and health services. Initial efforts at coordination and training of settlement house workers were described, which later gave rise to the profession of social work and to the New York and later the National Federation of Settlements.

To a family trained in the customs of small villages, the tenement house was a mysterious place. Settlement workers attempted to train new immigrants in tenement housekeeping:

> . . . a flat on Henry Street (NYC) has been taken and furnished with muslin curtains, . . . tables, plain, solid and stained, . . . a screen made from a clothes horse and hung with ten-cent chintz, towel rollers made of broom handles. Of course the beds are of white iron, easily washed; the chest of drawers without ornamentation and the chairs with no dust-collecting cushions.

> In this flat there are classes, very informal, . . . with the intention of teaching the neighbors how to make a fire in a stove which does not draw very well; how to wash and dry and iron with the disadvantage of a clothes line hung in a sunless air shaft, . . . how to keep the closets free from ants and cockroaches. . . .[2]

A money economy was also strange to many of the slum dwellers. The Consumers' League was founded to inspect the quality of goods available for purchase as well as the conditions of the workers who manufactured them. Adult education included practical matters but also music, art, and poetry. Cooper Union's evening classes were filled, and the Educational Alliance on the lower East Side had an enrollment of more than 5,000 men, women, and children.

Ethical Culture was involved with all these efforts. Adler and Elliott led many of the successful men and women from uptown into the work of helping people help themselves. The theme of the national convention of the Ethical societies in Philadelphia, April, 1900, was "The Function of the Social Settlement," and discussion ranged from practical needs to philosophy. "Hunger for beauty, the wonders of nature, the longing for music," "aid in foreigner assimilation," and enrichment of the public school curriculum—all were discussed. The

---

[2] *The Ethical Record,* February, 1903, p. 116.

headworker of the College Settlement described how it sought to "minister to the spiritual needs not available in the churches" with Sunday afternoon "ethical" talks. Others saw the settlement as a mediator between capital and labor. Adler spoke of the problems between the generations, between "Americanized youth and old world traditions."

In the work with settlements political reform was touched upon, but did not achieve the total program envisioned by Coit. Under the heading of "Current Comment" the following appeared in *The Ethical Record*:

> . . . the price of brutality abroad is paid in part here at home. The daily story of death and shame in our slums shocks . . . now one and now another public institution or body. It has lately been brought home to some of the churches; and there is more talk of a crusade against the forces—the foul political gangs of tribute-takers and the conniving police authorities—who are responsible for the moral ruin that is being spread among the young and innocent.[3]

The experience with social work had important effects on the development of Ethical Culture. Elliott was forcing a transition from Adler's aristocratic ideal toward a more democratic interpretation of Emerson's moral religion and Kant's categorical imperative. Especially among younger members, the opportunity to serve became the motive for affiliation. Another kind of Ethical Leadership arose along lines of social work to stand with those modeled after the scholarly, academic, and ministerial ideals.

If Elliott was unable to work out a philosophy of ethical idealism as a religion of democracy, he nevertheless suggested a number of ideas for the application of Ethical Culture to social work. Adler's doctrine of worth was, for Elliott, the essential postulate of social work: "The fundamental purpose of social work must be to give people self-respect. And to do this we have to begin by respecting them and then demonstrate this by our actions." [4] In the notes for a Sunday address in 1913, Elliott assimilated Adler's philosophic symbols to the practices of social service:

[3] October, 1900, p. 31.
[4] Notes, Ethical Culture Archive, c. 1905.

. . . it is the spiritual element that is lacking in our social reform work.
. . . I would call life spiritual where the . . . self-shaping element in
man takes the material things of this world and shapes them to some
noble end, adapts them to the highest human use, uses them in such a
way that justice comes to be done; . . . so I say that social reform will
never get on until the people who are interested in it go down deeper
than they are going now. . . . Now you want to approach these people
that are at the bottom. . . . You are not to teach but to learn from
them. . . . I will admit their ignorance, their pitiful weakness, the dirt
in which they often live, and the drinking in so many cases. . . . Among
the submerged tenth it lives, this spirit of holiness. . . . It lives there
among . . . the people of the abyss. We are insolent if we come forward with a bit of bread. . . . Organize . . . as though you were
dealing with people who have their contribution to make and give them
a chance to make it. . . . Only by a deeper conception of democracy
. . . will we get the vision which will make us able to help them. . . .[5]

It was against this changing background of Ethical Culture that the
Down-Town Ethical Society took shape. In December, 1889, a committee from the University Settlement met with Adler and Elliott to
discuss the start of an Ethical Society on New York's East Side. Because there was fear that uptown influence would not be well received in the tenements and because there was also hesitance about a
sectarian approach, it was agreed that the New York Society would
not "appear publicly as a patron." Initiative would have to come from
residents of the neighborhood, though Elliott was to conduct classes
for children; a class on the ethics of conduct was organized for young
men, and the New York Society stood ready to provide support as
necessary. In 1899 the East Side Ethical Club was organized on Madison Street with some forty members. The annual meeting of the New
York Society, 1901, heard that the venture was flourishing:

The Down-Town Ethical Society was organized to meet a vital need for a
new moral movement. . . . Our young people . . . have become so
absorbed in the social (i.e., the labor) question that they either neglect
the moral and spiritual problems or express an optimistic belief that
these problems will take care of themselves after a solution to the question of bread and butter is found.

[5] John L. Elliott, unpublished manuscript, October, 1913.

A considerable number of young men and women are passing through the period [where they try to] adjust the new with the traditions . . . of their parents. The Society has been active in the crusade on the east side. . . . We are establishing Residence Quarters which three of our members will occupy.[6]

The program tried to Americanize without destroying the traditions of the older generation. Adler addressed the Board in 1906:

The idea which is of particular interest to me in our work downtown is . . . that it is a harm to the East Side immigrant and especially to the Russian Jew to be Americanized by being taught to obliterate his race history and race consciousness. The aim at the down-town house is to develop the highest type of Americanization which shall develop race consciousness on its highest side and a feeling of race pride in the contributions of what is best in the Jewish race, making it all culminate in American citizenship.[7]

Adler was still responding to those who had accused him of treason to Judaism. Also, his interest in the validity of cultures contained an attack on left-wing reform, which he felt put too singular an emphasis on material improvement.

Henry Moskowitz, headworker of the Down-Town Society, was a native of the East Side, born in Rumania and brought to this country as a child. His mother had been educated in a convent; his father had been head of a Jewish congregation. An alumnus of the University Settlement, he was a member of its Social and Education Improvement Club, all of whose members went on to college and into the professions. Moskowitz was, therefore, a classic example of the success of second-generation immigrants. Following graduate study under the sponsorship of Adler and the New York Society, he became an Assistant and later an Associate Leader in New York, serving from 1899 until 1914. Though he taught in the schools, spoke occasionally from the Platform, and helped with weddings and funerals, most of his effort went into reform work on the East Side.

The career of Henry Moskowitz exemplified a newer turn in the Ethical movement; in a more complex world, specialization chal-

---

[6] New York Board of Trustees, Minutes, May 6, 1901.

[7] *Ibid*, November 6, 1906.

lenged the renaissance ideal of Ethical Leadership. Adler had spoken of specialization in ethics. It became evident, however, that the "specialist" in ethics, unless he were an academician, was inevitably forced to make a narrower distinction. Thus, Moskowitz was drawn to the new breed of politican who, unlike the reformers of an earlier day, was making over political machines for new purposes. An interest in housing reform led Moskowitz, together with Paul Abelson, also a member of the New York Society, to develop the East Side Civic Club. The cloak-makers' strike in New York City in 1910 found Moskowitz serving as secretary to the arbitration board for the industry. The Triangle fire in 1911 brought him in touch with Frances Perkins, later secretary of labor in Franklin Roosevelt's New Deal cabinet, and with Alfred E. Smith, later Governor of New York State and candidate for the U.S. Presidency.

Political realism—the "art of the possible"—even for the sake of reform did not sit well with the gentlemen of the Ethical Society. Independent idealism, which had motivated Adler's work with the Committee of 15 in electing a reform mayor for the city, was suspicious of all clubhouse politics. Increasingly, Moskowitz found himself at odds with the New York Board of Trustees and Adler. In 1915 when an opportunity came to take a post with the newly elected city government of Mayor Mitchell, he accepted and resigned his Leadership.

But we are moving ahead of our story. The Down-Town Ethical Society was flourishing. In its first years it was as much a religious movement as a settlement house. It conducted classes for children and adults in ethics, comparative religions, philosophy, the arts. It provided affirmative values for many who though Jewish by temperament and origin were at the same time utterly secular and often antagonistic to the synagogue and Hebrew religion.

> For the younger men and women the old faiths have lost their marrow and are regarded as lifeless creeds out of joint with present thought and conditions. Although eloquent . . . in destructive criticism, they have no religious faith to substitute for the old; the more thoughtful take refuge in a material skepticism . . . while others lack that courage and energy even to face the problem. . . . The integrity of the family is impaired . . . The helpless children are left alone with little conscious mora

guidance except the indirect moral training obtained in the public schools. . . .[8]

By 1911 the Down-Town Society had a membership of over 500 adults, some twenty-nine different clubs, and a summer camp program for boys and girls. Its headworker and staff were playing a role in the political and economic life of the city. But it was evident that the hope of marrying settlement house and Ethical Society was failing. Over the decade from 1901 to 1911 mention of the spiritual element in the program was increasingly rare. In 1913 the Board of the New York Society asked Moskowitz to give a report on changing the name of the Down-Town Ethical Society to Madison House.

The statements of Dr. Moskowitz show unequivocally that the Down-Town Ethical Society as an organic branch of this Society ceased to exist more than a year ago, . . . due to lack of financial support from persons interested primarily in the direct furtherance of the Movement for Ethical Culture. On the other hand, the . . . philanthropic work . . . set in motion by the Down-Town Ethical Society has engaged the interest and financial support of a number of persons, many of whom were either actively or passively out of sympathy with, if not actually prejudiced against the Society for Ethical Culture. . . . To retain such support it was necessary to dissever the organic connection between the practical work and the Society. . . .[9]

While this change was regretted, Madison House continued to grow and cordial relationships continued as well. The New York Society cooperated with the settlement's camping program, continued to assist in fund-raising drives, continued to supply leadership to its Board of Trustees, and from time to time encouraged one or another of its Leaders to work at the House. For example, Algernon Black was headworker at Madison House during his training for Leadership in the New York Ethical Society. Madison House itself began when alumni of University Settlement felt called upon to serve the lower East Side. In 1917 Arnold Toynbee House was founded by graduates of Madison House. Coit's initial importation from England in 1886

[8] *The Ethical Record,* February 1901, p. 144.
[9] New York Board of Trustees, Minutes, June 2, 1913.

was now in its third generation. The grandchild was appropriately named.

The city was a wilderness, but the city's children had little experience of natural wilderness. Milk came from bottles, fruit was stolen from a store, and green was the color of the sick and the drunk. About the turn of the century a fresh-air movement was developed to give slum youngsters some experience of the countryside. Southwark Neighborhood House, begun by the Philadelphia Society, founded Camp Linden to meet the needs of its city's children. In New York under the Presidency of Walter H. Liebman of the Young Men's Union, eighty acres of land was purchased in Orange County, New York, in 1901 and named Felicia in honor of Felix Adler. Children of the Hudson and Down-Town Ethical were sent there for summer vacations. By 1904, 485 children each had a two-week vacation there and by 1917 the camp cared for more than 700 children. Janet McClosky Robbins recalled the days when her father and mother directed the program for children who were Irish, Spanish, and Italian; Catholic, Protestant, Jewish; Caucasian and Negro.

> Camp Felicia had a sort of family feeling about it. . . . In those days they had counsellors who were . . . from the neighborhood and older adults who took their two-week vacation to be counsellors at the camp. . . . And so the counsellors all those years were either neighborhood children grown up or children from Fieldston School or colleges around, or children of members of the Society who were honored to do it. It was a wonderful mixture of Harvard and 10th Avenue and Madison Street.[10]

Summer play schools were started at the Hudson Guild in 1917. In March of 1918 the Federal Child Welfare Department expressed interest in the idea, declared 1918 "Children's Year," and attempted to open the public schools in summer on the model of the Guild program. John Elliott reported:

> The bad effects of the war had been shown so far in the very little children, the amount of crime in the Chelsea neighborhood has never been so great. There are probably many reasons for this among them the continued high cost of food and the very bad winter. . . . With the young people of an older age the question of the summer . . . is a very serious

10 Interview, 1964.

one. . . . It would seem a great mistake . . . not . . . to continue this very important work. . . . The social care of our young people is needed especially at this time. . . .[11]

Although troubled by financial difficulties as a result of the war, the societies nevertheless supported their projects. Under the direction of Dr. Benjamin E. Gruenberg, three play schools were organized in the summer of 1918 at Hudson Guild, Madison House, and Toynbee House to serve an average daily attendance of 380 children.

A miscellany of other social welfare efforts were undertaken by the Ethical Societies. The Children's Guild of the New York Society organized and conducted housekeeping classes for tenement house families; under the chairmanship of Mrs. Adler, the Guild to Visit the Sick supported district nursing services and helped introduce school nurses into public schools. A Guild for Aiding Crippled Children was organized and in 1904 established a permanent home for children at Hawthorne, New York, called Blythdale. Henry Neumann recalled:

When Eleanor [Adler] was one of the visitors to Blackwells Island . . . she found a young cowboy . . . who had lost both his legs. . . . She managed to have him trained . . . and got him a job. . . . She could go to the businessmen in the Society . . . as her father's daughter . . . [and] see if there was a place for a man with one arm, for example . . . best of all she went to John Elliott. He got a room set up at the Guild called the Bureau for the Crippled, an employment bureau. . . . It was distinctly understood that it was not a charity but a strict business. . . . The need was increased enormously with World War I. . . .[12]

The women of the New York Society established a sewing society for the employment of poor seamstresses, "regardless of creed, race, color." And in 1902 Mrs. Henry Ollesheimer, president of the Women's Conference, announced that the Manhattan Trade School for Girls would open its doors on 14th Street that fall.

Work in the city ranged from concern with one crippled cowboy to the troubled generations of immigrants. Deed was rampant, often to the exclusion of creed and eventually to the exclusion of Ethical Culture as well. The desire for human dignity was central to the works

[11] New York Board of Trustees, Minutes, May 6, 1918.
[12] Interview, 1962.

contributed by the Societies, but the emphasis on human need made it increasingly difficult to formulate a philosophic interpretation necessary for the continuing reconstruction of a moral religion. Adler was not intimately related to the settlement house efforts; much of the welfare work was regarded as a role for women of the Society; the experience of Moskowitz with the reformed political clubhouse and the insights of behavioral psychology and social psychology were alien to the philosophic idealism that still represented the symbolic and intellectual capital of the movement. The work was good, and its inspiration was drawn from the social idealism of ethical religion, but Ethical Culture was becoming fuzzy around the edges.

CHAPTER XIII

The New York Society: Like Topsy

From the first convention of the Societies in 1886 to the First World War, education, international organization, and community service mushroomed. But limitations began to appear too. The movement was paying a price for Adler's charisma. His disinterest in some of the major changes in the world around him and his hostility toward others could drive this price very high indeed.

Ethical Culture recognized and sought to overcome this weakness by nurturing a succession of "prophets"—that was the intent of a plural Leadership—and by institutional transformation. Adler was well aware of his blind spots and of the need to protect the movement from his own weaknesses. If he was conservative about institutional growth, it is undeniable that the Societies that he personally helped initiate—New York, Chicago, St. Louis, Philadelphia, Westchester, Brooklyn—survived, whereas those that began more spontaneously were but brief notations in the record, e.g., Wilmington and Detroit.

Adler could never escape the fact that he was the founder. Try as he might to do so, and he did try, he was the center of Ethical Culture. In consequence his colleagues seemed to direct their energies

133

outward in order to fulfill themselves. Some, like Moskowitz, matured in the movement but completed their careers elsewhere. Ethical Culture could not escape the chains in which movements are caught at their founding stages. A centripetal force pulled people toward Adler and a centrifugal force drove them away.

No clearer instance of this pattern existed than the New York Society itself. Adler, the New Yorker, was at the center of the movement; the founding Society was its locus and New York City its environment. While some might resent it (there is still half bitter talk within the movement about the "New York establishment") it was a fact of institutional sociology. To New York gravitated most of the wealth that was to accrue to the movement (though it was never very great). Leaders were trained there, and many of the innovations, like the schools and the settlement houses, were rooted there. If Ethical Culture had a national image it was in terms of New York and its Leadership. New York became the national headquarters and the most successful development of societies grew in the New York metropolitan area.

The New York Society added new services, projects, and functions each year. Programs proliferated without apparent control as Adler sought to make room for others and as others sought to give their own expression to the motivating idea. As early as 1899 the Directory of the New York Society covered two full pages under some thirty-six different headings. These ranged from the Sunday meetings to the Mount Pleasant Cemetery Society and included adult education, a normal school for teachers, a "bible" class conducted by John Elliott, the school on 54th Street with a branch on the East Side, various study groups in applied ethics, the child study group, the United Relief Works, the District Nursing Service, the young men and women's associations, classes for working women, a choral union. If the Society and the movement lacked planning and focus, they did not lack energy, leadership, or work.

In 1904 Anna Garlin Spencer called for a publication to define what the Society was doing—"The difficulty of getting together the material for this pamphlet should serve to convince us of the need for such a book." [1] Twelve years later Dr. Adler was still calling for coordination of the various branches of the Society.

[1] New York Board of Trustees, Minutes, November 7, 1904.

There is a sign of incompleteness in the workings of the Society. Some of the groups do excellent work, . . . yet they are not in touch with each other. It is very important that the Federation for Child Study be interested in the vocational ideals that are discussed in the Industrial Group. . . . The Women's Conference is giving a series of excellent lectures that all the groups ought to know more about. Dr. Adler's own group of thirty young men . . . has invited representatives of all the foreign nations in New York . . . to form a cosmopolitan club to stand for the best municipal ideals. . . .[2]

Many capable men and women participated in the planning and execution of the various projects of the movement. The presidency of the New York Society was held by men of genuine public stature— Professor Edwin R. A. Seligman, who was Professor of Economics at Columbia and heir to one of the great banking fortunes in the country; Robert D. Kohn, later president of the American Institute of Architects; and Herbert A. Wolff, son of Alfred Wolff and a partner in the New York law firm of Greenbaum, Wolff and Ernst. On the New York Board were people like Lionel and Florentine Sutro; Alexander H. Bing, a builder; Abraham L. Gutman, an attorney; Joseph M. Price; B. Edmund David, a manufacturer; and Sidney Blumenthal. The latter two were among the first businessmen to experiment with industrial democracy. A group of remarkable women gravitated to lay leadership in the movement, for example, Frances Hellman (neé Seligman), Jennie Fels in Philadelphia, Martha Fischel in St. Louis, and Miriam Sutro Price, who worked to improve the public schools of New York City.

Adler was not above political maneuvering. Florence Klaber recalled an experience of her father, Alfred Wolff:

. . . Before Professor Seligman became President, my father, who . . . had a feeling that only the people who were not only heart and soul in the thing but were the workers should be officers, . . . was approached by Dr. Adler. Dr. Adler . . . said that there was absolutely no question that he [Wolff] should be the next President of the Society. ". . . you will work just the same whether you are or not. But he [Edwin Seligman] needs a boost.". . . That hurt my father very much, not that he wasn't President but that Dr. Adler would take that kind of view and try to

2 *Ibid.*, December 11, 1916.

strengthen the Society by bringing in someone who although a member and supporter was not giving the fullest. . . .[3]

Adler was driven to make a thing work. He never stopped at the point of throwing off sparks of ideas. He gave equal thought to people to carry out the work and to sources of money for it. Some stories of Adler as fund raiser are so outrageous in their boldness as to sound almost apocryphal. Yet the following by Herbert Wolff may be taken to be accurate:

> In the old days, if there was a deficit . . . Felix Adler would be advised of the amount. . . . I remember one year . . . $25,000 was needed. Professor Adler phoned to people like Joseph Plaut, B. Edmund David, Mr. Berolzheimer, Mr. Oppenheimer, maybe one or two others. There was a command to appear at his office on a certain specified day at 5 o'clock in the afternoon. He . . . then told these gentlemen that the deficit was $25,000. . . . Each one—there were five present—said that he would undertake ⅕ or $5,000. . . . The other members of the Society were not involved. . . . Some of them didn't even know that there was a deficit. [4]

The movement took pride in its founder. On the occasion of the twenty-fifth anniversary of the Movement a $10,000 Felix Adler Fund was established for scholarship purposes in the school. A Chair in Political and Social Ethics was created at Columbia University, the funds raised by members of the New York Society, and Adler named to fill it in 1902. With the Society's program expanding and with Adler's interests leading him in differing directions and his age advancing, the question of new Leadership in New York had to be faced. The responsibility for finding and training leaders for the movement as a whole had to be settled too.

Stanton Coit, through his association with the idealistic young men who were founding Fabianism and fighting for social democracy in England, was more than helpful in suggesting candidates. One was Percival Chubb, an organizer of the Fabian Society who had worked with Coit at South Place in London. Born in an Espiscopalian home, he was influenced by Emerson Matthew Arnold, and T. H. Green. In 1884, at the age of twenty-four, he was a follower of Thomas David-

[3] Interview, 1962.
[4] Interview, 1964.

son and a member of Davidson's Fellowship of the New Life. He had listened to Moncure Conway at South Place. Active in British reform, he was inevitably drawn into assoication with people who were changing religion, philosophy, social thought. Coit arranged for young Chubb to visit the United States:

Mr. Percival Chubb, one of the founders of the London [Essex Hall] Ethical Society, . . . is spending a year in this country and has spoken for the Ethical Societies of Chicago and Philadelphia. Mr. Chubb is a philosopher of no mean ability, an earnest student of the social question, a man of letters who writes with something of the charm peculiar to cultivated Englishmen, and withal captivates those who meet him by his sweetness and simplicity of manner.[5]

A few years later Chubb returned to live in the United States. Starting as a teacher at Manual Training High School in Brooklyn, he soon joined the English department of the Ethical Culture School and in 1899 became principal of its branch school. Chubb's teaching stressed the moral importance of literature, the arts, the dramatic celebration of community values. Ruth Adler Friess recalled:

I loved Mr. Chubb and the wonderful Shakespeare course he gave . . . the thing I . . . enjoyed the most was Mr. Chubb [himself]. He had such enthusiasm; . . . he had a beautiful voice and read very well. . . .

The Christmas Festival was a big thing in the school . . . there were regular Christmas decorations of evergreens . . . e.g., a medieval Christmas or a folk Christmas. We . . . trooped down to the gymnasium . . . singing our own special carols. We had some presentations, usually some mummers, and St. George and the Dragon. . . .[6]

In 1905 Chubb was named an Assistant Leader of the New York Society. Not until he was named Leader of the St. Louis Society, however, did he have the opportunity of applying his aesthetic concerns directly to an Ethical Culture Society. While in New York, he, like Elliott and Moskowitz, accepted specialized responsibilities. Following Coit's lead, Chubb distinguished social reform from religion, see-

[5] *The Ethical Record*, Vol. III, No. 1 (1890), p. 57.
[6] Interview, 1964.

ing the former in political, the latter in philosophic, aesthetic, and even mystical, terms.

Ethical "mysticism" is rooted in that wonder of the self-conscious and creative spirit of man—whether in the dawning mystery of a child's soul or the twilight mystery of a body spent. . . . It is the sprit of life itself. . . . What is more bafflingly mysterious? Selfhood, character, personality, individuality—out of which issue all heroisms and discoveries, ideals and adventures, sciences and arts—here is the root of all mystery and all healthy mysticism. . . .[7]

To the gentlemen of the Ethical Society, this must have sounded esoteric. Yet they could not escape the validity of the man even if they found his expression unusual. Nor could they ignore his brilliance as a teacher. Personality overcame philosophy, and Chubb was accepted as a cherished co-worker, just as he came to accept, though not to agree with, these busy Americans. Chubb's openness was never more clearly expressed than on the occasion of the movement's fiftieth anniversary. Then sixty-six years old, he wrote:

The story I have sketched . . . is a story of "learning by doing." I had no academic education and no professional "preparation." Literature, philosophy, social reform, education, ethics—my life has been a ceaseless eager education. . . . I never expect to be quite ready. Equipment for so large a task as ethical leadership is an endless endeavor; . . .[8]

In 1904 the New York Society, on the recommendation of Dr. Adler, elected Anna Garlin Spencer as an Associate Leader. Trained as a Unitarian minister, she had been one of the young rebels who had heard Adler's criticism of the Free Religious Association. She was born in Massachusetts in 1851 and had been minister of a small church in Providence, Rhode Island. She was an advocate of women suffrage, a pacifist, and a vice-president of the Women's International League for Peace and Freedom, but her career in Ethical Culture was relatively brief.

---

[7] Percival Chubb, "The New Venture in Faith," *Fiftieth Anniversary Volume* (1926), p. 89.

[8] *Ibid,* p. 83.

Adler spoke highly of Mrs. Spencer for her work in philanthropy and the ministry and felt she could do much to organize the "women's work" of the Society. Apparently, he saw her as complementary to Elliott, working primarily with the distaff side of the membership. But she was not comfortable in the specialized role conceived for her, nor was Adler pleased by Mrs. Spencer's "unwomanly" strength or certain of the causes that she embraced. Sidonie Gruenberg said:

> . . . those of my generation were a little alienated . . . by the fact that he [Adler] didn't believe in women's votes and that he stood out for not marrying anybody that had been divorced. . . . He had a very patriarchal attitude toward women. . . .
>
> Anna Garlin Spencer . . . was a wonderful woman and a very good friend of mine. . . . She didn't feel that she was really *in* . . . a tiny little person [with] a very fine voice. . . . She cared about people . . . as did Doctor Elliott.[9]

Adler in recommending her was struggling to broaden the scope of his movement. The appointment of Mrs. Spencer was a victory for Adler; her resignation some ten years later, a defeat. Repeated attempts were made to find an appropriate place for her. She accepted responsibility for the American Ethical Union, for the women's organization, for propaganda work. But she left in 1913 to become Assistant Director of the New York School of Philanthropy (now Columbia University's School of Social Work) and later taught at Meadville Theological Seminary, a school for the training of Unitarian ministers.

Failure was no stranger to Adler and the movement. The effort had been made, even if unsuccessfully, and made at a time when professional careers for women were rare indeed. Even today when the ministry is open to women, more often than not they are restricted to religious education and work with children and other women.

Another unique spirit in the ranks of Leadership was Alfred W. Martin. Born in Germany in 1862, he was raised in Canada and educated at McGill in Montreal. On graduation from Harvard Divinity School, he was appointed minister of the First Unitarian Society in Tacoma, Washington, in 1892. A year later he removed himself and his church from Unitarianism to build a "free church movement,"

[9] Interview, 1963.

founding the first Free Church of Seattle, but continued working
with the Tacoma group. He was one of the liberals who sought to
establish free religion as a protest against more conservative Unitarian practices. Martin became a vigorous pamphleteer in the name of
"universal" religion, asserting that varieties of faith, rightly understood, were in basic harmony, and conflicts were only apparent. He
published such titles as *The Symphony of Faith, The World's Great
Religions, Fellowship of Faiths*. A colleague described Martin:

> . . . a life long . . . purpose of what he called "appreciation"—a
> word to which . . . he helped to give a place, and a high one, in the
> verbal hierarchy of the thinking mind. . . . Appreciation was the great
> instrument, the supreme means towards composing religious, philosoph-
> ical, ethical and political differences and arriving at syntheses above the
> dust of battle. . . .[10]

In 1901 Martin, in "The Ethical Culture Movement and Why It
Fails to Satisfy," [11] attacked Ethical Culture's "agnosticism." However, in 1906 he met Felix Adler.

> A recent conference with . . . Professor Felix Adler, has made it
> painfully apparent to us that we have seriously erred in our judgment,
> . . . and we take this first opportunity to retract our criticism. . . .
> The Ethical Movement is not an "agnostic" movement. It does not stand
> pledged to any of the various theories of the universe—theistic, aethe-
> istic, agnostic. It is peculiarly an ethical movement. . . .[12]

Adler invited Martin to give two lectures before the New York Society, informing the Board that if these were satisfactory he intended
to invite Martin to Ethical Leadership. In the following year Martin
was named an Associate Leader of the New York Society. His free
church movement in Washington state survived for a time and for a
brief period the group in Tacoma identified itself as an Ethical
Society.

In New York, Martin developed a regular program of Sunday evening lectures on comparative religion and the higher criticism. The
meeting hall was filled and gave promise of rivaling the Sunday

[10] George O'Dell, "Alfred W. Martin," 1932. Ethical Culture Archive.
[11] Ethical Culture Archive.
[12] "A Criticism Retracted," in *Universal Religion* (October, 1906), p. 133.

morning meeting. (Among those in the audience was John D Rockefeller, then teaching Sunday school at the Riverside Church in New York.) But, however large the audiences, there was little if any direct increment to the membership of the Society.

Martin began to turn toward a spiritualism radically different from Adler's transcendentalism. Adler insisted that differences had to be respected. Martin published two books on the subject, *Foundations of Faith in a Future Life* (1916) and *Psychic Tendencies of Today* (1918), maintaining that perfectability could not be attained and that what was worthwhile in human beings had to continue evolving. Thus whatever his differences from Adler, Martin accepted the concept of religious evolution.

In November, 1899, Dr. Adler reported on a young scholar named David Muzzey who was to give a course for the New York Society on the History and Significance of the Chief Sects of Christianity. Born in 1870 and graduated from Harvard, David Muzzey earned a degree at Union Theological Seminary in 1897 and a doctorate in history at Columbia in 1907. He became a teacher in the Ethical Culture schools (Adler used this means to test people for Leadership) and was named to Associate Leadership of the New York Society in 1905.

Muzzey's career in the Leadership was paralleled by an equally distinguished career as historian at Columbia University. Muzzey was one of several men in Ethical Culture who had multiple careers. Noteworthy in the Leadership were James H. Leuba, professor at Bryn Mawr and a leading scholar in the psychology of religion; and Nathaniel Schmidt, archeologist, linguist, and Professor of Oriental and Semitic Languages at Cornell. Adler, himself, maintained an academic career from 1902–1921. Keeping in touch with secular scholarship and secular institutions helped the movement escape the trap of sectarianism.

David Muzzey was a controversial figure for much of his life. Henry Neumann recalled:

> He [Muzzey] took part in the parade that some men got up . . . who favored votes for women. I remember his telling us that when the parade passed a street corner a man in the truck picked out Muzzey and yelled: "Hey Bessie, you're losing your sidecombs." [13]

[13] Interview, 1962.

Muzzey was a short man, somewhat shy with strangers, whose utterances were always precise and fact-filled. In striking contrast to the warm, blustery Elliott, and to the prophetic, fire-filled Adler, his preciseness had a cutting edge. In 1922 a citizen's association in Washington, D.C., attacked Muzzey for daring in a history text to deal with the American revolution more objectively than patriotically. Similar attacks were made in Georgia, Illinois, and New Jersey. The Hearst papers carried a cartoon depicting a "rat named Muzzey" gnawing at the foundations of the schoolhouse.

> History wasn't history in those days. It was just a soft public relations job. I used to get ten letters a day challenging me to duels for not being respectful enough to George Washington, Robert E. Lee, the Supreme Court and the original colony of Georgia which, I pointed out, had been started by James Oglethorpe as a haven for convicts. My, what squawks I got.[14]

While Muzzey seldom filled a pastoral role, he helped found the Westchester Society and served as its Leader for many years. When the movement organized its new publication in 1914, Muzzey suggested that its title, *The Standard*, be taken from a quotation from Washington's inaugural address: "Let us raise a standard to which the wise and good may repair." He contributed a scholarly tradition to a Leadership that blended the social worker's concern, the reformer's passion, the pastor's caring.

Thus the new generation of Leaders in New York were Elliot, Moskowitz, Chubb, Spencer, Martin, Muzzey, each with a particular talent and direction. Elsewhere Leslie Willis Sprague, Henry Neumann, and the Englishmen George O'Dell and Horace Bridges were working. Salter, Weston, and Sheldon were still active, though Sheldon died in 1907, leaving St. Louis without Leadership for five years. This seemed a large enough group of leaders for so small a movement, but the search for men continued, motivated by the movement's commitment to serve more than its parochial needs. In 1910 Elliott reported that he had visited Cornell seeking young men for the movement and that Adler had spoken at Yale for the same purpose. On the movement's fortieth birthday, Adler said:

14 Ethical Culture Archive.

. . . we must all face the fact that both School and Society are imperiled unless new Leaders are found. This is our weakest point . . . , for not only are we not responding to the demands from other cities but even our present Societies are running great risks. There is nothing to which we should all devote ourselves more than this providing for our successors. . . .[15]

Important as the search was, Adler and the others maintained their standards. A report in 1918 rejected a prospective candidate:

He [Adler] particularly emphasized the differences in point of view of [the candidate] and the Society, the former showing greatest strength in attacking the weakness of orthodoxy while the Society has tried to extract from it its contribution to human welfare. . . . [The candidate] wants particularly to enrich the mental life of those . . . people . . . crippled by barren dogmas while the Society has always made it its task to combat the great social sins, materialistic tendencies, etc., to change moral idols into moral gods. . . . Our Society did not start from the narrowness of people's lives but rather from the egregious shame of the social evils, the exploitation of the workman, and religion was needed as an engine to stop these outrageous things. . . .[16]

The internal life of the New York Society had found its pattern, paralleling the experience of institutional churches. The Sunday school (which Adler tolerated but never accepted) was highly moralistic. Florence Klaber said: "We have responsive readings. . . . almost always they were readings written by Dr. Adler . . . also during the Assembly period (we) would rise up and give the motto of the day." [17] The Sunday school was small in relation to the Society's membership—evidence that not everyone found it meaningful. Complaints were voiced about the lack of "poetic and emotional" elements in work with children. But despite opposition, scepticism, and indifference, the Sunday school grew, admitting the children of nonmember families in 1901, and by 1906 boasting of ten classes for children and six for adults. Each class, naturally, undertook some practical work of social service as part of its studies; Ethical Culture gave a special accent to even its most churchlike activities.

[15] NewYork Board of Trustees, Minutes, December 11, 1916.
[16] *Ibid.*, February 6, 1918.
[17] Interview, 1963.

Clubs for older boys and girls were created in 1899 to overcome "the difficulty of keeping boys and girls who have reached the age of fourteen or fifteen in the Sunday School. . . ." The teen-age program developed a unique approach and was the forerunner of later innovations in youth education. The formative influence of the clubs was due primarily to the adults who led them, e.g., John Elliott and David Muzzey. The clubs were modeled after the settlement houses but transplanted into a middle-class environment.

The Young Men's Union had some 200 members by 1901 and was engaged in programs of education and sociability, along with fund raising and social welfare. A characteristic meeting heard Rabbi Charles Fleischer of Boston on "Ralph Waldo Emerson." The women of the Society organized into the Women's Conference in 1891 "to encourage sound and practical efforts in the direction of social, educational and moral reform, and to promote union among the women of the Society." The group provided volunteers for the various settlements, supported the District Nursing Services, established the Manhattan Trade School for Girls, and the Crippled Children's Guild. The Public School Visiting Section under the guidance of Mrs. Price made major contributions to public education and was successful in instituting classes for defective children in the public schools. In 1901, twenty-five years after the founding of the movement, two women were elected to the New York Board of Trustees for the first time.

The separation between the prophetic and the institutional became more apparent. Part of the membership was motivated toward the service of others; another part was drawn toward satisfaction of personal needs. The demands of each, which found partial expression in the sense of disorganization, were increasingly difficult to satisfy. Two different memberships began to emerge, one highly autonomous and found primarily on the Board of Trustees, the other relatively dependent and found in numbers both at the Sunday meeting and in the organizations of the Society. The proliferation of programs was a symptom, too, of the change going on in the American way of life, the rise of a middle-class culture.

The attitude toward membership wavered between openness and restriction. Adler had always held that true membership in an Ethical society was always smaller than its apparent membership, for he defined true membership by inner consecration and commitment to

personal change through personal effort. In 1905 Adler told his Board
that admission to the Society ought to be "as free as they possibly
could make it" while encouraging the individual in growth toward a
"serious" sense of his own commitment. Yet in 1908 the Board provided for a membership committee to "investigate through the sponsors the qualifications of the applicant"; only after such investigation
would election to the Society be considered. In 1908 Alfred Martin in
a highly critical report called for more courteous reception of the
stranger, especially at the Sunday meeting. Mr. Chubb in a "plan for
propaganda" asked for greater militancy in attracting people. He criticized the Society and the movement as "too cautious and conservative . . . not having acted as people with the fire of a new faith
burning in them."

It was not until 1893 that formal provision for admitting women to
membership in the Society was made and an associate membership
for minors created. By 1894 the Society had 681 members contributing some $16,000 a year. In 1904 the New York Society, recognizing
its dual character as both local Society and national movement, provided for "non-resident" membership where no Ethical Society existed.

There were calls for "democratizing" the Society. A resolution was
adopted in May, 1907, "recommending abandonment of the former
policy of secretiveness with regard to the finances of the Society" and
calling for publicity about the discussions and actions of the Board.
Despite apparent agreement, practice by and large continued as before. Old habits were hard to break and possessiveness, justified as
guarding the "purity" of the movement, prevented basic changes.
Adler tried to remain above the battle, but his attitudes encouraged
those who took a more protective and conservative view. Yet Leadership, program, and membership reflected liberal transformation
made necessary by demographic and social change in the American
and world communities.

A climactic event was the building and dedication of the New York
Meeting House. As groups proliferated around the city—in New
Rochelle, Harlem, the Bronx, the lower East Side—sentiments arose
to situate the Society in a central and permanent location. As early as
1893 George Seligman had raised the question. Again in 1897 a com-

mittee was appointed to secure funds and a suitable site. In 1898 yet another committee was formed and by 1899 the building fund had reached the $350,000 mark. In 1904 the Society, aided by Henry Morganthau, Sr., purchased land on Central Park West between 63rd and 64th Streets in New York City for $250,000 and planned buildings estimated to cost some $600,000. Adler was unsure:

> It has been an advantage to the Society in some ways to be in a public Hall . . . the occupying of Carnegie Hall had probably helped to make the Society more all-embracing and cosmopolitan than it would have been if housed from the start in its own building. He felt that our influence as a Society would be less far reaching should we become a church among churches. . . .[18]

If the meeting house was a problem, a permanent home for the Ethical Culture School was not. In 1904 it moved into its new quarters at Central Park West and 63rd Street. Meanwhile, Adler wavered for and against a building for the Society. In 1907 he urged that "how to make this movement permanent" was the leading consideration:

> From the first, our Movement has been conceived with the aim of making it . . . stand upon its own feet. . . . Dr. Adler's interest in the new Hall is chiefly determined by the paramount consideration of its helping to establish the Society on a permanent basis. This is the reason why everyone should put his shoulder to the wheel, because this Hall would be one more assurance that the Society will continue.[19]

Adler resolved the question of the building in a highly personal decision about the meaning of the work he had begun. In his late fifties he alluded repeatedly to his own mortality and seemed haunted by the fear that with his death his movement might also die. In a letter from Germany, Adler echoed that thought,

> . . . the new interest in the building . . . has been exceedingly encouraging to me and I am happy indeed . . . that you seem to meet with a good response. "We must work while it is day for the night

---

[18] New York Board of Trustees, Minutes, June 5, 1905.
[19] *Ibid.*, March 11, 1907.

cometh when no man can work!" We must do what we can to make the
Society permanent, and certainly a Hall of our own is one of the principal
requirements.[20]

With Adler clear at last about the importance of a meeting house
and with much of the money in hand, work was begun adjoining the
school building. In 1910 the meeting house of the New York Society
was dedicated. Professor Seligman began the ceremonies with a brief
address on the significance of the Platform:

> Whatever honest ritual, whatever poetic symbolism may in time com-
> mend itself . . . now and doubtless as long as we shall exist, the spoken
> word will be the chief vehicle of inspiration, instruction and support.
> But . . . the Platform is subordinated as well as preeminent. It is
> placed low, the seats of the hearers rising in amphitheatrical shape
> . . .; the Leader who utters the word is not set up . . . high above the
> heads of his hearers, delivering to them a revelation from above . . .
> arrogating to himself supernatural powers of mediating in inexplicable
> mysteries. He is an interpreter. . . .[21]

The auditorium was large, and paneled with woods of various hues.
Above the speaker's platform was embossed a motto by Adler: "The
Place where men meet to seek the Highest is holy ground." It was
Adler's kind of place, symbolizing austerity, simplicity, almost spiritual nakedness. Some, at least, found it cold; too austere. The centrality of the word was evidenced not merely by the placement of the
platform, but by the fact that of the five floors of the building three
were given over to the meeting room.

The dedication of the meeting house was for that moment, at least,
a vindication of the adventure begun in 1876 and of the man who had
led the pilgrimage out of orthodoxy into moral religion. The ceremonies, begun with a Sunday meeting addressed by Seligman and
Adler, continued through the week. Adler's colleagues came from
Philadelphia, Chicago, and St. Louis, and Gustav Spiller represented
the International Ethical Union. Mayor Gaynor of New York, in a
letter, praised Adler and the Society for its good works. Lyman Abbot, successor to Henry Ward Beecher in Brooklyn, spoke, as did

---

[20] *Ibid.*, February 9, 1909.
[21] Dedication of the Meeting House, p. 19. Ethical Culture Archive.

Stephen Wise of the Free Synagogue. Adler in his dedication address
expressed the hope of the Movement,

> May it become a place where no consciously untrue word shall ever be
> spoken, no ungenuine symbol ever be employed! . . . may this house
> offer sanctuary to those who here seek refuge from the world's cares and
> the world's sorrows! . . . May this house become a center from which
> sound influence shall radiate far and wide into the community and may
> it continue to serve the same purposes for other generations that shall
> come hither when we shall long have passed away! . . .[22]

[22] *Ibid.*, pp. 39–47.

CHAPTER XIV

Out
from the Center

New York was the center, but the work of the movement was going on elsewhere, if not vigorously; Ethical Culture's
followers knew that moral religion could not survive with only a center; they had seen restricted movements come and go, and the
group around Adler were builders. Successful in their vocational lives,
they respected success and measured it in down-to-earth ways: supporters, dollars, and influence. If they held on where this was not
forthcoming, as did Salter in Chicago, it was the exception to the rule.
As businessmen, they knew of the need for investment. Thus, coupled
with the drive to achieve a permanent, well-founded movement, was
a generosity for experiment.

Typical was the fellowship granted to Morris Raphael Cohen, a
graduate of New York City College and later one of its great teachers.
On Adler's recommendation Cohen was awarded a $750 scholarship
for graduate study at Harvard in 1904. There Cohen started the Harvard Ethical Society, which by March 1905 had some forty members,
to "influence University sentiment in the direction of the highest
ideals in personal, political and social life." A description of that Society included:

149

The theme for 1904–1905 was ethics in the professions with Dr. Richard C. Cabot . . . speaking on medical ethics, Colonel Thomas Wentworth Higginson on ethics in literature and so on. Royce lectured on race prejudices and a discussion was scheduled on "The ethics of football" in the light of President Eliot's criticism. Louis D. Brandeis spoke on legal ethics.

At the meetings . . . current affairs were hotly debated; the labor problem, the peace movement, railroad rate regulations and municipal reform. Speakers included James Perry and Frank Taussig, the latter two being members of the Harvard Ethical Society's advisory committee on which Dean Briggs also served. Cohen's grand coup was bringing President Eliot to address the society on December 5, 1905.[1]

Adler had certain doubts as to whether Cohen's "physical appearance and careless dress would not be a handicap" to Leadership.[2] Moreover, the student was departing from Adler's neo-Kantianism. Hence, Cohen continued to have close personal relationships with David Muzzey, John Elliott, and his City College classmate Henry Neumann, but he did not become an Ethical Leader and soon after leaving Harvard even ceased identifying himself with Ethical Culture. At Harvard, Cohen was also vice president of the Semitic Conference and, though not a synagogue-goer, identified himself with Jewish causes. With a growing interest in Zionism, Cohen moved further and further away from Ethical Culture, and the Harvard Society did not survive Cohen's departure.

Brooklyn was more hospitable to Ethical Culture. In 1906 Leslie Willis Sprague, a former Christian minister and an Associate Leader of New York, started a Society in the "borough of churches." Apparently, he was of two minds both about the ministry and Ethical Culture. Walter Sheldon wrote to him in 1905:

> It would give me great pleasure to have you . . . in St. Louis for a Sunday. And yet . . . I should want to exercise considerable caution about presenting you. . . . Twice before . . . I have introduced men here . . . when they were at work with Professor Adler and presented them as new men in our cause whereas after that they have drifted

[1] Leonora Cohen Rosenfeld, *Portrait of a Philosopher*, p. 71.
[2] Max Grossman, "Morris Cohen, Felix Adler and the Ethical Movement," *The Ethical Outlook*, XLIX (1963), p. 122.

away. . . . For those of us who really have consecrated ourselves to the work it is like a thing of life and death. I think we were all misled by our experiences in New York. . . . Everything there is on a big scale. . . . But elsewhere, relatively speaking, the Ethical Societies are like dots on a big map with nothing else big . . . save the passion of enthusiasm in the hearts of the few men who are working in the cause.[3]

Public meetings were inaugurated in December of 1905 and by spring the Brooklyn Society had a memberhip of sixty-five people, with "very few persons of more than ordinary means." Most of Brooklyn's founders had formerly traveled to New York to hear Dr. Adler. A moving spirit in creating the society was Ralph Jonas, prominent Brooklyn attorney, who during his lifetime helped organize the Brooklyn Chamber of Commerce, Long Island University, and who was successful in bringing a branch of the City College to Brooklyn. But not many of the members were leading community figures. The Brooklyn Society was a forerunner of today's middle-class movement. Civil servants, teachers, social workers, housewives—the founding group greatly differed from the eminent men at the core of the New York, St. Louis, Philadelphia, and Chicago societies. The difference was also marked by the increasing number of members of middle-eastern European rather than Germanic backgound. Anna Garlin Spencer was in a "positive fury when she first encountered . . . the attitude of superiority taken by German Jews toward Polish and Russian Jews. It was news to her. She couldn't understand why it was that some Jews looked down on others." [4] Its founding group also included Edward Gross, a Lutheran and a civil servant, and Edwin Foster, formerly a Roman Catholic and a bank teller.

Organizing was unfamiliar to most of the founders of the Brooklyn Society, and much effort and sacrifice were required. When Brooklyn built its Ethical Culture school in 1922, heeding Adler's insistence that no Ethical Society was doing its job without one, the pennies and dollars were gathered slowly and painfully. Henry Neumann recalled:

I like to tell the story about Tom Doyle, an Irish house painter from Mount Vernon who used to come into Brooklyn . . . every Sunday.

---

[3] April 17, 1905. Ethical Culture Archive.
[4] Henry Neumann, interview, 1961.

When he heard we were starting the school, he took out . . . a workingman's policy where you pay 20¢ a week. . . . On his death we found that the school was the beneficiary. . . . I could almost see the smile on his face in the coffin when I went to his funeral, because the niece in Brooklyn had him buried as a Catholic. Then there was Rose Isaacs, a little lame hairdresser . . . who for years saved all her tips and gave us that in a lump sum for scholarships. . . .[5]

Sprague had struggled to resolve his own doubts, but in 1910 he returned to the Congregational ministry. To understand the Brooklyn Society, however, one must look to Henry Neumann.

Neumann was a New York boy, in background similar to Henry Moskowitz, who graduated from City College in 1900. During his senior year he had attended the New York Society's meetings, and a classmate had introduced him to the Down-Town Ethical Society. Neumann was seeking to make up his mind between Reform Judaism and Unitarianism, and settled on Ethical Culture instead. Remembering himself during his early twenties, Neumann said:

I had gone through a state of disillusionment . . . when the world looked utterly grim and hopeless—idealism was nonsense. I was very fond of Thomas Hardy's novels. . . . I can remember how finally when I read *Jude the Obscure*, I touched bottom. . . . Then I heard John Lovejoy Elliott [quote] Thomas Carlyle [who] had gone through the same experience of . . . despair. "It may be true that the devil rules the universe, but there is always one spot over which he can have no control so long as I . . . say no!". . . I found . . . it meant so much to me that I wanted to pass it on to these young fellows [in the clubs]. . . .[6]

Neumann completed a doctorate in 1906 and was appointed instructor in English and education at CCNY. At the Down-Town Ethical Society he met and married Julie Wurtzburger, whose parents were ardent admirers of Felix Adler. For a time he served as assistant headworker to Moskowitz. More and more familiar with Ethical Culture, it seemed natural for him to take up the Leadership in Brooklyn. Meetings there were conducted at a Masonic Temple, the Aurora Grata Cathedral. At first the Society seldom drew more than a hun-

5 Interview, 1961.
6 Interview, 1961.

dred people, but gradually the audience grew and in 1912 moved to the Brooklyn Academy of Music, the borough's equivalent of Carnegie Hall.

Neumann, a life-long socialist, often recalled listening to the returns on election night: so and so many for the Democrats, so and so many for the Republicans, three for the Socialists—Henry and Julie Neumann and Dr. Neumann's mother. His own Leadership incorporated a bit of the Adler prophet, some of Elliott's social work, scholarship in literature and the arts. From the outset Brooklyn's was a family society, with a program of parties, picnics, and outings. Neumann was a fatherly personality, a bit old-fashioned and demanding on occasion. A continuing interest in teaching carried him to nearly every state in the union. His daughter, Ruth Hand, recalled:

> The summer Dad's harem [Mrs. Neumann and their three daughters] drove to California, we stopped for gas at a tiny crossward in Montana. The attendant seeing our license plate [said] he knew a man from Brooklyn. We three sophisticated teen-agers shrugged that one off, but Mother . . . discovered it was Dad he knew. He and his wife had been pupils of my father's in a summer session. From then on the frequent use of the initials P.O.M. for both Mother and Dad, meaning of course, Pupil of Mine.[7]

Neumann's special style as lecturer and raconteur stood him in good stead. And he was a worker. Indeed, to his death in 1966 Henry Neumann continued to speak from the Platform of the various societies, to counsel people, to marry them, to be available to them at time of death.

Not for Neumann was the specialization of interest or the freedom to explore within the security of a well-endowed institution. He became, in many ways, what traditional faiths call a pastoral figure, though on his Platform he never avoided difficult issues and in his teaching he found doorways to the wider world. The demands on him were quite different from those made in even the smaller societies like St. Louis and Philadelphia.

While Brooklyn and Henry Neumann were giving omen of what was to come, Chicago, St. Louis, and Philadelphia were experiencing

---

[7] Script on the occasion of Henry Neumann's eightieth birthday party, New York, 1962, p. 6. Ethical Culture Archive.

change and growth. Chicago, hard pressed for survival after Salter's unpopular defense of the anarchists, struggled on. By 1900 attendance was down and the membership widely scattered. An active women's club led by Lydia Coonley and Mary Wilmarth kept much of Chicago's work alive.

To make matters worse, Mangasarian, whose outspoken anti-Catholicism had caused his resignation from the movement, organized an Independent Religious Society in 1901 with a membership of over 500 and regular Sunday attendance of more than 1,500. Of its nine trustees, six had been members of the Chicago Ethical Society. Its statement of purpose gave answer to Adler:

> Recognizing the right of private judgment, the sacredness of the individual conviction, and the moral obligation to one's best thoughts, we require no assent to any theological or philosophical doctrine as a condition of fellowship but cordially welcome all who desire to promote the religion of truth, righteousness, joy and freedom.[8]

Chicago's Henry Booth House continued to flourish. About 1900 Nathaniel Schmidt took up residence there and from this association joined the Fraternity of Ethical Leaders. In 1905 a new building was dedicated for Booth House—although at the annual meeting of the Society only forty-two were present. The Society's Bureau of Justice merged with the Women's and Children's Protective Agency and became known as the Legal Aid Society. The Platform was continued, as was Salter's scholarly work.

By 1907 Salter resigned to devote the remainder of his life to his philosophic interests and to teaching. The conflict between moral religion and institution was clearly illustrated. If Mangasarian had been permitted to continue, he would probably have built a popular and viable institution. A majority of the members had flocked to him or just stayed away from Ethical Culture. Yet Judge Booth and other Chicagoans had rejected Mangasarian and supported Salter. Adler arranged a university post for Salter when the Society could no longer provide support.

Adler and his colleagues were convinced that the movement could not survive without representation in the second city. A staff of lec-

[8] Ethical Culture Archive.

turers began serving the Chicago Society in 1908, including Salter, Jane Addams, Nathaniel Schmidt, and Charles Zueblin. The tide began to turn. In 1909 the Society reported 189 members; in 1910, 194; and by 1913, 296. From its Platform John Dewey spoke on "Some Leading Ideas in Modern Education," and among the themes to which Chicago addressed itself repeatedly was "the Negro problem." In 1913, turning to another of the Englishmen whom Coit had won to the idea of moral religion, the Chicago Society named Horace J. Bridges as Leader. Bridges, a newspaperman in England, had joined the South Place Society in about 1899. Raised in the Church of England, he had flirted with the Baptist church while in his teens but found Coit's attempted revision of the Church of England more congenial. In 1904 he was invited by Coit to work with the British Ethical movement. Although with little formal education, he was a widely read and highly literate man and became a prolific author and a highly popular lecturer. During his first months in Chicago, attendance on Sunday mornings jumped to over 300 and until the 1940s Bridges filled the lecture hall. From a youthful Fabianism, Bridges had moved toward conservatism which became pronounced enough to attract support from some of the leading businessmen of Chicago, including General Wood of Sears-Roebuck. He also became the despair of the reformers who had looked to the Ethical Society for support: Jane Addams was alienated from Chicago, although she continued her friendship with John Elliott and Henry Neumann.

Bridges was proud of his American citizenship, but always retained a little of the Englishman, which led to conflict with his colleagues of German background on the advent of the First World War. For all his conservatism, the race question evoked Bridges's deep concern, so much so that he was a founder and first president of the Chicago Urban League in 1917. A strikingly handsome man, his journalistic skill appealed to a wide popular audience, unlike the philosophic subtlety of Salter, Adler, and the others. Whatever his departures from many of the attitudes of the Leadership, Bridges did cause the struggling Chicago Society to grow and for a time even to flourish.

In St. Louis, Walter Sheldon devoted himself to his interpretation of ethical religion. For him social reform began with personal change through education, and to this purpose the Self Culture Halls Association was created in 1888. Beginning with free reading rooms, lectures on a variety of themes were added, and branches sprang up throughout the city. Literature and civil government were discussed, but there were classes in cooking and dressmaking too—the settlement house idea with a heavy educational accent and minus the social reform ideology of Coit. The aim, as expressed in its strange, clumsy name, was to provide "opportunities for general self culture among workingmen and their families." Roger Baldwin, key figure in the organization of the American Civil Liberties Union, was among those who began their careers by teaching in the Association; he served as one of its directors. He recalled:

> It had been a sort of adult education institution and the professors of Washington University were primarily the people who were depended upon to teach as volunteers. . . . There were no public school evening classes at the time [1906] . . . so the Self Culture Hall filled the vacuum. . . . There were a number of [settlement] houses in St. Louis but none of them pretended to give what might be called University Courses in higher education to people who had only finished high school. It was a very lively center. . . . Located in a mixed Irish-Jewish district, . . . it was also a recreational center. . . .[9]

By 1893 the Self Culture Halls were separately incorporated, following the New York pattern, but the St. Louis Society continued to provide support. William H. Leighty, assistant lecturer of the St. Louis Society, served as director of the Self Culture Halls Association. Later, at the University of Wisconsin, Leighty drew on his experience in St. Louis to help build the University's extension program, one of the country's major ventures in adult and community education. He continued his interest in the Ethical movement, presenting a plan for a correspondence bureau to the American Ethical Union in 1911 and offering to direct it from Madison, Wisconsin. He hoped to develop an extension program for people who could not attend Ethical Societies. Unfortunately, the plan was never implemented.

The Self Culture Halls program grew. By 1899 it had over 250 members and by 1906 more than 350 members. As part of its work the St. Louis Society undertook in 1901 to found the Colored People's Self Improvement Federation, offering adult education courses to more

[9] Interview, 1963.

than two hundred people. This early venture followed the lead of such Negro spokesmen as Booker T. Washington, aiming at the tedious process of overcoming the handicaps of hundreds of years of slavery through education. The venture, as with much of Sheldon's work, lacked the militancy of social action, opting instead for gradual accomplishment.

Among the Society's lecturers were Nathaniel Schmidt, John Dewey, Warner Fite, Josiah Royce, and a host of other leading figures in the academic and intellectual life of the country. Roger Baldwin said,

> The Ethical Society in St. Louis was quite different from those I have seen elsewhere. . . . Its membership was very varied, very diverse. It was scattered all over town. . . . It was essentially a society of intellectuals who had not found satisfaction in any of the established churches. . . .[10]

Characteristic of St. Louis' intellectual air was the organization of a Political Science Club and somewhat later (around 1900) a Men's Philosophical Club. Led by men of genuine intellectual reputation such as Professor Frank Thilly of the University of Missouri and Professor A. O. Lovejoy of Washington University, it devoted attention to such themes as the history of philosophy and experimental psychology.

In May of 1896, when the St. Louis Society celebrated its Tenth Anniversary, a local newspaper reported:

> St. Louis is essentially a conservative city and does not take very kindly to anything strikingly new or radical. Yet it seems to have practically adopted this Society as one of its permanent educational institutions. . . . Happily the name has been changed, and that has made a difference. At first it was "The Society for Ethical Culture." That formidable title exists here no more. It is now plainly and simply, "The Ethical Society." [11]

Sheldon had within him the fire of the reformer. His emphasis on learning was a matter of principle, a decision as to method rather than

[10] Interview, 1963.
[11] *The Criterion,* May 29, 1896.

an expedient concession to the climate of St. Louis. In a moving address he described his conception of patient dedication:

> It means most of all to be willing to work for an outcome that a man will never see, to be willing to walk blindfolded all his days, to work for the vision within and to go down in death while the work is not yet done, while the battle is going on, while not one gleam has come to him of the fruits of his labors.[12]

These words were particularly poignant for in 1907 Sheldon died immediately following his return from a visit to Japan under the auspices of the Japanese Ethical Society. In memoriam, William Salter said of his colleague:

> We have been pioneers together in two western communities. . . . I think of that face with the deepset eyes, with the arching dome above them, with the firm tense mouth, yet so capable of sweetness as vanished, gone irretrievably gone! Mr. Sheldon . . . would not follow another's lead . . . he had his own peculiar ways of formulating things. . . . He spoke in an early lecture of an "ethical church" and later of "we, the clergy" an expression . . . that grated on me. . . .
>
> He wished above all to have his own life right. I feel this personal note in a very early statement he made. . . . "We shall not reform the world unless we are reforming ourselves. The most perfect man is never more than half perfect in comparison with what he might become. . . . There is not a day nor an hour when we do not need to be in a process of inward refining. . . ."[13]

For nearly five years the St. Louis Society continued without full-time Leadership. Like Chicago, it managed by filling in with guests from the movement and the community, and by the hard work of its membership. In 1911, Percival Chubb was asked to come to St. Louis as its Leader. Temperamentally akin to Sheldon, he found St. Louis congenial. In 1912 a memorial to Walter Sheldon was dedicated in the form of a permanent home for the St. Louis Society. By 1913 Chubb was firmly established in St. Louis, a gain of more than a

---

[12] "What It Means to Work for a Cause," reprinted in the *Fiftieth Anniversary Volume* (1926), p. 70.

[13] "Memorial Address for Walter Sheldon," 1907. Ethical Culture Archive.

hundred members was reported, and the Sunday school was enrolling 150 children.

While continuing Sheldon's educational emphasis, Chubb added his own aesthetic interest and began to introduce more formal church-like elements. For example, he instituted "recognition day" for students of the Sunday school on which those who had completed the course of study were recognized by the Leader as potential members. The Society began its "twice a year" festivals with the Children's Sunday Assembly (the Sunday school) as a "means of propagating our ideas on moral and religious education." In 1917 Sheldon Day was established to commemorate the founder of the Society. Chubb's innovations were not greeted with unanimous approval; in 1916 he asked his Society for "an open mind . . . on . . . the form that Sunday Meetings should take." He saw himself both on the frontier of American and of religious life, although certain of his ideas seemed to look to the past:

> The fellowship meets in a quiet place. The walls do not speak loud. They are a shell for silence and tempered speech and the tones of music . . . the pleasant plainness says . . . "I favor the meditative mind and I am a background of tranquility for it." Here the shy voice of the soul, lost amid the noises of the world outside, may be heard and heeded. In this still atmosphere the folded self may unfold to the light shed from communing minds and to the warmth of intimacy. A choral silence reigns here. . . . There is no cramped pulpit. . . . And so the many are made one in visible presence.[14]

On the East coast, Philadelphia continued on a steady course, buffeted only by the brief storm when Horace Traubel led the followers of Walt Whitman out of the Society and the Ethical movement. Philadelphia had the smallest membership of all the Societies. Its Platform, however, continued to be quite influential in the city and attendance at lectures, though not formal membership, continued.

During Salter's Leadership, one of the publications he edited reported:

> Occasionally those far away from Philadelphia come to know of the Society and are attracted to it. Professor and Mrs. William James of

14 *On the Religious Frontier,* pp. 68–69.

Cambridge, Mass. and Miss Perkins of Concord, Mass. have recently become members. . . .[15]

In 1899 a branch was organized as the Kensington Ethical Society, with a membership made up entirely of "working people." Philadelphia's program included a Sunday school and Sunday evening lectures, a philosophy section devoted to the study of religion under the guidance of Dr. Morris Jastrow, a business section, and a young people's section with lecturers on such themes as "Mind in Nature," "Emerson," "Single Tax Theory."

By 1906 the twenty-one-year-old Society was an established institution in the city and celebrated its anniversary by founding Southwark Neighborhood House, later enlarged by the purchase of three adjoining houses. To dedicate the venture, the Platform was manned on May 13, 1906, by social welfare workers from New Orleans, Washington, Cleveland, New York, and Philadelphia.

Philadelphia and Weston continued to serve as Ethical Culture's publishing house and source of propaganda. In the fall of 1914 the Society purchased a meeting house on Spruce Street. It reported that during its third decade the membership had doubled and the Society had "renewed its youth."

The founding Societies managed to survive and grow, and Brooklyn joined the ranks. But Harvard was not the only place where organization was tried and failed. In 1895 a Society was organized in Milwaukee under the Leadership of Mr. Duncan. In order to support it, the national conference was held there in 1898. Property was purchased and a program developed, but by 1910 Mr. Duncan had resigned and Anna Garlin Spencer reported,

. . . [I] attended three meetings at the home of Mr. Charles Scheuster of the remnants of the Ethical Society of Milwaukee. . . . It is thought that this small group could unite with one led by Mr. A. Dee Brown, former Baptist Minister who calls his group The Christian Socialist Brotherhood, and which is now using the Ethical Hall. . . .[16]

In 1915 Horace Bridges visited Milwaukee and spoke to a large audience. Nothing came of this and the Society died out. Similar short-

[15] *The Cause*, Vol. I, No. 5 (May, 1895), p. 23.
[16] Ethical Culture Archive.

lived efforts were made in Baltimore in 1904 and in Elmira, New York, in 1905. In 1915–1916 an Ethical Lecture Society existed in Wilmington, Delaware. Martin tried to reestablish his free church movement as an Ethical Society in Tacoma and Seattle in 1915, but without success. The First World War brought many members of Ethical Societies to the nation's capital, and they organized a Washington Ethical Society in 1918. After the armistice, these members returned to their homes and that Society ceased to exist. George O'Dell, serving as Secretary of the American Ethical Union, organized an abortive Society in Newark, New Jersey. Another unsuccessful attempt was made there in 1915 under the presidency of the Dean of the University Law School.

Perhaps symbols meaningful to the immigrant did not come across to the emerging American middle class; perhaps a Leadership conceived as embodying reformer, scholar, and prophet lacked necessary organizing and pastoral elements. Then too, other institutions were grasping the message that had seemed so fresh when first uttered by Adler. Social Gospel was at its height in Protestantism; Unitarianism was moving in ever more liberal directions. The younger radicals were finding a hold on the world in Marxism and socialism. Adler, who might have promoted reinterpretation and fresh insight, was in his late fifties and unable to escape his own past.

One may speculate on the reasons that prevented significant growth. Certainly a genuine national movement was never organized, which was a strategic error of major proportion. No movement could hope to grow in twentieth-century America if it remained a haphazard collection of regional organizations, which is what the national federation of Ethical Societies, the American Ethical Union, amounted to.

Organized at the end of Ethical Culture's first decade, the American Ethical Union sponsored periodic meetings and publications. Modeled after philosophic conventions, the subject matter was likely to be of a theoretical concern: in 1890 the proposed theme was "The Relation of Religious Teachers to Controversies of the Day Involving Moral Questions," and various prominent clergymen of different denominations were invited to participate. Occasionally a subject of some practical interest would be included, but little if any attention was given to institutional growth or its problems. The presidency of the national movement quite naturally fell to Felix Adler. While leading figures of the various Societies played an important role—Seligman, Wolff, and Klaber for New York, Dr. Frances Emily White of Philadelphia, Dr. and Mrs. Fischel of St. Louis—each remained identified with his local organization.

Adler was suspicious of too much popularity. His followers and colleagues believed in doing their good work quietly. Numbers were not regarded as significant. Indeed, organization, itself, was under a cloud—it might endanger the very freedom of the movement. Resistance to becoming a "sect" justified the group in its anti-organization philosophy, and turned them instead toward the study and application of ethics on a more broadly cultural and social basis. Thus the discussion at the first convention of the Ethical societies concerned a college for the study of ethics, the development of the Summer Schools of Ethics, and so forth. Similar motivation underlay the founding of the *International Journal of Ethics* in 1891. Adler's description of the journal corroborated the anti-institutional thrust of the movement:

. . . desire to spread ethical science among men and not simply to voice the views of our societies. This effort to increase the world's knowledge of ethics should be considered a permanent feature of interest by our Movement.[17]

Anna Garlin Spencer and Percival Chubb vigorously but unsuccessfully opposed this institutional "altruism." Sporadic efforts were made to reach out to people in various cities, to establish "bureaus of propaganda" and the like, but these were never seriously organized. In 1913 George O'Dell was appointed to the dual job of editing *The Standard* and serving as AEU Executive Secretary, the latter office unfilled for several years following Mrs. Spencer's resignation.

O'Dell was born in England in 1874 and came to the British movement in 1903. Of Episcopalian background, he visited the West London Society in 1895 with his sister and soon joined. He once revealed the origins of his ideology:

. . . the road by which any man travels from . . . orthodoxy to . . . an Ethical Society begins earlier than he can recall . . . my own steps

[17] Meeting of October 22, 1910, *AEU Records*, Vol. I, p. 14.

. . . date back at least as far as the age of nine when I was shown a copy of Herbert Spencer's *Study of Sociology* and was asked what I supposed the word, Sociology, to mean. I replied that it seemed to have something to do with going to balls and parties. The natural hilarity of my questioners at this answer hurt very sorely, and created a determination someday to read this book and *know*. Alas, it supported the doctrine of evolution and was anathema. But at the age of fifteen, I borrowed it surreptitiously, read it eagerly, and through it became aware of a new world.[18]

O'Dell became active in the British Labour Movement, serving as a labour member of the Municipal Council of Kensington from 1906–1909, financial trustee (treasurer) of the National Union of Clerks and Administrative Workers from 1906–1912, and its President from 1912–1913. An unassuming man, he was never accepted by Adler into Leadership, but served the movement all his life in a kind of administrative limbo. While some of the other Englishmen in the movement were boasting of their patriotism, O'Dell quietly enlisted in the Canadian Army in 1917.

His father conducted a free forum in London in the 1880s and much of O'Dell's education came from attendance at this intellectual free-for-all. He recalled his father inviting Bernard Shaw to speak:

Shaw replied "I will speak for you," he wrote, on "How to Become an Atheist!" Fireworks! My father . . . had for a while peddled bibles in Ireland from door to door. "Very well," replied Shaw to his protest, "I will not talk on that subject. Put me down to speak on 'How We Become Atheists,' instead." [19]

O'Dell was invariably described as a gentleman. It was a personal tragedy that he was never granted the recognition that his dedication and, indeed, his ability warranted. Serving the AEU as field secretary he was the national "office" in his own person for some thirty years, but had to carry editorial responsibility as well. He returned to England after the Second World War and died ten years later in 1957.

That Adler and his colleagues allowed O'Dell such a history in the movement had serious implications. The national organization of Eth-

---

[18] *Fiftieth Anniversary Volume*, p. 165.
[19] *Some Human Contacts*, p. 113.

ical Societies remained the part-time effort of a man whom the founder of the movement regarded as unqualified for the accolade of
Leadership in Ethical Culture. The failure to grow institutionally was
apparently a consequence of policy at least as much as a failure of
effort.

CHAPTER XV

An Ethical Platform for Social Reform

The turn of the century was a time of dissent and dreams and of the death of some precious "veracities." Workingmen were decreasingly contented with dictates from their employers. Women were demanding equal rights. Education was no longer the prerogative of the wealthy. Even the approaches to reform that had seemed so promising during the 1870s and 80s already seemed outdated.

The United States, while pretending to virtue, was following imperialist ambitions in Latin America. After a century of continental conquest, the heartless destruction of the American Indian, and the indecency of slavery, the record was not one of high morality. It was the "gay nineties" only if one did not look too deeply, and the new century of progress beckoned if one did not ask for whom.

A prophetic response was heard clearly from the Ethical Platform. Like the Protestant pulpit in form, colored by the spirit of Hebraic prophecy, benefiting from the lecture platform style of America, it became a place for significant utterance. That pattern was molded by the personality and genius of an Ethical Leadership led by Adler. If

Ethical Culture was frequently unable to transform the promise of the Platform into the reality of the institution, the questions raised on the platform were nonetheless urgent. The young Negro revolutionary W. E. B. Dubois, Booker T. Washington, Abdul B'Ha, founder of the BaHai Faith, William James, Josiah Royce, John Dewey, Jane Addams, and Senator Robert La Follette were among the guests on the Ethical Platform. The issues were interpreted in the light of cultural transition and measured against a moral standard. Nor did the Platform succumb to oversimplified solutions. Little naiveté was evidenced about the complexities and contradictions in human beings, individually or collectively. The call of conscience seldom rested on a sentimental appeal to a hazy sense of virtue.

In 1899 in New York, Mrs. Percy Waddington spoke on "The Moral Issues of the War in the Transvaal." It was the first time that a woman had been permitted to speak at the weekly meeting of that Society. Joseph Price speaking on "The Young Man in Politics" in 1900 attacked the spoils system and the businessmen who created and supported machine politics. In 1908 when Adler was in Germany, Elliott reported:

> . . . a number of brief speeches will be made [to open the year], . . . and the attempt will be made to follow out Dr. Adler's custom of having a question of national importance discussed in a competent manner from the Platform immediately before election.[1]

The New York Platform was not alone in its outspoken courage. Salter in Chicago and Weston in Philadelphia were creating a community Platform along the same lines. In 1900 Philadelphia sponsored a debate on the "Ethics of Expansion." In St. Louis more muted voices expressed concern with labor, with Negroes, with the educational revolution. Franklin Giddings spoke one week on "Malthusianism and Working Women"; a week later, Morris Jastrow delivered a lecture on "The Ethics of Assyrians and Babylonians." Chicago heard Paul Carus give three addresses on "Is Ethics a Science" in 1890 but was also treated to an appearance by Jane Addams speaking on "Democracy and Social Ethics." The Leadership similarly addressed itself

---

[1] New York Board of Trustees, Minutes, October 5, 1908.

to a vast array of problems, weaving a tapestry of perennial, personal, and topical themes. When David Muzzey was marching for women's rights, he also found time to share his latest insights on American history from the Ethical Platform.

Attendance remained high. New York, for example, reported regular audiences of 1,000 to 1,500 in 1914; Philadelphia, Chicago, and St. Louis were filling their meeting halls. Brooklyn, too, was reaching a good many people from its Platform. The large audiences did not represent membership. Many of those who came of a Sunday—indeed, who came Sunday after Sunday for years—never dreamt of joining the Ethical Culture movement. This puzzled and troubled the Leaders and the Boards of Trustees. Nevertheless all took comfort in sharing a point of view widely, responsibly, and without sectarianism.

The Platform was indeed free. The speaker spoke for himself. But when, if at all, did Ethical Culture as an entity enter the arena? Adler and his followers had set out to establish a moral consensus within a metaphysical and theological pluralism. Some thirty years later, with the movement more diverse and with the nation and the world undergoing radical change, moral consensus was elusive. Ethical Culture demanded respect for the integrity of the individual. Adler and his followers wanted to cry out against injustice and speak together for the moral conscience of men, yet to do so proved impossible.

The Platform, by its very nature, was antithetical to consensus. In 1906 the New York Board recorded:

> . . . the last Council Meeting had been occupied with . . . the question whether it would be advisable on occasions like the discussion of the Insurance Investigation at Carnegie Hall by Mr. Hughes to call a special meeting of the Society for the purpose of putting on record the opinion of the Society. . . . [Some] feared that it would establish a precedent in the direction of crystallizing a moral code . . . that the first step might [thus] be taken towards formalism and towards externalizing the spirit of our new Movement. . . .

> Dr. Adler expressed his belief that the Society as a whole . . . could not exclude . . . any of its members on grounds of opinion; that the Society cannot, as such, pass a Resolution which would excommunicate those who disagree . . . the Society should have it out . . . not shirking the issue, never passing a Resolution which would excommunicate

any member but passing Resolutions signed by those who wish to stand publicly as in favor of them.[2]

Yet when Adler spoke many felt, and rightly so, that he spoke for Ethical Culture, no matter what disclaimers were made. And such seeming resolution jeopardized the hope of ever achieving moral consensus. The problem was to appear more clearly after the death of the founder, for in Adler's lifetime the policy might be ambiguous but the voice was clear.

Adler had described the Sunday address as the "flame burning on the altar." Inevitably, such high intent was not always matched by performance. The integration of intellect and commitment, of emotional fire and analysis, of contemporary relevance and philosophic perspective was an ideal which burdened and drove the Leadership of Ethical Culture. Hopefully, too, the audience was more than passive listeners. At its best, a communion was established between speaker and auditor. There were recurrent stories of men returning from the Sunday meeting to share point by point what they had heard with their families. Often the Platform stimulated significant behavioral changes in business, in private life, in career. For all its dependence on language, the Platform did serve as symbol of unification and as stimulus to change. It was, paradoxically, for many people an active experience. Its weakness and its strength were the same. It depended on a particular person and lacked the "insurance" added by ritual.

Scarcely any issue was neglected. The age-old maxim, "nothing human is alien to me" was the guide. Week after week, politics mixed with personal life, issues of international affairs shared the stage with the "higher criticism," with pedagogy and the educational revolution, with attitudes toward death and immortality. Ethical Culture made clear that no area of life was religious or secular *per se*. The task of the Ethical movement was to "ethicize" *all* the relationships of life and the Ethical Platform was to lead the way in this process.

Concern with education was a priority of the movement. Mangasarian said:

> To teach means to lift another . . . to provoke thought and action. . . . The teacher therefore is . . . a builder of men. We often hear it

[2] Board of Trustees, Minutes, March 5, 1906.

said that, "it is one thing to know and another to teach." To know and to teach mean one and the same thing. . . . Teaching . . . is the convincing evidence of knowledge. . . . To give dignity to knowledge and force to method, the teacher must possess character. To lead, one must be in advance; to lift another, one must stand upon higher ground; to guide one must know the way; to enlighten, one must possess light.[3]

Symptoms of Victorian moralism and classical bias were abundant. Yet the insistence on an integration of knowledge, method, and character revealed the Platform's intent to transcend a merely technical view of education.

Much of the social criticism from the Platform had devoted itself to the city. With America looking more and more to the rest of the world, attention began to focus on national and international affairs. The United States' troubled relations with Latin America cried out for comment, but few voices were raised in protest against jingoist adventure. Among those few was the Leadership of the Ethical Societies. In 1896 Adler spoke on the "War Spirit in the United States:"

A wave of war feeling has swept the United States. . . . A democracy is more exposed to sudden eruptions of emotional excitement. . . . One cause is the teaching of history in the public schools. . . . The second cause of the war feeling is the restlessness of democracy. . . . Individuality tries to assert itself in miserable external means, in small contemptible ways, in titles and publicity. Thus, war offers the individual a chance for notoriety and distinction and excitement. We want sensation, . . . which war promises. The United States lacks grandeur in its psychic life. . . . At its founding we believed ourselves the political Israel. . . . But today, we no longer believe in a humanitarian mission.[4]

In Philadelphia, Salter was speaking on a similar theme. Denying that the Platform was "religious or political" he affirmed its dedication to "those abstract principles of right and justice which we call ethics": ". . . let us examine the Venezuelan question not in terms of my country right or wrong, but in terms of the right and wrong of the situation." Salter, like Adler, supported the Monroe Doctrine as a

[3] "Teaching and Teachers," in *Ethical Addresses*, (first series; 1895), pp. 143–44.

[4] "The Monroe Doctrine and the War Spirit in the United States," in *Ethical Addresses* (third series; 1897), passim.

"sound political instinct" and called for impartial arbitration between Venezuela and England. He criticized President Cleveland's "twenty-inch gun" message which could make the United States partly responsible for the conflict by arousing all of the emotions of the "war spirit." Like Adler, he concluded his speech with a call to the American ideal and a commitment to "world citizenship." [5]

Weston also commented on Latin America. Again the moral nature of politics was the basis of the criticism: "The state, as well as the individual, is a moral organism, and the commandments of morality are no less applicable to the former than to the latter. . . ." Weston held that we were justified in warring with Spain as a way of freeing the victims of Spanish tyranny—the war was a holy war:

> If any one can read the reports . . . submitted to Congress without being filled with burning moral indignation against the Spanish government his heart must indeed be made of stone, his soul composed of clay.

> If I believed, as some do, that intervention was brought on merely to aid the sugar and tobacco trusts; if I believed that it was the result . . . of jingoism . . . with a view to territorial aggrandizement; if I believed it was a mere scheme . . . to influence the next election; I would denounce the government . . . even though I knew I would be denounced as a traitor. . . . Let not our utter hatred of war blind us to the true causes of this one. . . . It was the terrible conditions which existed close to our own territory that aroused the conscience of the entire country. . . . [6]

Adler, Salter, and Weston were all interventionists in the name of principle. The state was a moral agent or it had no right to exist. And an Ethical Platform was obligated to judge the state and society.

Another theme was race. In 1895 Elliott commented that America had gone back on the promise made after the Civil War. The more alert and sensitive were aware that the war was over, but the struggle for racial justice was only beginning. In 1900 Felix Adler and three guests (Messrs Baldwin, Taylor, and Fisher) spoke on "The Future of the Colored Race in America." Reporting to the Board, Adler said:

[5] "The Venezuelan Question," in *Ethical Addresses* (third series; 1897), passim.

[6] "Our War with Spain," June 1898. Ethical Culture Archive.

The Sunday Platform seeks to formulate a philosophy of life, to clarify the mind as to what is right, to quicken impulses to do the right and to sustain man in the battle of life. To broaden the influence of the Platform . . . there should be more discussions like that on the Negro question, held on April 8.

in 1904, on the publication of W. E. B. Dubois' *The Souls of the Black Folk*, Adler spoke on "The Negro Problem in the United States." In 1905 Booker T. Washington was invited to the Platform. In 1906 Josiah Royce spoke on "The Race Question and Race Prejudice," and in 1907 W. E. B. Dubois himself addressed the New York Society. These lectures helped toward convening the International Races Congress in 1911—an instance of the relationship of Platform to action. In 1909 Henry Moskowitz, Mary Ovington White, and William English Walling, speaking on "the spirit of the abolitionists," issued the call to organize the National Association for the Advancement of Colored Peoples. Among the Ethical Leaders who signed that petition were John Elliott, Anna Garlin Spencer, William Salter and, of course, Dr. Moskowitz. The relationship of the Platform to social reform was not a sporadic affair. Education and the Ethical Culture School, social reform and the settlement houses, equal rights and legal aid—the record was long.

The growing movement for women's rights ran head on into Dr. Adler's attitudes, but others in the societies were sympathetic. One theme of the 1896 assembly in St. Louis was "Women's Influence in Public Affairs," and the meeting houses were made available for suffrage organizations. In 1918:

> Mrs. Politzer presented the request of the Women's Suffrage Party . . . for an information booth for the instruction of foreign women of the district, not only for the purpose of instructing them in the matter of suffrage, but for getting to them information in regard to government war activities, food conservation, and the like. . . .[7]

If there was conflict on equality for women, there was none on the rights of the child. The crowded slums of the major cities were vast factories which produced the goods demanded by a growing American population, and a number of the laborers were children. In 1894

---

[7] New York Board of Trustees, Minutes, May, 1918.

Adler joined with the Reverend Edgar Gardner Murphy and others to form the National Child Labor Committee and served as its chairman for many years. Adler returned over and over again to the question of child labor, education, the family.

For the reformer of that day, the social question was the rights of labor. Upon it depended all other community issues. Ethical Culture, not unexpectedly, opted for meliorism, seeking to affect both the conscience of the employer and the condition of the worker. And the worker was to be improved morally, culturally, and intellectually. St. Louis's Self Culture Halls and Salter's conferences between business and labor were efforts toward those ends. In New York, with so many of its members active in the business world, the appeal to conscience could be tested. The labor question was discussed from the Platform and also by the Board:

> . . . an Industrial Section should be organized . . . [to] discuss what the employer, what the wage earners themselves, and what the public can do to improve the . . . welfare of the wage earners. . . . Mr. Reichow and Mr. White, both labor union workers and members of the Society, had . . . asked . . . why the Society did not help. . . . A letter written by Mr. White [was read]:

> ". . . the members of the Ethical Societies can be of service in mitigating the intensity of the industrial strife which the struggle for a living wage and shorter work day involves . . . by endeavoring to conciliate differences, by helping to maintain higher ethical standards in the conduct of unions, and also by impressing employers with the responsibilities which their position imposes upon them.

> "The Workingman's Lyceum, . . . in the early days of the Society, included some of the finest men in the Delamater Iron Works. At that time there was no platform in the city to speak for the Labor Movement . . . to awaken the public conscience. . . . In our Society we have employers who desire to be just, wage earners, and representatives of the Unions, and Professor Seligman—an expert on sociological questions; in fact, all the elements to make . . . an Industrial Ethics section successful and helpful." [8]

The Board did establish an Industrial Section, whose members included Alfred Wolff, James Klaber, Emil Berolzheimer, Louis Seligs-

[8] New York Board of Trustees, Minutes, April, 1900.

berg, Henry White, and Arthur Reichow. Professor Seligman led the planning committee. The Young Men's Union investigating labor conditions in 1906 heard from Edward Gould of the International Brotherhood of Teamsters and Timothy Healy of the Stationary Firemen and Engineer's Union. For men isolated from the lives and problems of laborers, it was an education to learn about hours of work, working conditions, the need for a compulsory day of rest, the problem of the non-union shop. The result was support for labor legislation and labor health services. Dr. George Price, a member of the New York Society, worked with both labor and management to develop the Unity Health Center, which provided free care for working men and their families.

The meliorist stance of the movement led occasionally to roles in labor arbitration. Henry Neumann recalled,

> One of the members of our Brooklyn Society was a neckwear manufacturer. He asked me whether I would become impartial chairman for a group [of manufacturers]. . . . I accepted . . . [and] served for about three years, until I was obliged to hand in a decision against the workers. . . . One worker had falsified his production slip. . . . He was discharged and . . . the employers also discharged the foreman on the ground that it was [his] business to protect the industry against that kind of dishonesty. . . . The union protested . . . [and] . . . because it was a split, the decision was left to me. I decided the employers were right. . . . That so angered the union that my appointment was terminated with a gift of a dozen neckties. . . . For once in my life I had more neckties than I could wear at one time. . . .[9]

New York's garment industry had for some years enjoyed labor peace under its famous "protocol"—a joint agreement between management and labor on working conditions, methods for settling disputes, and legitimacy of union organization. However, in the summer of 1915, a strike appeared imminent. Mayor Mitchell appointed Adler to the mediation committee. Julius Henry Cohen recalled:

> Hillquit [Morris Hillquit, lawyer for the union] and I [Cohen was lawyer for the employers] with the approval of our clients, both agreed

[9] Interview, 1961.

that Felix Adler was the one man ideally suited to sit as Chairman of that Council [the mediating committee]. On my part, I counted on his business sagacity to understand the employer's side. Hillquit relied on his sense of justice. Both of us were right.[10]

Adler had just returned from presiding at a Child Labor Conference in San Francisco and from lectures in other western cities and had gone to St. Huberts for a vacation. He was tired. The call back to the city was not welcome. Cohen continued:

> We believed it was imperative that we should get him back to New York. I recalled one of his own stories. . . . A colored man went out into the wood to pray . . ."Lord please come down to help this sinner. Please Lord, come, but come yourself. Don't send your son. This am no child's play." I wired the Doctor . . . supplementing Mayor Mitchell's call: "Come thou thyself—this is no child's play." He afterwards told my wife the telegram did the trick. He loved a joke, even if it was at his own expense.[11]

Ethical Culture taught that reform meant changing the reformer himself. Good works were not enough. The attorneys in the movement were motivated to develop an ethical code for the bar in 1905. And in an unpublished paper, Robert Hirsch spoke of the businessmen's group:

> I placed before Dr. Adler the need of ethicizing our economic life. I strongly believed that the businessmen belonging to the Society ought to clarify and define [their] ideal of . . . service. . . . I pointed out that the great difficulties to be overcome in the industrial field would prove the supreme test of his ethical philosophy. Here there were mountains of selfishness and acquisitiveness to be moved and he gave us the driving force that brought the Businessmen's Group into existence. . . . One large silk manufacturer (Sidney Blumenthal) introduced industrial representation in his plants. Another businessman (Alexander Bing) created a new type of dwelling and settlement for the working classes. Still another started a Cooperative Marketing System for Farmers. . . .[12]

[10] *They Builded Better Than They Knew*, p. 40.
[11] *Ibid.*, p. 40.
[12] "The Most Unforgettable Character I Have Known," unpublished essay.

From this grew An Ethical Program for Business Men, which asked the businessman to "put himself on salary" and thus avoid being trapped by the profit motive. Included was discussion of the public interest:

. . . in certain kinds of private business—the railroad business is an obvious example—the amount of profit to be allowed to the owners is to be strictly limited on the ground that the private business is affected with a public interest. The same principle is applicable to house renting in cities . . . and to the fearful problem of unemployment. The employment of wage earners may be a private transaction, but the laying off of laborers . . . is certainly a matter profoundly affected with a public interest. . . . From the point of view that profit making is the be all and end all of business, it is indeed perfectly logical to employ the laborer in times of prosperity and to dismiss . . . all thought of him in times of industrial depression. But if, on the other hand, the employment of workers is a private transaction affected by a public interest, then ways and means must be found of bridging the industrial and commercial gaps, either by creating reserve funds, by unemployment insurance, or by other methods. . . .[13]

The appeal to conscience thus took practical turns, forecasting in a sense some of the philosophy of the New Deal.

The question of prison reform also occupied the movement. Spencer Miller, assistant to Thomas M. Osborn and George W. Kirchway at Sing Sing Prison, spoke of this:

I had the opportunity . . . to know something about his [Adler's] deep interest in prison reform. . . . [He describes a meeting at Carnegie Hall.] Dr. Adler took the chair. . . . Dr. John Elliott . . . was deeply interested [in prison reform]. Mark McClosky . . . [and] Robert Kohn were also there. Also Dr. S. Whiten and Dr. Seligman, all of whom were members of the Society for Ethical Culture. . . .

Out of it all came the formation of what became known as the Mutual Welfare League which was the self-governing organization of the prison. It was a pilot experiment begun first at Auburn, then carried into Sing Sing and then taken by Osborn to the Naval Prison at Portsmouth. . . . The Columbus State Prison had had a tragic fire in which some 300 of the prisoners had been burned to death. . . . [I] had a long talk with

13 An Ethical Program for Business Men, c. 1915.

Dr. Adler about the possibility of holding some kind of mass meeting . . . , [and it] was held at the Ethical Culture Society.

. . . one other recollection I have of Dr. Adler and that was his unalterable opposition to capital punishment.[14]

John Elliott gave much of himself to men in prison, especially to those who had come to the Hudson Guild as boys. The abolition of capital punishment remained an active concern of Ethical Culture.

From the outset, members of the Ethical societies had been concerned with the ethical dimension of politics. Few could accommodate themselves to the clubhouse which had become the arena for the new political reformers, but they nevertheless pursued both a practical and a theoretical interest in political reform. Adler helped organize the Committee of 15, which led in 1902 to the election of Seth Low as reform mayor of New York. In the eighties he had supported Henry George (although he opposed George's Single Tax Theory) because he felt that George represented a genuine moral force in political life. In 1899, Adler called together a political ethics circle "to meet the difficulties experienced by independent citizens in determining . . . how they ought to vote." A distinction between religion and politics was impossible for the Ethical Movement. The effort to "ethicize" all the relationships of life led inevitably into the muddy waters of politics.

> . . . It is because politics is usually regarded as outside of religion . . . because the churches divorce the two; because political service is not regarded by them as part of the "divine" service . . . that our political morality is so low, the political conscience is scarred, and the body political mere carrion for spoil. . . .
>
> . . . a recognition of the need for widening the scope of man's religious duty to include his political obligations and privileges has been an important factor in bringing the Ethical Movement into being. . . . There has been struggling into expression that supreme regard for the commonwealth, for the general well-being of men. . . . It is in this sense that there is a religion of politics and a political piety.[15]

[14] Interview, 1962.

[15] "Political Degeneracy and Its Cure," *The Ethical Record*, Vol. VII, No. 1 (October, 1900), p. 7.

If religion and politics could not be seperated, church and state must be. Aid for the Schools had been rejected. In 1916, there occurred one of the first of many inconclusive debates on the question of tax exemption for religious institutions.

Professor Seligman held that these institutions accomplished for society at large quasi-public functions—. . . .

Dr. Adler called attention to . . . the fact that the State by this tax exemption supports ideals and methods to which a part of the community does not and cannot subscribe.[16]

The keynote of the Ethical Platform was its attention to the world; its self-imposed task was to point directions of transforming the secular into the sacred.

[16] New York Board of Trustees, Minutes, April 3, 1916.

PART THREE

Ethical
Culture
in the
Twentieth Century

CHAPTER XVI

The End
of Innocence

As Ethical Culture reached its fortieth year in 1916, the war in Europe was bringing death to tens of thousands. Wilsonians were campaigning for his second term with the slogan "He kept us out of war," but a year later the United States declared war upon Germany, and many members of Ethical Culture, however loyal to America, could not forget their German heritage. As these men and women illustrated so well, the First World War cut deeply into the meanings of American life. To members of the liberal reform community and inheritors of the enlightenment, war, especially this war, seemed a direct and brutal denial of everything they had believed.

Celebrating the fortieth year was tragic irony for moral religion. The decision to affirm the possibilities of the future was a remarkable testimony—to either irrational stubbornness or spiritual courage and probably a bit of both—but the decision to go on was made. For many liberals and reformers the war was an excuse for retreat. Self-help philosophies and psychologies began to replace social ethics. Eric Goldman writes:

Reform in the Seventies and Eighties had the buoyancy of a movement that was just taking the offensive. Progressivism of the Twenties was a beaten army. . . . As the new era opened, so the story goes, Herbert Croly (of the *New Republic*) went home and refused to see anyone for three days. On the fourth day, he summoned his editors . . . and told them that progressivism was finished. "From now on we must work for the redemption of the individual."

Thousands were like the progressive . . . in Muncie, Indiana. With witch hunters thrashing through the state, this man was no longer signing petitions or making speeches at the town meeting. "I just run away from it all to my books," he explained resignedly. Still other progressives turned to the cushion of cynicism or to expatriation which offered the delights of disillusionment on a devaluated franc, or to the exhilaration of Socialism or Communism.[1]

To the generations who know the horrors of the Second World War, the first "great" war seems tame. But this is to miss its impact. It was a shock to those who, from the enlightenment onward, expected progress, organized democratically, to stretch inevitably before mankind and be led by science, technology, and education.

Adler's philosophy remained unshaken:

How do you manage to support your confidence and belief in humanity, seeing that all civilization has broken down? It is a trifle trying to one's patience to hear these weak meowings that civilization has broken down. No, civilization has not broken down. The war has demonstrated that *what we believed was civilization was not civilization.* . . . And the challenge of the War is that we should now get together and try to build up a real civilization instead of trying to build up a money civilization and power civilization.[2]

Ethical Culture was not drawing back. The task was to reaffirm its mission and apply it with greater wisdom and insight. Never was the movement's prophetic character more evident, its insistence on facing the new while affirming essential continuities more strongly. Before America entered the war Adler had said,

[1] *Rendezvous with Destiny,* p. 223.
[2] Adler, "Ethical Prerequisites of Personal Peace," December 16, 1917, p. 16.

. . . when future generations look back on 1915 and 1916—heaven knows! 1917 and 1918 possibly, or all of the twentieth century, humanity will sit in sackcloth and ashes. . . . The whole world seems to have dropped. . . . And among those . . . none present a more melancholy spectacle than the . . . intellectuals, . . . the scientists and the thinkers who unfortunately did nothing to check the passions of the multitude but echoed them, outscreeching the universal shriek and did their best to lash into fury the raging waves. . . .[3]

Ethical Culture refused to yield to social radicalism on the left or to retreat to personal security on the right. Yet the middle road, never easy, was even more difficult in a time of crisis. It was chosen with full knowledge of the price.

Debates raged within the Societies over the questions of pacifism, neutrality, and the limits of warfare as America neared entry into the war. The "German question," the assignment of war guilt, wracked Ethical Culture and drew public hostility toward the movement. By 1916 most Americans had taken sides. Anything German, from symphony to sauerkraut, was suspect. Any effort to assess the causes of conflict objectively was rejected as war hysteria mounted. Doris Stein, daughter of one of the early members of the movement, recalls:

I remember the German teacher, Mr. Euster, told me many years later that whether he could get a salary three times as big or not, he would not leave the school. . . . During World War I everyone had cut their German classes, [but] Dr. Adler had insisted that learning had nothing to do with feelings toward the government and kept him all the way through . . . , and he would never forget this.[4]

The German question took many forms. The school had to face it in its curriculum; individual Leaders faced it from the Platform and in their dealings with members and the wider community; the institution was forced to make decisions too. In December, 1914, the New York Society was asked for the use of its meeting house by the German Academic Union for a memorial meeting in honor of German

[3] Adler, "How to Keep at the Level of One's Best Moments," January 16, 1916, p. 12.
[4] Interview. 1962.

professors who had died in the war. Extended consultation followed by lengthy debate in the Board ended finally in granting permission— but hesitation and fear are written between the lines of the non-commital secretary's note.

For most Americans the problem of the war was abstract prior to 1917. Comforted by physical and psychological separation from Europe's struggles and convinced of the security afforded by the Monroe Doctrine, they saw war as another Old World aberration. The various Indian wars, the adventure against Mexico, the Civil War, the abbreviated skirmish with Spain were somehow different in the American's eyes. He saw himself as the peace-loving man of virtue in a jungle of conflicting national interests and imperialisms. If Teddy Roosevelt carried a "big stick" it was only for the sake of justice. Fighting for power was not suited to America's idealized image of itself.

The beginning of the end for this illusion was the First World War. 1916 drew to a close with the election campaign turning on the question of war. Submarine attacks and trade necessities revealed that America was not really separated from the rest of the world and its problems. And moral religion was not above the battle. A start had been made at the turn of the century with the various Platform attacks on America's imperialistic adventures. Now the war question came to preoccupy everyone.

In his traditional address just before the 1916 election, Adler spoke on "The Principles Which Should Guide the Citizen in His Choice of a President." Mindful of his audience, he cautioned German-Americans to think twice before voting against Wilson because of the President's sympathy with the Allies. His vote would go to Wilson. In February, 1917, Adler spoke of the growing hysteria he saw all around him. To the Board of Trustees in New York, he said:

> . . . In case . . . war be declared it would be the duty of the Society for Ethical Culture to contribute its mite to calming the excitement aroused. . . . I have been overhearing the most ridiculous hysterical emotional utterances in regard to internment. . . .

At that same meeting Adler commented on Wilson's plan for a League of Nations, calling it an appeal to a state of things that obtains nowhere. "As President, it was his part to suggest something—not the ideal of the far future but that next step that would lead in the ideal direction." Adler went on to criticize England for not being a beacon of liberty and justice with its record in Africa and Asia and its behavior toward native populations. He warned that America's entry into the war should not be based on the illusion that it was joining an alliance of principle. Entry, if it occurred, must be understood as a political necessity and as a defense against German attacks on American life and property. Adler ended his commentary,

> . . . going into the war, we should not go in on the side of the Allies on the ground that we stand with them on the everlasting principle of virtue . . . as far as political issues are concerned. . . . I doubt whether it would be possible for us to go in pro tanto and not pro toto. . . . These spectres [of militarism] haunt me; first, the strain in the population; second, the feeling of the German-Americans that they must excuse themselves for living.[5]

Adler was always aware that no decision rests purely on principle, an unadorned instance of the struggle between good and evil. He was more perceptive than most Americans, more realistically critical than many liberals who responded to Wilson's dream of a League and the plea to make the world safe for democracy.

War and its meaning occupied the center of the stage. In January, 1916, Adler discussed the dangers of war to children and the way in which war erodes relationships between the generations and weakens family life. He also criticized the revivalism of Billy Sunday, characterizing him as "The man who does good to individuals and does, at the same time, great general harm." [6] He saw that reawakened fundamentalism was a response to fear and anxiety—which, apparently, was a problem not only for the unsophisticated. To the Board Adler spoke of attendance at Sunday meetings "being large when religious subjects are discussed."

In April, 1917, America entered the war, and on April 8 Adler addressed his Society and the movement through *The Standard* on "The National Crisis." Rejecting pacifism he called for acceptance of war as "the duty of a nation to protect the rights of humanity." He said that

[5] Citations above are from New York Board of Trustees, Minutes, February 5, 1917.

[6] *The Revival of Revivalism,* January, 1917.

the highest loyalty was to the sovereign will of the people. A conservative with respect to the state, he added "It is better that bad laws should prevail than that individuals should be free to decide which laws they will obey and which not." Behind his unequivocal assertion of loyalty, no doubt, was the German-American trying to demonstrate his allegiance.
Hysteria in America now reached a fevered height.

> . . . persons indicted or imprisoned included a woman who had received a Red Cross soliciter in a "hostile" manner, a socialist who had written a letter to the Kansas City Star charging wartime profiteering, and an editor who had printed the statement: "We must make the world safe for democracy even if we have to 'bean' the Goddess of Liberty to do it." A Californian went to jail for laughing at rookies drilling on San Francisco's Presidio, a New Yorker served ninety days for spitting on the sidewalk near some Italian officers. . . . Ministers were unfrocked for emphasizing the Sermon on the Mount, clubs expelled members who questioned the omniscience of the Administration, college professors were dismissed or bludgeoned into resigning for pacifist leanings or for ardent pro-war statements that also criticized the home front.[7]

John Elliott was Chairman of the Emergency Peace Federation, which tried to keep America out of the war. Failing this, its attentions shifted to the defense of conscientious objectors and victims of the country's hysteria. Dr. Neumann recalled:

> . . . a poor Italian who had a junk cart. He knew that if anything projected from the wagon you had to attach a red flag to it; but because red was beginning to be a dangerous color in 1917 (the Menshevik and Bolshevik revolutions had taken place in Russia), someone advised him to put an American flag instead. The flag was upside down . . . [and] he was arrested. The judge, instead of telling him that because it was war-time he must be careful, fined him the maximum of $25. [8]

For the liberal community, including members of Ethical Culture, taking sides seemed necessary. Adler had no illusions about war—he analyzed it in terms of a *realpolitik* worthy of a hard-headed prag-

[7] Goldman, *Rendezvous with Destiny*, pp. 196–97.
[8] Interview, 1961.

matist—but nevertheless believed it could be justified on moral grounds. John Elliott called for mediation up to the moment America entered the war and thereafter took a pacifist position. Henry Neumann pleaded for the United States to stay out in order that it might be more effective when peace came. Prior to America's entry, David Muzzey joined Neumann and Elliott in pacifism, but afterwards, with some hesitation, supported the U.S. effort in Europe. In Chicago Bridges, loyal to his British ancestry, was a vigorous proponent of American intervention while O'Dell resolved to join the Canadian army. But it was not only the Leadership that was divided by conscience. Members were torn as well. Some left the movement in protest at John Elliott's and Henry Neumann's pacifism. Shortly before America entered the war, a Mr. Rosenblatt introduced a pledge of loyalty at the New York Board meeting:

> Resolved that we pledge our loyalty to the Government of the United States and our support to all measures it may take for the preservation of the nation's dignity and the protection of its lawful right.[9]

He argued that the pacifism of three of the Leaders had committed the movement unfairly and had misrepresented Ethical Culture. Members needed an opportunity to express their views since the Leadership had had its chance. Adler asked if his intent was to foreclose criticism of the government after it had acted. He anticipated that freedom of the Platform could be curtailed. The debate was inconclusive, but the issue was not put aside. It was revived over and over again, though the Platform did in fact remain free and a loyalty oath was never required.

The Leadership nevertheless felt called upon to make an affimative statement on the position of the movement toward the war. In the fall of 1917 a "declaration" was submitted containing these three points: members and Leaders were encouraged to undertake "patriotic service"; loyalty to constituted authority was urged, but at the same time the effort should be made to promote "a loftier and more inspiring loyalty by giving in [the] Schools and on [the] Platform the highest possible spiritual interpretation of the ideal of America"; and

[9] New York Board of Trustees, Minutes, April 2, 1917.

the ideal should remain a united humanity, the goal "amity to follow the enmity, of a comradeship of justice." [10] The declaration was not intended to bind all members but only to express a consensus for those who wished to accept it. Adler stressed the need for safeguarding even the tiniest minority. "There must not be an attempt to introduce a majority resolution in a matter of conscience. There must be no strait jacket of moral creed, no force, no coercion." He was mindful of the drive for unity that was part of the war spirit and recognized the attempt to manipulate and coerce conscience as one of the significant threats of modern warfare.

The conflict between individual integrity and social ethics was not resolved. Forums, debates, discussions, and declarations could not unify the two. With the breakdown of the common sense of liberalism came too the first overt sign of the malaise that was soon to afflict the entire liberal community. World war marked a turning point for the inheritors of the enlightenment, not only psychologically but philosophically too. For Ethical Culture, it marked a time when concentration on this or that social issue replaced a coherent philosophy of social reform. Adler continued to insist on the centrality of the moral ideal, but was forced to rethink the meanings of that ideal. His words in this period are more problematic than affirmative, raising more questions than answers. Almost in despair Adler turned backward, seeking to recapture an earlier wisdom. His master work, *An Ethical Philosophy of Life,* dates from this period. In a chapter on frustration, he reveals a sense of unfinished business and a feeling that for the time at least the business of making ethical sense was suspended. A hint of this appears in his comments to the Board in the fall of 1917:

> We are a Society for Ethical progress . . . , but in relation to the great issues as they arise, we should not take one side or the other but should assist in the formation of a new conscience by inviting the views of each in a spiritually tolerant manner. . . . The Society is not helpless [sic] . . . but rather acts as an accoucheur bringing ideas to birth. . . . The Society stands for something after all that is more lasting than these issues of the day. It stands for the personal life, the family life, life and death, the friend and counsellor of man from birth to the grave.

10 *Ibid.,* November, 1917.

It seems wise to give to the members in the midst of the present emotionalism an opportunity to speak.[11]

The debate on loyalty took many forms. There was the discussion of raising an American flag over the meeting house as was the custom of other religious organizations. Adler felt this would be a mistake: "A religious society should fly its own flag—the flag of humanity is wider than that of any nation." Members of his Board disagreed but the issue was tabled in May, 1917. However, by November, American troops were fighting in France, and Adler changed his mind: "We too might say [to the public], 'Look at the record. We have been working for the highest interests for forty years. . . . We of the Ethical Culture Society have made a contribution to America. We have a civic record in many movements.' But people do not look up records. . . ." A flag was raised above the meeting house; the absence of a symbol spoke louder than the record.[12]

Henry Neumann recalled:

A very significant incident as a result of our entrance [into the war]. . . . Somebody noticed that the flag was not flying over the school building and complained. Adler's answer was, "Our patriotism is unflagging."

But . . . at an assembly of pupils . . . , after Adler had said a few words about the duties of citizens, the chairman of the student body came forward to take the flag. . . . But Adler himself took it and led the procession. I still see it flash across my mind—he carried the flag as, in the Bible, Jesus carried the cross. He didn't walk proudly. He walked like a very old man feeling its weight.[13]

If the issue of loyalty left the patriots unhappy with Ethical Culture, the refusal to adopt a clear, critical stance against the war seemed to others a betrayal of the Ethical ideal. Oswald Garrison Villard, a long-time member of the New York Society and its Board of Trustees and the very influential editor of *The Nation*, resigned because the Society had not expressed support of pacifism and opposi-

[11] *Ibid.*, November 5, 1917.
[12] *Ibid.*, November 5, 1917.
[13] Interview, 1961.

tion to the war. Much later in *The Nation* (October 25, 1933) Villard still criticized Ethical Culture for not urging nonparticipation in the war. To this John Elliott replied,

> . . . you wrote some very earnest words of regret because the Ethical Society as a body had not declared itself as opposed to the War and because Dr. Adler and the other Leaders had not spoken and acted vigorously enough against it. May I remind you that three among our Leaders were outspoken pacifists? But even these believed that it was wiser to continue the policy of the Ethical Society not to commit itself and thereby all its members to positions on specific issues . . . it does not declare itself as a body for the reason that many persons whose consciences are their guides differ on many important questions, not merely on how to get peace.[14]

After the war some of those who had left returned—but most did not. The middle way exacted a heavy toll, while other institutions seemed to flourish on unambiguous and often simplified rallying points.

Civil liberties also suffered during the war. Loyalty, hysteria, and flag-waving were a poor environment for the Bill of Rights. Dr. Neumann recalled another incident that came to the attention of the Emergency Peace Federation:

> There was a poor old German, a consumptive, who was arrested because his neighbor heard him, on waking from a nap, say in German, "Goddam Woodrow Wilson." . . . One of the women . . . got a portrait of Woodrow Wilson and hung it in the poor janitor's apartment so that when they came in and asked this poor fellow about it it was enough for him to show that he had the portrait on the wall. I wouldn't like to discuss the ethics of that. . . . The Emergency Federation was raided by the police. . . . They took all our books—the names were nothing secret—took our money and all that.[15]

A National Civil Liberties Bureau was created, and Roger Baldwin recalled that Dr. Elliott was one of the most faithful on the "directing committee." He was "one of the standouts, a man who never failed us. . . . [He] took an active part in the defense of conscientious ob-

14 Ethical Culture Archive.
15 Interview, 1961.

jectors and the rights of freedom of speech. . . ." From the Bureau grew the American Civil Liberties Union with Baldwin its first Executive, John Haynes Holmes, Elliott, and others in its founding group. Elliott's activity for civil liberties was not unanimously approved within Ethical Culture. In April, 1919, a resolution was introduced by the ubiquitous Mr. Rosenblatt requesting a specific demurrer from the Platform that no speaker was uttering an official position of the Society or the movement. The resolution was motivated by an address Elliott had given denouncing the Espionage Act, deploring the conviction of Eugene Debs under the provisions of that Act, and expressing resentment at the affirmation of that conviction by the Supreme Court. Elliott portrayed Debs as a martyr worthy of admiration and respect. Once again the Board affirmed the freedom of the Platform; the resolution failed with four in favor and twenty-one against. Consistent support of freedom was a testimony to the affirmative values of Ethical Culture and its depth of commitment. It would have been easier, and more popular, to be circumspect. It was painful to see long-time supporters and friends drop away and in some instances, as with Villard, to do so publicly.

The work nevertheless went on and assumed new chores as a consequence of the dislocation and suffering brought by war. Relief work was organized for Belgian and Polish victims of war under the guidance of Mrs. George O'Dell and Mrs. Robert Kohn. An information bureau was established where those interested could learn about the possibilities and needs for service. Entertainment and dinners were organized for servicemen. Extensions of community work included a kitchen in the domestic science room of the school to prepare hot lunches for the children in the play schools, in Brooklyn a co-op.

Though the war overshadowed other issues, it did not erase them. Premonitions of the meaning of the Russian revolution were heard. Muzzey, still faithful to the rights of women, took issue with an editorial in *The New York Times* which called for a vote against women's suffrage as "an impertinence, a distraction, and diversion when the country should be united on the cardinal and sole purpose of winning the war." Adler, troubled by the technical innovations of war, addressed himself to the problem of science and technology: "The time will come when that scientist will be considered and will consider himself a disgrace to the human race who prostitutes his knowledge of Nature's forces for the destruction of his fellow men." Concerned with the rights of labor, John Elliott spoke out "whenever any attempt shall be made, under the pretext of national necessity to destroy or weaken those legal restraints upon the unfair exploitation of human labor. . . ."

A year and some months of war, not Europe's four long years of torture, had been enough to bring radical change to the American continent. Armistice now posed the question of reconstruction. Governor Smith appointed Felix Adler to the New York State Reconstruction Committee as chairman of its subcommittee on Americanization. The Housing subcommittee had as its secretary Clarence Stein, architect and member of the movement. Gathering strength for the more subtle task facing the liberal community, Adler put an agenda of concerns before his Board early in the fall of 1919: "The great living questions . . . such as the League of Nations, the labor unrest, etc." He insisted that response to these questions be consistent with an ethical point of view and that the Society "not shirk meeting [them] for fear of creating division in the ranks." Out from under the cloud of the "German" question, Adler was apparently able to deal more forcefully with problems of social reform and social criticism.

In January, 1920, Adler reported on collections taken to help the impoverished societies abroad. The British, German, Austrian, and Swiss movements still survived though in much weakened condition. Elliott had gone overseas as soon as the war ended. Returning in the fall of 1920, he reported on his two and a half months in Europe:

> He was profoundly impressed with the strength of the foreign Ethical Societies and how those little struggling groups held on through all the years, how their Leaders, hungry themselves and speaking to their hungry people came through with heads held high and a profound belief in the Ethical Movement. Most feelingly, he spoke of Snell struggling in London, of Wagner in Lausanne eagerly drinking in all the news of the American point of view . . . of Boerner in Vienna, of the continued publication all through the war in spite of the difficulties . . . of *Ethische Kultur* and then of the grand old Geheimrat Foerster, 88 now, and making his lecture trips twice a week from Potsdam into Berlin.[16]

16 New York Board of Trustees, Minutes, October 5, 1920.

Arrangements were made for Snell and Wagner to visit the United States in the fall of 1920. Adler at that meeting called attention to the "necessity for gathering all the forces of the Society for a forward look . . . it was the time, not to look back but to look and forge ahead. . . ."

Ethical Culture had been created with the city in mind, against the backdrop of industrial organization, a growing labor movement, the admission of more and more people to equality. It was an inheritor of the enlightenment and of nineteenth-century idealism. Now the war was over, and the innocence of liberal progressivism was over too. The city, like so many other things, was losing its former boundary lines. Among the first actions of the postwar movement was to look across the ocean and bring representatives to America. The city of man was now the world and Ethical Culture would have to change its perception if it was to be meaningfully engaged with the twentieth century. Looking forward meant seeing differently, and behind Adler's exhortation to forge ahead was the question of whether moral religion could encompass a world environment and could absorb the shock of the destructiveness revealed by the war. Rudolph Penzig, from Berlin, stated the challenge:

> . . . after this war there will be . . . neither victors nor vanquished. . . . The task of Ethical Societies . . . will not be merely to act as a "Society of the Red Cross" for the social struggles of mankind. In their work of healing the wounds which morality, justice, humanity, mildness, and mutual respect have suffered, they must bear in mind a still higher purpose, the creating of a union of mankind which will make impossible the inflicting of such wounds in the future and forever.[17]

[17] "Ethical Culture in Germany After the War," quoted in *Essays,* Horace Bridges, ed. (1926, but written in 1915), pp. 369–70.

CHAPTER XVII

There Is
No Peace

The war was over, but the disease lingered. Adler addressed himself to "The Reconstruction of the Spiritual Ideal." More than cities and economies had to be rebuilt. The ideological, spiritual, and moral life of man was in disarray. The liberal community was in fragments—some retreating to individual self-help, some enamored of the new totalitarianisms of left and right, some uncomfortably caught up in the Wilsonian crusade. Fear drove people to the banner of virulent jingoism. Opening Pandora's box, war let loose uncontrollable forces which peace treaties could never control. The "clear" vision of wartime—the confident goals and slogans—turned out to have been false visions. Allies became enemies, and enemies, friends. Revolutions in Russia, Italy, and Germany were to create new tensions for the twentieth century.

Ethical Culture found itself suddenly without moorings. It had rehearsed the experience on a lesser scale in 1876, what Adler had spoken of as the "temple in ruins." Now, much more was in ruins. Former allies in the struggle for reform were running toward new salvation in totalitarian experiments. The churches, caught up briefly in the affirmative though somewhat naïve efforts of the Social Gospel, were rediscovering sin in neo-orthodox form. Those intellectuals who did not succumb to Marxism were enamored of a mythical Freudianism and a value-free scientism. The very idea of morality seemed outdated. The good people were on the make; their children were singing the tunes of the jazz age; everyone played the money game in the market and toasted success with bathtub gin. Everyone, that is, except Negroes, workers, American Indians, and a few others who experienced the "return to normalcy" as depression, deprivation, and broken heads on picket lines.

Ethical Culture turned to the question of peace and the League. The reformers saw the treaty of Versailles as moral treason. Elliott, following a visit to Vienna, wrote:

> . . . this terrific crime in the heart of Europe is not the work of war but of peace, not of men blinded by the savageries of organized war but of men sitting securely around a table in Paris deliberately assassinating a nation and plunging the whole of central Europe into a wreckage unlike anything which the infamies of men have perpetrated in the past. If Vienna had been blotted out from above or swallowed up from beneath it would have been a more merciful fate than the mutilated life and lingering death to which the peace criminals of Paris have doomed it.[1]

Elliott repeated over and over again his horror at the effects of total war: the shock of sixty houses left standing where 14,000 had stood before in Rheims; "of weeds that now cover the foundations of what were formerly . . . cities and villages, where not one single stone is left upon another above the ground and where the stones themselves are not visible because they have been beaten into the dust . . ."; of cemeteries and barbed wire everywhere.

Adler, now sixty-nine years old, was harshly critical of the peace negotiations. In the spring of 1920 he said:

> I wish to say here to you that the twilight of the Gods has come. There must be a new God if there is to be something more solid, more worthy of respect than that flimsy thing which they framed in Paris. . . .[2]

[1] "10 Days in Vienna," *The Survey*, October 2, 1920.
[2] April 4, 1920.

The old political habits had taken over the treaty discussions and had sabotaged the League before it had even begun. To the moralist, crime was piled on top of crime. For Adler, the League was a basis for neither justice nor peace. "It was a league of victors" with the interests of the smaller states unrepresented. Its control was in the hands of "professional politicians" whose main concern was personal power. David Muzzey reported that after a meeting at which Adler spoke in this vein one of the supporters of the League said to him ". . . in a voice trembling with indignation, 'I will never set foot in this building again.' "

A moral faith forced its supporters to seek an affirmative platform, not just criticize. On the political side, Ethical Culture called for a genuine parliament of nations and, ultimately, an international representative government, disarmament, a world police force, world law. On the educational front, it attempted to find a method of dealing with the class struggle and the shift to a technical culture. For Adler, however, programs and plans began with a philosophy. In his seventieth year he set himself the task of defining his ultimate views of life and man more explicitly than he had done in *An Ethical Philosophy* and *The World Crisis and its Meaning*. He began with the Kantian distinction between the empirical and the ideal. Human nature, he believed, allowed men to show bestiality toward fellow beings while remaining loyal to the ideal at the same time. The interplay between ideal and real continued to be the dynamic element in Adler's philosophic thought. In a series of addresses early in the 1920s he spelled out this philosophy:

> . . . how can you attribute such royal . . . grace and authority to a human being . . . when you . . . see how far they differ from any such ideal conception of them? . . . of course one must distinguish between two selves in everyone, between the animal self and this divine unclouded self. . . . Those instincts, those sensual infirmities, those rages, those passions, those flaring irascibilities, those cruelties, those crushing instincts . . . are part of our animal heritage . . . , but the other is what has been put by Stevenson . . . "a rising radiancy in man. . . ." [1920]

> A certain madness has seized people. . . . Had not the world behaved as if it were insane? And what hope of better things can you have if the

human race is subject to fits of insanity? . . . victors and vanquished are alike the loser. . . . [1922]

There is . . . at times, a morbid tendency just to hurt yourself, to dig into your vitals. . . . And . . . you find among humanity at large the same fact that you see in individuals—alternating periods of depression and elation. . . . Mankind has the blues; at times whole nations have the blues. . . . And then these periods of depression are followed by the opposite. [1923] [3]

The climax of this reasoning process came in the Hibbert Lectures delivered by Dr. Adler at Oxford in May, 1923, as *The Reconstruction of the Spiritual Ideal*. Reviewing the war and its meaning, its effects on personal and public life, the failures in politics, in international affairs, the rising rate of divorce, and so forth, Adler took the tack that these were effective demonstrations of a basic moral error. "[C]ivilization was not what we thought it to be. . . ." In the framework of his empirical/ideal analysis, he could once again speak of progress:

> Standing then at the terminus, I should say that one guiding thought for me would be continued interest in the progress of the human race to which I belong. . . . Progress means advance toward a society which shall more adequately reflect in all its relations the pattern of the spiritual world. To see God as reflected in the face of Christ is the theological way of putting this idea; to see the world of spiritual perfection as reflected in the face of humanity is the turn I give to the same thought. . . . [4]

Spiritual immortality was distinct from personal immortality. In a revealing footnote, he commented:

> That there actually is progress in human history it is impossible to prove. I rest my belief in progress not on the fact that it is demonstrable, for it is not demonstrable, but on the moral pronouncement that it ought to be, that therefore it can be and must be. . . . [5]

Progress, no longer the evident historical process of the enlightenment, was a moral commandment guiding personal and social ethics.

[3] Ethical Culture Archive.
[4] *Reconstruction of the Spritual Ideal* (New York 1924), pp. 215–16.
[5] *Ibid.*, p. 216 n.

It was a necessary attitude, not a discernable process. Thus, its heroes were prophetic rather than scientific, and progress required not so much an act of knowing as an act of will. In this Adler set himself in direct opposition to both Freudian and Marxian determinism and to what came to be called existential despair. Choosing to go counter to the prevailing intellectual currents of his age, he reinforced the minority status of his movement and almost guaranteed that advanced thinkers of his period would by and large turn their backs on Ethical Culture as a survival of an outdated, nineteenth-century philosophy. On the other hand—and in this he may have been right even if impolitic—he laid the basis for a philosophy of hope and of ethical freedom for all its metaphysical peculiarities and linguistic archaism.

Others in the Leadership were also seeking a basis for reconstruction. Alfred Martin addressed himself to the question of developing an international "mindedness" as the prerequisite to peace, ". . . America cannot ethically be divine except as a member of an international society. . . ." The test of such an achievement was in the old ideal of justice:

> . . . moral standards applied to the international actions of states are on a lower plane than the moral standards required of individuals in their dealings with one another. . . . One of the radical defects of our present civilization is the lack of a grip on the most elementary idea of justice between people and people. . . . Every honorable individual feels what is called a duty to himself. . . . He would be ashamed to steal from or lie to or seriously injure a weak neighbor. Ought not a nation have a like sense of duty to itself? [6]

In notes, John Elliott in 1931 listed as subjects for a speech: the disarmament conferences, the state of the League, the World Court, the Kellogg Pact (on armament control) and—still a pacifist—Remarque's book, *All Quiet on the Western Front.*

In 1928 an International Conference was proposed to consider how various religious denominations could contribute to world peace, and Alfred Martin was designated to attend for the Ethical movement. Martin reported that the meetings had excellent publicity, that at his

[6] Alfred W. Martin, "An Ethical Code of International Relations," October 22, 1922. Ethical Culture Archive.

suggestion similar meetings had been held in this country, and that each religious group had agreed to give attention to its position on peace. However, the onset of the Great Depression, the attacks on China and Ethiopia, the war in Spain, and the rise of Hitlerism made the hortatory process of traditional religions irrelevant.

For all its dependence on words and ideas, Ethical Culture was never contented only to speak. The call for the deed created Ethical Culture, but deciding upon deeds and finding men and women willing and able to commit themselves was problematic. Examining the decade following the end of the First World War, one is struck by the fact that, consciously or not, the patterns of the founding years recur: attempts were made to found a new school to answer the "social" problem and to reconstruct a purely ethical basis of faith; popular trends were criticized; Kantian idealism was reasserted. An abortive attempt tried to reestablish under a new name and with a different membership the Union for the Higher Life, the core group that in the earlier days had provided the nascent movement with the strength and funds to get on with the work. In 1919,

> Dr. Adler reported briefly on the Conference [of Leaders]. . . . He told of the discussion in regard to the proposed formation of an inner fellowship of the Ethical Society composed of men and women who will work out for themselves a certain way of living, this group to form a sort of nucleus within the Society without in any way attempting to impose anything upon others, but rather with the idea of giving a greater definiteness to the ethical ideal in regard to one's vocation, to money gain, to one's colleagues, to one's clients; also the attitude of mind at time of bereavement; the relation of young men and women, old ethics in fact with the new standards. The proposed order—Companions in the Spiritual Life—will be created within the larger community. . . .[7]

Reminiscent of Adler's youth, the desire to establish such a vanguard had within it the elitism implicit in Adler's view of the movement—the prophetic, chosen, dedicated few. Some months later at the convention of the American Ethical Union in Philadelphia, he said:

> . . . there is too much pressure toward the practical. We are living in a period of excitement when people want palpable results. . . . This is

[7] New York Board of Trustees, Minutes, October, 1919.

good, but it is only one side of life, and there is little tendency toward self-recollection, inwardness, and the quiet things. . . . Now, I am trying to build up a path to the inner life and while I think it is likely to appeal only to a minority, it is that minority which I think is going to be the soul of the Society. . . . We must have a central group. There must be a heart in the Society. The blood could not go through the veins without the heart, and without a soul the society itself would be a pretty dry affair. . . .[8]

But Adler was no longer a young man leading his peers, and the 1920s were not the 1870s. His movement had attracted members from many walks of life, and the Leadership was by no means united in support of Adler's idea. Like so many postwar proposals, the idea was there but the execution was missing. These years were tragic and frustrating to Adler, and he interpreted such negative experiences as the inevitable consequence of the interplay of the real and the ideal.

The ideal which I have enunciated has been accused of over-emphasizing frustration, of leading to a depressing view of life. If to stand at the brink, as it were, of the finite and to look out upon the solemn serenity of the external order is depressing then the accusation is just. But frustration is only the stepping stone. The accent of my view of life is on that which lies beyond the frustration—frustration being the inevitable means to the holiest vision.[9]

The attempts to recapture past insights in newer form was part of the seach for meaningful ends in a world that seemed to have lost all order. Nor was Adler alone in this. William Salter, at the fiftieth anniversary of the movement expressed his moral anguish:

. . . there is tragedy in life. . . . The happiest of us, the securest— those who have come safely out of every accident and recovered after every illness—have yet something to face from which there is no escape no recovery. For this is the final meaning of tragedy: no change for the better; there is the solemnity of the irreparable, the unalterable about it . . . , somehow the heart sinks within us. . . . Some of us acquire a more or less constant undertone of melancholy in contemplating this side of things—the zest and joy of life have passed now that we have felt the

[8] May, 1920.
[9] *Reconstruction*, pp. 210–11.

shadow of the end. . . . From habit, or mere animal shrinking from death, we may go on with our daily tasks, but the heart is sick.[10]

Gone were the common-sense acceptance of a religion of duty, the good will, the conviction of common ground. Salter sounded what was to become the basic tone of existentialism. Others turned to good works, to specific attacks on this or that social problem. But idealistic philosophy was vanishing, and, from Adler's point of view, its place was being taken by false gods and illusions. At the end of his life, and despite failing physical powers alert and sensitive, Adler was restrained by self-discipline and supported by philosophic trustfulness. Nevertheless, he too came near to expressing desperation.

> Out of the depths into which it has fallen humanity cries today for help. But as yet there is no response. There seems in fact to be moral retrogression all along the line. . . . The horror of the recent war is still felt in our bones, and yet it seems as if mankind could not take to heart the most drastic lessons, the most condign punishments. For alongside of the pacifistic current, preparations for new wars to be conducted by still more terrible methods are proceeding apace. Above all, there is one fact that strikes every observer: the so-called moral forces seem to have failed in the great crisis through which the world is passing.[11]

Never was the need for moral commitment and insight greater, and yet the spark that would ignite the moral imagination could not be found.

A miscellany of problems presented themselves, and the moralist bereft of ideological security was forced to attend. The growing struggle for the rights of workers, the organization of labor unions, and the increased success of communism received attention on the Ethical Platform and in the work of the various groups within the movement. Alfred Martin spoke of the lack of a moral sense in industrial relations:

> The prevailing conception of industry is no different from what it was in 1760 when the great industrial revolution occurred. . . . Then as now,

---

[10] William Salter, "Tragic and Heroic in Life," in *Aspects of Ethical Religion* (1926), p. 56.

[11] *Reconstruction*, pp. 1–2.

industry [was] conceived as a revenue-producing process only. . . .
Hence the spectacle . . . of guerilla warfare in which capital is seeking
to increase profits at the expense of labor, and labor is seeking to increase
wages at the expense of capital. . . .

What the industrial world needs . . . above all else is vision, the conception of industry as a form of social service. . . . It needs a new
paramount object to take the place of the present sordid object of money-
making.[12]

Others found possibilities in socialism for an ethical society in
which the cash nexus and the profit motive would both disappear.
Some found hope in the Russian revolution and in the militancy of
labor organization. For this group, growing in number but as yet not
able to assert leadership, Ethical Culture and socialism were interwoven, each complementing the other. A few recalled as a precedent
the close ties with Fabianism in the early days of the British expression of Ethical religion. Beneath the surface a basic rift began to separate those who, following Adler, were essentially conservative and
reformist and those who took a radical view of society and looked
toward democratic revolution. Coupled with the latent conflict between democratic and elitist views, these antithetical positions served
to paralyze the movement's development for many years, particularly
in the absence of a centralizing ideology and a unifying personality.

To the end of his life, Adler spoke against communism. In a 1930
address he said:

Marx made an invention . . . society [as] a kind of mechanism that
will produce more in quantity, that will stimulate production to such
a degree as to swamp and beat out of the field the capitalistic states. . . .
Then the immensity of products will be divided, of course, among the
proletarians. . . . The radicals are wrong, the sympathetic are wrong
who believe that the heart beats so warmly within the masses. The
Marxian[s] . . . disclaim moral ideals as nonsense, rubbish, sentiment
. . . the result of all this . . . is . . . the robot idea. The object is not
to uplift all the proletarians to a human way of living but the use of
the proletarian mass . . . as so many parts of this machine. . . . It is
the most terrible, freezing, shuddering sort of conception of society. . . .

[12] "Where There Is No Vision the People Perish," October 17, 1920.

Nowhere is liberty more outraged or more disdained than in Russia . . . the nine demigods who govern Russia today with the one man who really rules the others—the man of steel—they are not insane. They are all too sane in their fashion . . . constructing a machine in which you fit men. . . . a sort of Procrustes bed idea—the consequence . . . is the loss of liberty.[13]

Although the ideological center had disintegrated, the social work, the settlement houses, and the schools went on. Algernon Black, beginning his career with Ethical Culture at Madison House, reported to the New York Board in 1927 on a campaign to build a new home for that settlement house. At the Hudson Guild, Elliott announced to the Board that Mark McCloskey was joining him as assistant headworker and expressed gratification that both Black and McCloskey were graduates of the Ethical Schools. The play schools begun during the war were flourishing, and Joseph Jablonower reported:

. . . on the million children who such schools do not now reach . . . for whom and for whose parents the summer is a purgatory. He said that the work done so far was . . . important because . . . of the leverage it exercised. There are now 19 schools whereas ten years ago there was only the one belonging to the Ethical Culture Society.[14]

To the more radical critics, much of this activity seemed pointless. It did not reach the roots of the problems, and was even dangerous, since patching over some of the worst failings gave the illusion of progress. But others saw modest achievement. Edith Goldwater said: 'People used to say to me, can you notice any lasting influence? . . . But all I can say is that I know that we enriched their lives while they were here with us. . . ." [15]

Social reform became limited to personal social service; the time had passed when a Coit could envision the settlement house as a valid alternative to revolution. With the death of philosophy, social service justified itself by a kind of personalism and even sentimentality. In the face of increasing professionalization and expertise, the amateur

[13] "Humanity Uprooted and Humanity Regenerated," April 20, 1930.

[14] New York Board of Trustees, Minutes, November 1926.

[15] Interview, 1963.

was displaced by the "volunteer," and his role often reduced to fund raising or envelope stuffing.

Throughout the twenties the interests that had formed the movement continued. In 1927 the legislative committee of the New York Society addressed itself to Albany, calling for New York State's ratification of the proposed child-labor amendment.

The specter that had appeared during the war continued to haunt the councils of liberalism—the problem of loyalty and subversion. The first attack came in the schools. Elliott, in an address called "Junkers and Bolshevists," criticized the attempted domination of the schools by "alleged patriotic organizations" and the intimidation of teachers. The pulpit, too, was intimidated by superpatriots. In 1920 the New York Society debated the "Lusk bills" then before the state legislature in Albany, which would have mandated licensing of all schools by the University of the State of New York. The intent of such rigorous licensing was the state's effort to insure the patriotic bona fides of the various schools, public and private. Opposition was voiced ". . . on the ground that it would put a curb on educational and intellectual enterprises and throw the power of control of school in [to] the hands of politicians." [16] In a discussion of the legislation after its passage Adler said,

> The great tendency of American life is to disinfect what is diseased. Suppression never suppresses but drives inward to secret machinations and intrigue. If we once begin to interfere with liberty of conscience we cannot stop.[17]

The group was by no means unanimous, but they agreed to a position on the question and selected representatives to the Governor. One of the Trustees questioned the competence of that group to deal with anything other than the "business management" of the Society. That Trustee's objection was overruled then, but it was prophetic of a problem that much later was to dominate the institutional structure of Ethical Culture—the division of labor between lay and professional leadership, its manifestation of the "lords temporal and the lords spiritual."

[16] New York Legislative Committee, Minutes, March 30, 1920.
[17] New York Board of Trustees, Minutes, May 3, 1920.

A still unresolved question was whether and how an Ethical Culture society could take action. Seeking to safeguard the individual
conscience, the Society found itself often paralyzed; yet granting
freedom of the Platform, the societies often found themselves identified with public positions since the community did not make the fine
distinction between a Leader's private views and his symbolic and
representational character. In 1923 the Board of the New York Society once again returned to the question of how to guide action
against the hysteria of superpatriotism and jingoism. The freedom to
speak and debate any and all issues was unquestioned, but the sticky
point was action. The Society feared for its reputation and was concerned about public misunderstanding.

> The Board was reminded that they were not only Trustees of a plant or
> institution, but Trustees of an ideal,—of a view of things,—of a seed
> come to fruition later,—and if Dr. Adler's position was rightly under-
> stood, his unwillingness to pronounce on controversial questions was not
> conservatism but the fruit of a constructive idea—that it was more im-
> portant to keep an ideal pure than to speak on a particular subject at a
> particular moment. . . . That is why the Society is unwilling to enter
> the arena and pronounce.[18]

Adler was not present at the meeting and was cited freely for all positions. Remaining above battle might be a proper stance for the Society as a body, but the groups within the Society must be free to speak
and act on their own. They had been organized to provide centers of
common concern within the overall embrace of the Society. Adler had
often used the analogy of the cathedral and its chapels for the Society
and its special groups. A procedure was adopted of granting group
autonomy within the framework of the society; however, the freedom
of the groups increased the already evident fragmentation.

The movement's concern for its image and for the clarity of its purposes was repeatedly challenged by events. No sooner would one issue be resolved (usually by an uneasy compromise) than another
would appear. Elliott had spoken out for Eugene Debs and criticized
the Supreme Court for arming Debs' conviction. In the mid-twenties Elliott repeatedly visited the Governor of Massachusetts to urge

[18] New York Board of Trustees, Minutes, February 5, 1923.

freedom for Sacco and Vanzetti. In 1922 the Society was among those who petitioned the President for executive clemency for some seventy persons still in prison who had been tried and sentenced during the war. Even the "communist" question was aired in the Meeting House, to Adler's displeasure:

> Dr. Adler expressed his displeasure that the use of the auditorium had been granted for a meeting with Mr. Scott Nearing as speaker on the subject of communism. . . . We do not dispute the right of anyone to have his opinions and to have convictions different from ours [but] . . . this auditorium is said to be holy ground to those who seek the highest. Those who seek the highest, therefore ought to be welcome—not those who seek other than the highest . . . ! Dr. Adler added, however, that he would be satisfied to have other convictions expressed at forum meetings, provided always both sides of the question were presented.[19]

The climax was the Great Depression. To the problems of an Ethical Culture movement seeking to focus itself anew, to a liberal community caught up in crisis over its reason for being, to threats from left and right, was added the brutal question of economic survival. In a series of letters, Adler and Elliott addressed themselves to the problem of unemployment and how Ethical Culture might counteract its intensity. In New York the Hudson Guild was playing a major role with the unemployed. In Chicago a workroom for unemployed women began. An emergency work bureau and sewing shop were organized. Relations with relief efforts of various state and federal governments were developed as the reformers responded to a challenge that was familiar but now on a massive scale. John Elliott commented on,

> . . . an overwhelming sense of the inadequacy of the attempts to stem the tide of poverty and fear and uncertainty that has swept so many thousands about us from their work and left them struggling for life. . . .
>
> Perhaps next to men selling apples the most familiar sight is that of the breadlines. . . . I was walking by one of these breadlines with a friend. . . . After the first glance he never looked again but walked with his

---

[19] New York Board of Trustees, Minutes, January 6, 1930.

eyes straight ahead. . . . He couldn't look on the indignity of men standing in line for hours waiting for a bowl of soup and a piece of bread. To see prisoners is hard. To see the sick is pitiful, but to see men physically . . . fit for work standing there to be given bread was a sight that a person socially, humanly, spiritually sensitive could not look at without a sense of shame.[20]

The societies found the depression hard going. In 1931 the Leaders unanimously asked for a ten percent reduction in salaries. This was refused when the Trustees agreed to find the funds somehow. Those few who could gave willingly. Typical was a letter from Mrs. Lionel Sutro offering $50,000 to help the School survive. But most of the membership could not respond. B. Edmund David reported in 1932 that there had been a sharp drop in the number of members who could make any contribution to the Society—from 949 contributing members in 1931 to 816 in 1932. Other societies were harder pressed. Julie Neumann wrote to John Elliott:

I imagine that you must be as sick of all of this money raising as I am. It has come to discolor life so much that the various schemes, not only of our organization, but of all others are like red flags to me and I long to get away where I would never hear another word about a benefit performance. Nevertheless, as you know to your sorrow too, we have got to keep on.[21]

Henry Neumann wrote: "Brooklyn unfortunately is in no position to increase its budget. Three months salary is still unpaid to me in spite of good hard work by a lot of people like Joe Lichterman who have far graver worries of their own just now." [22]

The tragic decade was over, the peace that was no peace revealed in all its emptiness. More than the temple, more even than the common sense of liberalism and enlightenment was in ruins. The high hopes of reform were clouded by a sense of doom. Reconstruction was Adler's rallying cry, but revolution seemed much more likely in the light of the apparent failure of the liberal, capitalist, industrial system.

[20] *The Standard*, XVII (1931), p. 130.
[21] Letter, March 17, 1932.
[22] Letter to John Elliott, June 24, 1931.

CHAPTER XVIII

The Fieldston Plan

To anyone visiting the Fieldston School in Riverdale, New York—its buildings, laboratories, studios—or meeting members of its highly qualified faculty, its rather precocious student body, its successful graduates, Fieldston must seem a success. Yet, measured in terms of Adler's intent, praise must be qualified. Instead of an agency of social reform and transition Fieldston became an excellent college preparatory school. Instead of an instrument for change what evolved was a part of contemporary culture, a response to the pressures and interests of the educational and social establishment.

By the 1920s Adler was harking back to the pattern of the founding years and to the idea that religion must be integrally related to education. He had envisaged that by its hundredth anniversary Ethical Culture would have twelve societies, each with its own school, located in twelve major urban areas of the country. The Ethical Culture schools began for workmen's children but had gradually integrated the children of the rich as well as students of all races and religions; it had extended to an open-air school, a normal school for teacher training, and an arts high school. Those Ethical Culture members upon whom

208

Adler counted most sent their children to the schools and thus developed closer ties to each other and to the movement. The schools complemented the Society, making Ethical Culture a place for young and old, for Sunday and weekday, for social service and personal growth.

With the war, revolution abroad, and latent revolution in the United States, the question of the nature of education was raised anew. All of Adler's thinking now—about the crisis, the failure of civilization, class struggle and the industrial process—pointed to the need for new educational ideas. Moreover, the idea of character formation as the end of ethical education needed reformulation. In the 1890s a concept of "organic" education was germinating which confronted the "atomistic" (or specialized) education of the day. A forerunner of the matured idea of vocation expressed in the Fieldston Plan was Adler's philosophy of education, which drew upon the related themes of natural capacity, individual difference, and cultural necessity. Now he was seeking empirical expression in the educational process.

In 1913 the Arts High School was established, and Adler was soon speaking of the need to expand the experiment. In 1926 he formulated "ideals for the new school":

> . . . the principle of the preeminence of values must be adhered to
> . . . we go through the whole history of commerce and the commercial
> class—the kind of government it has promoted; and how it has influenced science and the arts; . . . how far commerce was the accomplice
> of tyranny; how far commerce today is a menace in the Far East. . . .
> We give the young business men . . . an idea of the man of business
> considered as a member of the commercial group, of the policies to be
> favored in national and international life, of the attitude to be taken
> toward fellow-workers . . . we endeavor to implant in them the principle of watching their lives and estimating their own value by the way
> in which they affect other people, to bring that principle into the very
> market place.[1]

In 1923, commenting on a report of Dr. Pritchard, head of the Carnegie Foundation, Adler challenged the notion that education for

[1] Felix Adler, *Ideals for Our New School*, February, 1926.

most students should be limited to narrowly conceived fundamentals and trade school training. Efficiency and economy should not be the criteria of schooling. In contrast, "The Ethical Culture Schools stand for a certain tenderness toward the human creature . . . so as to . . . make [its life] as complete as human lives can become for the sake of the development of personality." [2] Adler invoked his older idealism—"Give the children a touch of that bigger life in such a way that they will live it"—and calling on the Society to establish a series of "pre-vocational" schools in business, art, science. For Adler, vocation meant life career, a way of focusing individual talents in an integrated personality and of building a more meaningful social order in which each individual contributed to "orchestrating" an evolving culture.

That same year, 1923, Adler was in England for the Hibbert Lectures. At Oxford he spoke on "Culture and Education" and sought to make explicit the essential relationship between ideal, empirical reform, and educational preparation. Criticizing Matthew Arnold's and Goethe's concepts of culture, Adler set forth his alternative:

> I have said that our educational system . . . is pointless . . . [and] have traced over-specialization back to provisionalism. I have said that provisionalism arises from teleology being confounded with theology. . . . We can advance educational theory and practice by setting the example of a teleological system (as opposed to the pragmatist tendencies and mere efficient ideals) . . . [Lecture I]
>
> . . . culture . . . shall be accessible to the manual worker or the man in the shop . . . it shall not be the property of the elite. . . . [Lecture II]
>
> What we have in Arnold is culture confined to the elite. . . . The humblest seamstress is cultured insofar as she is the typical cutter of gowns . . . but we have a kind of frozen world, each specialist in his place. . . . The next step . . . and by that I understand the ethical conception of culture, is to thaw out this frozen world. . . . It is the relation between the special vocations and the spiritual rule . . . so act on others as to promote the sense of life in them and by repercussion to arouse the sense of life in yourself. . . . Culture is to be the . . . antidote of specialism. The ethical relation is the cross relation. Ethics is the sense of action and reaction. . . . [Lecture II]

[2] New York Board of Trustees, Minutes, March, 1923.

While Adler was planning a new departure in education, the times insisted upon change as rights of minorities became current. In 1920 *The Nation* published an article on "Democracy Worthy of the Name," in which the Ethical Culture schools were cited as the "one place where colored children are freely admitted, in some cases on scholarship. . . ." [3] The school's Board of Governors faced another difficulty when a Negro youngster applied for admission to the school's new summer camp. It was feared that an open admission policy would jeopardize the financial success of the project. A few were apprehensive that intermarriage would grow out of the coeducational nature of the camp and the intimacy of camping experience. "After very thorough consideration, the vote was almost unanimous that colored children should be admitted and from the start, even at the risk of not making the camp a financial success." The Board of Trustees accepted their decision with applause and congratulated the Board of Governors on the stand that they had taken. [4]

The concept of integration, of which the question of race was only a part, became the guiding idea of the new school. Robert Kohn said: "We believe that all these groups (men, women, workers, business men, professionals, scientists, artists, rich, poor) should be kept together and that the effect of each will be broadening to all." At the same meeting Adler let loose his imagination:

. . . we should . . . give rein to our vastest hopes . . . , think of the future graduates of this business school as playing a great role in the world. . . . The white races are one third of the population of the world; the colored races . . . are showing their restiveness under the domination of the white. . . . The commercial spirit is everywhere breaking the hearts of the races. . . . The greatest change that the world needs today is the creation of real men. . . . We must dedicate our pre-vocational school . . . to the future civilization of this planet. [5]

So the Fieldston Plan grew. Early in 1927 a booklet was published entitled "A New Departure in Education," describing in some detail a school aimed at educating "a generation of specialists" whose effectiveness would be judged by their contribution to the general

---

[3] December 1, 1920, p. 147.
[4] New York Board of Trustees, Minutes, January, 1923.
[5] New York Board of Trustees, Minutes, November, 1925.

advance of humanity. The first step was to be the pre-professional school of business. By "the commercial class" was meant both worker and employer. Robert Kohn and Clarence S. Stein, both members of the Society, were the school's architects. Herbert W. Smith, a faculty member, believed the Plan could forge new tools:

> As soon as we can we intend to educate in one administrative and social unit general professional students, artists, homemakers, industrial executives, and business men, carrying our work through what are now the freshmen and sophomore years of college and feeding many of our graduates directly into the professional schools. . . .[6]

Smith's article made clear that Fieldston was not to be just another high school but a six-year program incorporating the first two years of college.

The Fieldston idea sought to bring together under a common educational and moral ideal the disparate strands of a culture in disarray. Democracy was to mesh with competence, specialization with generalization, the American ideal with the needs of world culture, industrial requirements with classic style. The conception was worthy indeed of Emerson's moral religion and Adler's genius. Philosophy came alive again to demonstrate how a bridge could be built between the old and the new, and to Adler nothing less than civilization was at stake. A good society was found by making good people.

The School was to stand out against both private and public education, being neither "class schools" (Adler's words for private education) nor "mass schools" (his description of public education). The plans for the school described an ethical personality—humane, free, efficient, cultured, forward looking. Leading educators of the day supported the plan, including James R. Angell, President of Yale; Frank Aydelotte, President of Swarthmore; Nicholas Murray Butler, President of Columbia; Livingston Farrand, President of Cornell; Glenn Frank, President of the University of Wisconsin; Frank J. Goodenow, President of Johns Hopkins; Ernest M. Hopkins, President of Dartmouth; Henry N. McCracken, President of Vassar; and William Allan Neilson, President of Smith.

Adler's talent for bringing institution and idea together, his ability

6 "A Teacher Forges New Tools," *The Survey Graphic*, June, 1927, p. 256.

to stir support and excitement, was still evident. He was in his seventy-fifth year when the Plan was completed. Yet, while he drew on the resources of his colleagues, his members, and his fellow educators, Fieldston was essentially his, nurtured over fifty years of effort. Could the means be found for giving it reality and would the older Adler be able to sustain the necessary drive? Not the least of the questions was what would happen to the idea when its originator died. Because these questions were very much in the minds of Adler and his inner circle of supporters, the effort to describe the Fieldston Plan was extensive. The long period of discussion (from the end of the War until 1926) was probably an effort to create understanding among those who would have to carry on. The meticulous attention to the educational philosophy of the school was, no doubt, intended to leave behind a guide to its development. The school was to be both the fulfillment of a promise made in 1876 and the next step in the evolution of a movement committed to working out moral idealism.

Even as Adler mustered public support for his idea and worked out its philosophic and cultural meanings, he gave attention to the means. The existing schools contained a core group of competent faculty for the new program. The various efforts with secondary education within the movement (the Arts High School, the ethics classes, the camps, the normal school), combined with the newer ideas in progressive education and educational psychology, gave promise of a meaningful and exciting course of study. Idea, manpower, and aim were available. Attention turned, naturally, to money.

By 1922 the deficit of the war years had been eliminated and the schools were self-supporting. Scholarship funds were raised and teacher's salaries were on a par with those in public and private schools. Requests for admission outnumbered places for students; the days of wandering the streets of New York looking for pupils had long since passed. Thus, the Board of Trustees felt justified in approving plans for the new school, and by May, 1927, a million dollars had been raised.

The list of donors to the Fieldston project revealed that Adler had not lost his ability to reach men and women of eminence and wealth. The largest single gift came from John D. Rockefeller, Jr., who gave $250,000 on condition that $750,000 come from other sources. Herbert Wolff recalls:

. . . Dr. Adler recalled that he had worked very closely with John D. Rockefeller Jr. in connection with better housing and various other civic and communal projects. They were good friends. Dr. Adler decided to telephone Mr. Rockefeller . . . for an appointment. . . . Mr. Rockefeller said that he would come to see Dr. Adler since Dr. Adler was the older and more important individual. . . .

Mr. Rockefeller . . . told Dr. Adler that he was very much interested but that he would like to have a survey made . . . by his own people with respect to how this school was functioning, what its reputation was, its history. Dr. Adler readily acceded to this and at the end of 30 days, Mr. Rockefeller came again to see Dr. Adler and told him that he had gotten an excellent report, that he was very excited about the plan . . . , and that he would be glad to contribute one quarter of the necessary amount.[7]

In 1928 the cornerstone of the Fieldston School was set in place in Riverdale, New York. Academic buildings on a large open campus were planned as were apartments for faculty members at the western edge of the property. Because the apartments were to be operated as a business venture separate from the school itself, tax exemption was voluntarily surrendered on that part of the property.[8] The Board consolidated its school programs on the Fieldston campus, closing the branch school which had been meeting in two rented houses in midtown Manhattan. A lower school was planned for the Fieldston property, too. By 1932 the basic physical plant was completed, though additions were made over the years.

The idea, the money, the place were in hand. The task now became working out a specific program for implementing the Fieldston Plan in the classroom. Dr. V. T. Thayer was appointed Educational Director in 1928. Earlier he had served two years as principal of the high school after the retirement of Henry Kelley in 1922. One of the pioneer group of progressive educators, Thayer had been a university professor, an author, and a secondary school teacher. Basically, he was Deweyan in his approach to education. Understanding Adler's differences with Dewey, he struggled to adjust himself to the idealism which differentiated Adler's thought from the "process" approach of the progressivists.

[7] Interview, 1963.
[8] Board of Trustees, Minutes, April, 1929.

In organization and administration the Fieldston School resembled other secondary schools, but the mood was different. The faculty understood its role on the edge of a new experiment and was versed in Adler's concept of the school as an ideal community. An ethics department was established at Fieldston:

> Ethics was really more like current events with a philosophic undertone. . . . All through the ethics classes we talked about behavior, attitudes about things that happened, tolerance, about war and peace rather than . . . doctrinaire ethical discussions or even any systematic review of ethical philosophy.[9]

John Elliott, Henry Neumann, and Algernon Black helped build the ethics program, and Mark McCloskey was a teacher.

> . . . you had in him . . . a person who could understand the background and environment of these youngsters but [who] also brought to them an experience of other environments. . . . My own son, Robert, was in the school . . . and . . . less academically inclined than some of his classmates. I remember his coming home one day and stating with a great deal of satisfaction that Mark McCloskey in the Ethics class had gone down the line and asked all the boys to open their hands. He wanted to see if they had calluses . . . or not . . . and Bob could show calluses. . . . This was McCloskey's way of trying to give these youngsters an understanding of the dignity of the callused hands as well as the hand that does not have them.[10]

The ethics program related Ethical Culture to the work of the school. The Leaders of the Society became active in the school's life, introducing into it the problems of social and personal ethics central to an evolving movement. Alumni of the school say that the ethics classes were often significant in determining vocational and avocational choices. The school as well maintained a classics department, shops, laboratories, and art studios. "Learning by doing" complemented but did not replace the humanistic tradition. The school had the best of both worlds—the traditional and the contemporary. Social service was encouraged in the school, as is revealed by a 1921 report:

[9] Interview, Janet Robbins, 1964.
[10] Interview, V. T. Thayer, 1964.

The Board approved of the resolution of the School Council to the effect that the Neighborhood Service Work became an integral part of the School's educational work. . . . Dr. Adler approved the Council's recommendation with the following remarks:

1. . . . one learns by doing, and hence acquires the spirit of service by rendering service;

2. . . . one learns by teaching and hence that our high school pupils will themselves profit by acting in the shop and elsewhere as teachers of . . . boys and girls in the neighborhood.[11]

A curriculum for ethics, the classics, social service, and usual subject matters was ready; new materials and new sources were examined. Fieldston reported to the General Education Board, a Rockefeller philanthropy, in 1934 on some of the teaching research in process. Mr. Klock of the Fieldston science department was partially freed from teaching duties in order to visit industrial plants and research laboratories to bring the latest work in science and technology into the school. For English and literature, Mr. Lenrow had developed a bibliography and library to allow students to follow their own special interests and to keep abreast of recent literature. Mrs. Koch and Miss Day were working on material about the influence of women in the history of civilization (required by Adler's notion of the vocation of womanhood). Similar efforts at research and curriculum were undertaken by Mr. Jablonower in mathematics, Mr. Hanchett in business and economics, Mr. D'Amico and Mr. Mangravite in the arts. A sense of what all of this hard work intended emerged in the following description:

. . . Dr. Kelly in his course on Biology and Human Life . . . has selected . . . facts and principles that help a student majoring in euthenics to understand herself and others; and in a way to form something of a tentative philosophy of life. By its many-sided treatment of man, his relations with the lower animals, his geological history, his development of a social life, his differentiation into races or types, his embryological development, the laws of his heredity, the problems of eugenics and euthenics, his emotional and intellectual development, he has made extraordinary progress in finding teaching material of great value. This

11 New York Board of Trustees, Minutes, November, 1921.

work, with its excursions and its laboratory procedure seemed particularly significant for the non-verbal type of girl. . . . Moreover, by bringing into his course pediatricians, psychiatrists, and anthropologists, by clinical work and by bringing these concrete experiences to bear on large general problems he has contributed toward a sound and liberal education.[12]

The school was in close touch with others on the educational frontier. It was one of thirty schools participating in the Progressive Education Association's experiment in sending high school graduates to college without traditional grades, course credits, and so forth. The school arranged for consulting psychologists and psychiatrists to determine "whether our new procedures did in fact promote easier and more complete integration of personality during adolescence, did diminish frustration, and in general met better the emotional and personal needs of the individual." [13] The consulting specialists responded that the school offered a "total environment which is more stimulating and more encouraging than teachers of equal ability and originality could produce if they were isolated from each other. . . ." [14] On the question of "vocation" and the integration of specialization, the report seems affirmative too: "We thus envisage as a final outcome an educational program designed for a democracy of interests in which the established abilities of students are placed at the center of the school program—but used in such a way as to combine at once a thorough grounding in one field with definite lines of transition to other areas." [15]

Although, in all likelihood, no one perceived it at the time a subtle shift is evident in Thayer's report which was to jeopardize and ultimately defeat the Fieldston Plan. Instead of specifying the "needs of civilization" as an objective for the school in accordance with Adler's concept, first place was given to the individual student's needs, abilities, interests. More and more emphasis shifted to the "development of the unique potentialities of the individual child." The reciprocal nature of Adler's social ethic and the cultural concept of vocation

[12] Letter to General Education Board, from V. T. Thayer, November, 1934, pp. 4–5.
[13] *Ibid.*, p. 7.
[14] *Ibid.*, p. 8.
[15] *Ibid.*, p. 10.

were missing. College entrance requirements became important, although this resulted from pressures of the American culture, not from the search for an ideal. Social criticism and social reform, which had been the core of the Fieldston Plan, were now peripheral and restricted to discussions of social ethics in the classroom and social service projects. The school had been drawn into the orbit of existing practice.

> Dr. Adler never developed, or never succeeded . . . in having the Fieldston School or schools in general carry out logically his concept of education. I am not sure after all . . . that conditions in American life would have made it possible with or without college entrance examination requirements.[16]

In fairness, it should be noted that Thayer and others, guided by newer insights in developmental psychology, probably had serious doubts about the desirability of urging vocational choices upon high school students. On the other hand, the New York City Board of Education did successfully develop a remarkable group of specialized schools that were quite in line with Adler's basic idea—the High School of Music and Art, Brooklyn Technical High School, the Bronx High School of Science, and others. In place of Adler's pre-vocational education, a first-rate private high school developed. In the case of the Progressive Education Association experiment requirements were modified; however, the goal of college admission took the center of the stage as it did for nearly all secondary education. The concept of a six-year school, in part modeled after the European gymnasium, was not tried at all. By ordinary educational criteria, the school could certainly be regarded as a success, though it is doubtful that Adler would have been content. Thus, Thayer reported:

> A group of visitors to Fieldston . . . looked at the course of study and said, "well, this is just the conventional curriculum." But after having spent several days at the school, they expressed their astonishment at the experimental work that was going on and at the richness of every one of the subject matter fields.[17]

[16] V. T. Thayer Interview, 1964.
[17] Interview, 1964.

The school was distinguished for the number of men and women it contributed to the arts, the sciences, social service, and politics. Victoria Wagner, Educational Director of the Schools and former teacher and principal as well, said of the graduates:

> Lincoln Gordon, for example, an ambassador, is one of the graduates, [as is] Adam Yarmolinsky. . . . Joseph Kraft is . . . in Washington and has written quite widely on political matters. Bernard Nossiter . . . writes on political science . . . J. Robert Oppenheimer, a remarkable person . . . both poet and scientist, was in the school. People in the theatre arts as well as painting. . . . In the field of music, Deems Taylor [should be] mentioned. . . .[18]

A good many other well-known figures could be named, including Henry Dreyfus, the designer; Babette Deutsch, the poet; Joseph Margolies in the arts. V. T. Thayer, commenting on the alumni, noted:

> Well, I suppose any good school can produce a list of its distinguished alumni, but I think the distinctive thing in our case is the number of people who would otherwise not have had the advantages of this education. . . . The scholarship principle in the school made it possible for Joseph Margolies, Henry Dreyfus and others to . . . receive a type of education that they particularly needed and which they might not have received elsewhere.[19]

To the school's credit, whatever its failure in carrying out the more imaginative implications of the Fieldston Plan, enough social idealism persisted to ensure a vigorous scholarship program. It was endangered and to some extent curtailed by the Great Depression, which produced a financial imbalance from which the school did not recover until well after the Second World War. By then it was much too late to recapture the initiating insight of Adler's.

The relationship between the schools and the Ethical Culture movement was problematic. Never intended to be sectarian, the personalities and interest of Adler, John Elliott, Henry Neumann, and

18 Interview, 1964.
19 Interview, 1964.

others in the Leadership created an informal yet very real tie between the work of the schools and the movement. However, interpreting that tie was left to personal style and choice, and to many of the student body the relationship was mystifying or not apparent. Janet Robbins recalled:

> . . . I never had any religious feeling for the Society. I am sure this is an answer you get from many graduates. . . . *I don't think the Society was ever discussed* and I think this was one of the things that was very good about the Society—that it supported the school, founded it and ran it but that it didn't proselytize.[20]

It is difficult to estimate how much of Ethical Culture was indirectly and implicitly communicated. While no one wanted the school to be parochial, Adler at least intended that the values and goals of the Ethical Culture movement pervade the school and its work. The narrow question of institution was no problem; converts were not desired. But the broader question of teaching from a basic point of view became less and less clear after Adler's death. Adler had repeatedly tried to interpret his ideal of the school. One of the last occasions was in 1928, when Fieldston was about to open:

> The new educational experiment . . . should be considered as the very fibre of the Society's life. The possibility of making an ethical impression upon this generation must never be abandoned. . . . On the whole we realize that the current is not going our way. . . . We are passing through a period of great uncertainty. . . . The foundations are rocking. . . . In looking to the future we . . . plant the seed in the next generation that will produce the fruit that we hope for. . . . The mind of youth, of America, of the world will make a beginning of a change of direction. And that is what the experiment at Fieldston means.[21]

To the very end, Adler preached his vision of reform, his belief that civilization demanded and individuals responded. That was to be the pedagogical theme of the schools, the crux of an education in ethical culture. But each of these notions gave way under pressures which seemed irresistible or in the name of educational viewpoints different

20 Interview, 1964.
21 New York Board of Trustees, Minutes, May 1928.

in spirit from Adler's. It was not simply the dollar dilemma, college admission requirements, or the progressivist ideology of individual potential and needs. The confluence of these forces, together with Adler's death soon after the school's opening, insured that the Fieldston Plan would not be implemented. In 1927 Herbert Smith had written,

Colleges . . . are specializing more and more narrowly in the education of those boys and girls who are academically apt. Yet, so long as American parents believe that the only way to give their children a chance in modern American life is to send them to college, no administrative device can withstand the power of money and social position to force into college boys and girls who are intellectually unfit. Some one must open [other] roads that lead to success with equal directness.[22]

Gradually the student body of the school became academically elite; more and more the ambitions of parents and the admissions policies of the colleges narrowed the range of acceptable experiment. Attention to the individual student and a respect for differences remained but steered a new course. Dr. Thayer commented,

. . . We do have a high IQ. . . . The parent who wants his child to attend . . . a good private school . . . has, at least, an appreciation of the importance of education. . . . In the course of times the child who is not necessarily college material, as we use the phrase today, may find it somewhat difficult to keep up with the increasing number of ambitious children and ambitious parents. And so there is a process of natural selection that takes place even before the school becomes aware of it. And when the school becomes aware of it the faculty begins to ask the question: here is a child that's having increasing difficulty—is it really to the best interest of that child to remain in a competitive position with other children, struggling to maintain [a] pace . . . that is too high for him?[23]

Mrs. Wagner rounded out the picture:

They all go to college. . . . They do not all go to the Ivy-League colleges. . . . A large percentage of the boys, particularly, go on to grad-

[22] "A Teacher Forges New Tools," *The Survey Graphic*, June, 1927, p. 258.
[23] Interview, 1954.

uate school and many girls go too. You know, when they finish high school, this doesn't mean that they are finished with their education. Even the girls who get married before they graduate from college . . . somehow they feel that they want to go on and finish their degrees.[24]

Perhaps Dr. Adler had been foolish, perhaps out of tune with his time, too early or too late with his educational ideas. Speculation does not help. Thayer maintained that Adler's ideas could not work in the America of the 1930s, 40s and 50s. But we will never know, for those ideas were not really tried.

[24] Interview, Victoria Wagner, 1964.

CHAPTER XIX

The Movement
in the Twenties

Prohibition symbolized a schizophrenia in American life during the twenties—an appearance of virtue glossed over behaving as one pleased. For some the decade was one of great economic success, for many it was a time of serious deprivation. Young intellectuals were running away physically to the Left Bank or spiritually into Freudianism. Politics was at a low ebb; the Wilsonian crusade and its idealism was laid to rest.

Adler was growing older, and many of his early colleagues and followers were dead or dying. Inattention to organization was now beginning to exact its price. The societies in New York, St. Louis, Philadelphia, Chicago continued as did Dr. Neumann's in Brooklyn and, tentatively, Dr. Muzzey's in Westchester County. Other societies appeared and disappeared with disturbing frequency. The international movement scarcely existed, though the British Ethical Union was recovering from the war and the Vienna Society was at work.

Adler had pictured a very conservative institutional growth for the movement. Others, including Chubb in the United States and Coit in England, envisioned a popular, and thus greater, expansion. A letter

from Anna Spencer to Mr. Chubb on the occasion of the fiftieth anniversary predicted that the movement would die if Adler's view pre-
vailed. However, the question that really had to be faced was posed
by Dr. Adler—what relevance had an Ethical Culture movement in
the postwar world? The answer seemed self-evident prior to the war;
now it was no longer clear. Adler, unlike many of his colleagues, knew
that reform without a philosophic basis would rapidly deteriorate into
fragmented experiences.

The reconstruction of an ethical philosophy has been the paramount problem of the movement from the postwar period to the present. Meanwhile, cultural changes were making the need more pressing and more difficult to fill at one and the same time. Most evident,
especially as it affected Ethical Culture, was the trend toward a bour-
geois culture in the United States, which was reflected in the changing nature of membership in the Ethical societies. Successful and
autonomous personalities were becoming rare. Thus, Elliott spoke:

> . . . I want to say that most of the people who come here lately do not
> know what the Ethical Society is about. . . . Feelings, yes. General
> feelings. But if we want to build a place, we have got to see the plan, to
> understand, we cannot just feel . . . a plan. . . . It is the fire that
> gives light.[1]

Alfred Martin, on a more prosaic level, described the newer membership:

> During the past 8 years . . . 700 applicants for membership have been
> interviewed. . . . Fully 80% . . . are people of modest circumstances
> . . . one in every eight has taken occasion, following the interview, to
> confer privately at my study regarding some personal, domestic, or
> business perplexity upon which help was desired. . . . Thus a distinct
> department—what the churches call pastoral work—has grown.[2]

The Leadership was to find fewer and fewer recruits for the creative and innovative task of reconstructing Ethical Culture. Demands
for "servicing the membership" frequently overshadowed all else. A

[1] John L. Elliott, "The Young Rebel of 1920," March, 1920.
[2] Alfred Martin, Special Report to the New York Board of Trustees, November,
1920.

few of the older, more independent spirits remained in the twenties—
the Seligmans and the Sutros, the Bambergers and Morgenthaus, the
Kohns—and a few recruits were added to this group. V. T. Thayer
recalled of Robert D. Kohn:

> . . . he [Adler] influenced Robert Kohn who organized the building
> industry for a time . . . along these lines [Adler's ideas of business
> responsibility] when he was President of the American Institute of Ar-
> chitects. . . . He succeeded for a time in bringing together contractors.
> architects, electricians—all the people who are really concerned with
> the construction of a building. He tried to have them become the force
> for raising the level not only of business practice . . . but also to de-
> velop closer relationships between labor and capital.[3]

The Kohns, Robert and Estelle, close friends of the Adlers, became
part of his inner circle, the "true" Ethical Culture society. Another
member, B. Edmond David, a silk manufacturer in Paterson, New
Jersey, applied the idea of cooperative relationships between capital
and labor in his plant, encouraged the development of unionism, and
arranged for employees to be represented at the management level.
Similar attempts to apply an ethical view of business were undertaken
by other members of Adler's inner circle. While Mr. David was encouraging organization in Paterson, New Jersey, Sidney Blumenthal
was doing the same with his textile mills in the South. But men and
women with the power and position to influence policy directly were
becoming scarce within Ethical Culture societies.

The conflict between a conservative and expansionist view of the
movement was accompanied therefore by a drastic change in the nature of the membership. Adler's image of an Ethical movement as the
vanguard of reform for the larger community was betrayed by a shift
making the membership of that nucleus institutionally less capable.
Nevertheless, Adler continued to fight for his aristocratic interpretation. To his Board, Adler made the problem explicit:

> . . . He had been thinking about the membership. . . . In the early
> days there was a strong contingent of men of substance, of maturity, of
> influence, and while many are still here, others have gone and many of
> the new members seem to be of a different status. The Society seems to

[3] Thayer, interview, 1964.

be weakening in the calibre of the inner nucleus. . . . The Society needs reinforcement and Dr. Adler asked that the Chairman of the Nominating Committee put himself in communication with him in regard to a reinforcement of the Board of Trustees.[4]

This effort seemed certain to fail. The days of the bureaucrat, the functionary, and the pragmatist made the ideal of a nobility of behavior seem romantic and foolish. The problem of excellence was not peculiar to the movement, but characteristic of the culture itself.

The Leadership was changing too. Henry Neumann, in Brooklyn, was a forerunner of the pastoral and familial Leader. Other changes revealed that Adler's tight hold on the movement was weakening. In New York the Board of Leaders requested that it be designated a Council of Leaders. In Chicago Horace Bridges was ordained a Unitarian minister, ostensibly in order to perform marriages in the state of Illinois. The Leaders in the summer of 1923 concluded that while the freedom of members for multiple affiliation was unimpaired, "so long as a man is a Leader of an Ethical Society, he cannot at the same time be [Catholic priest, rabbi, Protestant minister]." Latent in the debate about Bridges' action were the issues of clericalism and the distinction between laity and ministry. As a larger number of members sought what Martin correctly identified as a pastoral relationship, two kinds of Ethical Culture became distinct. The older type, still present but rare, was a partnership of equals within an elite; the newer type, infrequent in the past but now becoming the norm, followed the traditional relationship of minister and congregation.

John Elliott, who had never fully accepted the elitist ideal, resolved his differences by developing parallel careers at the Hudson Guild and in the Ethical Culture Society. By the mid-twenties, however, Elliott raised the issue directly:

> . . . Years ago when I first heard Dr. Adler at Cornell, he made a deep impression on me when he spoke of the "new profession of teaching people how to live." I would change that phrase now to the "profession of living with people," with people of all kinds, in sickness, people in trouble, in the most soul-searching kind of trouble.[5]

4 New York Board of Trustees, Minutes, October, 1923.
5 New York Board of Trustees, Minutes, December, 1925.

Adler interpreted this as a matter of personal inclination, not institutional change: ". . . as a matter of fact, Dr. Elliott is doing the work of a priest in a new fashion, by entering into the very lives of people with whom he comes in contact." [6] Earlier that year, however, Adler had acknowledged the issue during the American Ethical Union Conference at Philadelphia:

> There has been a feeling of dread of a new clergy, a dread of entrusting to the Leaders of the Society anything like sacerdotal powers and that must be respected, that is a very proper misgiving. The world has suffered too much from priestly organization, priestly arrogance.[7]

However Adler might protest, in some sense at least the priestly had come about, not by design but out of a changing cultural and social environment. A shift in emphasis disturbed Adler and the nuclear group, probably without their being quite aware of what had changed. The Leader had been envisaged in rabbinical or Socratic mold—teacher, scholar, critic, and prophet. With the increased demand for a response to "spiritual" needs, Leaders assumed a pastoral image—the caring, nurturing, forgiving, supportive father. Percival Chubb in a plan for the training of Leaders tried to define the Leader's function. He made explicit the confused image without recognizing its ambivalence,

   a) To teach the ethical philosophy of life so that the will is stirred to conduct and aspiration kindled

   b) To minister to the special needs of the bereaved, the sick, the morally perplexed, the tempted, the penitent, etc.

   c) To take part in the machinery of organization for this purpose.[8]

Even more problematic than the shifting perspective on Leadership is Chubb's unabashedly bureaucratic statement. The very attempt to describe a "job function" was evidence of how far the movement had

---

[6] *Ibid.*

[7] Adler to the Philadelphia Conference of the AEU, May, 1925.

[8] Tentative Plan for Training of Leaders, AEU Records, May 21, 1929.

come from the days when Adler addressed himself to a "new vocation" on philosophic rather than administrative grounds.

This trend did not go unchallenged, but the ambivalence of role has
not yet been resolved. Making explicit the bureaucratic requirements
for the career shaped the lives of Adler's successors and the societies
which they led. The conflicting views of prophecy and institution
now became a highly personal debate within the movement itself.
Against Chubb's job description, Adler continued to fight for a different ideal:

> What is needed in a Leader is scholarship. A man should be versed in
> religion and in philosophy, for our religion is a way of life and to be a
> Leader is to know what people in the past have found or thought that
> they have found and expressed in their philosophies and their religions.[9]

However, the very nature of the struggle changed as Adler's hold
on the movement loosened and as institutional formalities replaced
his authority. In addition to a changing membership and an ambivalent image of Leadership, another trend was added—institutional instruments were created to do by regulation what had been done for
many years in a personal, informal way. Typical of this trend was the
establishment of a Committee of the American Ethical Union to pass
on the qualifications and suitability of Leadership, which was approved at the Philadelphia Conference in May, 1925. Dr. Adler supported this proposal before the New York Board, which criticized the
action as unnecessary and an infringement on a society's freedom. John
Elliott supported Adler on the grounds that: "There is danger that if
[the Societies] cannot get their Leaders [from the training program]
they will look to some other group which may or may not be in harmony with the Movement." [10]

However, institutionalism didn't win a clear victory, as was illus-
trated by the fact that in 1928 Professor Horace Friess of Columbia
University was asked to undertake the training of young men for
Leadership with the assistance of James Gutmann, an Associate
Leader in New York and a teacher in the schools. Both men were by

[9] New York Board of Trustees, Minutes, November, 1925.
[10] *Ibid.*, December, 1930.

temperament the opposite of bureaucrats; their appointment insured continued tension on the question.

Meanwhile, Stanton Coit proposed to revive the Ethical Lecturer's Fund, a scholarship source which had existed in England from 1899 to 1904. Coit wanted to encourage young students to study ethical philosophy and to create thereby a core of men and women from which Ethical Leadership might be drawn. Coit proposed that the committee for the Fund be "primarily to represent the general educated public and the Universities in particular, the actual Leaders of Ethical Societies should not be a majority on it." [11] He had comfortably accepted different roles for the university, the Fabian movement, the Ethical Church. Within the movement he also foresaw a division of labor for Ethical Leaders; specialized functions would allow both a parish ministry and a scholarly cadre. In a letter to Dr. Adler he tried to soften his position: "The last eight years have strangely strengthened my love for the Ethical Movement as a whole, for the Ethical Movement as it is, and I wish no longer to work exclusively for my own particular branch of it." [12] Adler was unconvinced of Coit's change of heart; he wrote to Chubb:

. . . I understand he has written . . . urging the use of the theological vocabulary, and his reference to the "lines which I indicated at the Glenmore Conference" suggest at least the possible intention of formulating a metaphysical creed. Both constitute serious objections. Though the metaphysics were my own, I should dread nothing so much as to see it imposed. The Ethical Societies must have for their unifying principle a way of living.[13]

Coit's plan for an independent fund raised another unresolved question—should the "new" vocation of Ethical Leadership be filled by the amateur or the specialist? The strengths of individualistic and prophetic Leaders had to be balanced against the need for an ongoing objective and secure institution. Adler had managed by sheer force of mind and personality to hold the conflict in check. Now in his

[11] Statement by Stanton Coit, Ethical Lecturer's Fund Committee, September, 1927.
[12] October 16, 1924.
[13] October 20, 1924.

seventies, he was too weak physically to give dynamic attention to his movement. The tensions became open, but the solutions remained elusive.

Nevertheless the work had to go on, and new Leadership was needed. A young teacher named Roy Franklin Dewey came to work with Mr. Bridges in Chicago but after several years returned to academic life. Dr. David Hanchett edited *The Standard* from 1917 to 1924 and tried to organize business courses for the schools, but left to become Dean of Men at Antioch College. James Gutmann became an Associate Leader of the New York Society in April, 1927. He had graduated from the Ethical Culture schools and Columbia University. Before being named to Leadership he had edited *The Standard* and taught ethics at the schools. A member, with Horace Friess and John Herman Randall, Jr., of Dr. Adler's Ethics seminar at Columbia, Gutmann resigned in 1930 to become a university teacher and later Chairman of Columbia's philosophy department.

Henry S. Golding, from England, gave promise of being one of the permanent successors. As a young man Golding had planned to join the British Navy, but he was rejected on medical grounds. He entered the insurance business instead and remained with it for more than twenty years. He moved from an early childhood Episcopalianism through an attraction to the Society of Friends to affiliation with the British Ethical movement. His autobiography[14] reveals that Locke, Spinoza, and Kant were his philosophic heroes. Attracted to the Fabian Society he became an active member of the British Labour Party. At the invitation of Harry Snell, a Labour M.P. and also President of the British Ethical Union, Golding lectured for the Ethical Church. Reading Adler's *An Ethical Philosophy of Life* was, apparently, the final goad to his decision to give full time to the Ethical Movement.

In 1921, on the occasion of the forty–fifth anniversary, Adler arranged for Golding to visit the United States to spend a month or two lecturing to the various societies. Following that visit, which was apparently a success, Adler recommended that Golding be appointed to travel around the country lecturing on the philosophy of the Ethical movement and also to prepare materials on comparative philosophies

[14] See Fiftieth Anniversary Volume, pp. 177–81.

for young people. In October the New York Board unanimously approved this proposal and cabled an offer to Golding. Unfortunately, at that time Golding's wife had taken ill and was unable to travel. It was not until the fall of 1923 that he finally accepted the offer. This was greeted with great satisfaction, not the least of its causes being Golding's willingness to leave a lucrative business career for the precarious work of Leadership.

In October, 1923, Dr. Adler introduced Golding to the New York Board as a man who "had left an assured position in London, had burnt his bridges behind him . . . had come to a foreign land to preach the religion that is to him the dearest thing in life. . . . " Golding replied:

> . . . my resolve to abandon security and comfort and to throw in my lot with the Ethical Movement was due to a spiritual impulse which gathered head and finally became irresistible. Judged from the standpoint of worldly success it was doubtless imprudent. . . . I endeavored to bring into life a new spirit based on our ethical principles. . . . Shortcomings in that, there inevitably were. . . . But it was the overwhelming moment of my life when I found that the very proclamation of that ideal and the imperfect actualization of it . . . had gained me the esteem and respect of my staff . . . when I severed my connection with the Company for which I had worked for 29 years, when the staff had nothing to hope from me, their warm-hearted demonstration of affectionate regard and good wishes magnificently justified the ethical faith.
>
> Men, in my experience, do not esteem mere orthodoxy. . . . My opinions were well known. . . . I only cite this incident to show that men respond as to a new gospel to the message of the Ethical Movement.[15]

Plans were made for Golding to lecture in Boston, Philadelphia, Brooklyn, Chicago, and St. Louis. Assignments in adult education and on the New York Platform were added. Two years later, in 1925, Golding was elected an Associate Leader of the New York Society. He seemed well on his way to taking his place in the succession of Leaders who would carry on the work of moral religion. In 1931, Golding took ill with scarlet fever, and the disease, relatively minor in childhood, proved fatal to the man. Golding's death was a severe

15 New York Board of Trustees, Minutes, October, 1923.

blow; it left a gap in the generations of succession and a void in that part of the Leadership which saw itself in intellectual terms.

Another younger man was gradually inducted into Ethical Leadership. Algernon Black, born in 1900, was a child of New York City and the son of working-class parents. An unfortunate incident in public school encouraged his mother to request a scholarship at the Ethical Culture schools, and Black completed his education there. He was awarded a scholarship at Harvard and was graduated with honors in 1923. Returning to New York, he began teaching economics at the School for Printer's Apprentices at the Hudson Guild (remaining at it for fourteen years) and working at the Madison House Settlement, where he became Headworker in 1926. Black also began part-time teaching at the Ethical Culture schools in 1924; he served there for forty years, first as faculty member and later as Chairman of the Ethics Department. He also worked in the youth and Sunday school programs of the New York Society. From 1923 until 1934, when he was elected to Leadership, Black held a training fellowship during which he acted as secretary to the Leader's seminar and to the Business Men's Group.

Black recalled Dr. Adler,

. . . once in Seminar, he gave a paper in . . . which he criticized an ardent socialist, and as the youngest person [there] I couldn't very well say anything, but I just shook my head. . . . He stopped the talk, pointed his finger in great wrath and said, "Shake not thy gory locks at me," which brought a howl from the whole seminar. . . . When it was over he came to me and said, "what did you differ with me about?"

In the period before the Roosevelt election . . . the head of the History Department at Fieldston . . . thought she would teach about American political life by having the students put on an . . . election rally. They had posters all over for the different candidates. . . . The faculty were in the dining room because it was a rainy day . . . and he [Adler] walked in with his hands behind his back. . . . His eyes were blazing like coals and he said, "who has put these posters up of politics? Politics is dirty and it's soon enough that our children will learn about the realities. . . ." I was the only one at the table who was working at the Society. . . . I said pointing my finger at him, "You know, the trouble with the world is that old men like you go around tearing things down." Instead of fighting back, he said, in a quiet way and twinkling,

"You wouldn't put an old man out in the rain would you?". . . . Everybody laughed and it relaxed the tension. . . .[16]

Black quickly revealed the tremendous energies of which he was capable. He revealed, too, his impatience with abstraction, preferring the direct activity of social reform and the direct relationship of social work and classroom. His own man from the beginning, as the recollections about Adler illustrate, Black was modeled more in the mold of Elliott than Adler. Like Elliott, he was capable of great human warmth and of evoking responses of trust and friendship from young and old. And, like Elliott, he could arouse equally strong opposition in a very personal way. At the annual meeting of the New York Society in November, 1934, he was unanimously elected to Leadership; the long apprenticeship was over.

Black's democratic socialism remained, although it was based on ethical idealism rather than materialistic determinism. Active in behalf of civil liberties, Black worked with Roger Baldwin to secure the rights of workers. As a young man he helped the strikers in Paterson, New Jersey, to organize the silk mills, engaged in the battle against Mayor Hague of Jersey City when the CIO (Congress of Industrial Organizations) was trying to organize the food industry, and fought for the right to picket when cafeteria workers were organizing in New York City.

His concern for social justice led him to condemn fascism in the mid-thirties before that became popular. His interest in ethical education motivated the founding in the late thirties and mid-forties of the Work Camps for Democracy and later the Encampment for Citizenship. Added to his complex career were efforts for racial integration long before the civil-rights revolution was born. Chairman and founder of the Citizens Committee for Harlem in 1941, he was a prime mover in the development of the New York State, and later the National, Committee Against Discrimination in Housing. An active member of The National Association for the Advancement of Colored People, he was elected a vice president in 1950.

Black was prophetic; repeatedly he came to grips with issues and attitudes long before they were popularly debated and discussed. Some of the more affluent and conservative supporters of Ethical Cul-

[16] Interview, 1963.

ture saw in this younger man a threat to the stability and "soundness" of the Ethical movement. As Black became a public figure, be became a figure of controversy within the Movement. Unlike Elliott, he did not have the protection of age and long association with the founder. His approach was a mixture of prophetic criticism and intuitive response to felt injustice. He lacked too the academic credentials which, though seldom used, gave Elliott a certain claim on the intellectuals. Finally, the sheer number of concerns to which he attended gave the impression of a kind of superficiality. However his research was careful, and, if not of a philosophical temperament, he nevertheless drew strength and coherence from a central ethical idealism.

The work of those long in the movement continued, too. Dr. Neumann remained in touch with Salter, who, having left the active Leadership, was teaching and writing. Neumann wrote to Mrs. Salter: "On page 81 of the enclosed, you will see that Gandhi makes reference to his debt to Mr. Salter's *Ethical Religion*. I am afraid that if I sent this directly to Mr. Salter himself, he might perhaps not tell you about it. . . . " The work to which he referred was Gandhi's *Young India*.[17] Muzzey was continuing to achieve eminence in his academic career. But honors and recognition in the world of letters was not the stuff of which movements were built. More to the point was a series of letters among Elliott, Neumann, and Chubb initiated by Chubb's troubled concern with the movement's deliberate self-limitation under Adler's Leadership. In a sour humor, Neumann sent a brief note to Elliott,

> . . . Chubb sent me a few of his usual lamentations—this time a bit more so—and now if Coit, from whom I have not heard for a long time will only write me one more of his complaints for not moving faster, I shall begin to feel really cheerful or maybe even spiritual. . . .[18]

Elliott almost pled with Chubb for a more affirmative mood; "I don't propose to scold and I don't want to be a pollyanna, but I do think you stress very hard the negative side of things and I don't think this is the time to do it, even if it should be done sometimes." [19] But

[17] Letter, May 20, 1925.
[18] June 24, 1931.
[19] August 27, 1931.

Chubb would not accept the advice; he felt that the issue of Adler's age and authoritarianism could not be avoided:

> . . . The Chief . . . has kept the Movement isolated, detached, lacking in friendliness and appreciativeness. He has been so keen about being "unique"—different—superior . . . I really think he does not know the contemporary world. He is so intent on the eternal. . . .
> We none of us want to hurt the Chief's feelings. There is no personal issue and yet it would be taken personally. The Chief is touchy, shies at dissent, and is very self-opionated . . . the spirit of freedom is lacking. . . . We are suffering from frozen assets. But as this conviction of mine is frowned upon all around, I'm going to quit. . . .[20]

Chubb was not alone in this. Martin and others had apparently expressed their discontent to him but felt unable to speak openly. The perennial conflict between popularity and purity, an elite and a mass view, smoldered on. Not wishing to lead an opposition party, Chubb wrote to Elliott in the fall of 1932:

> Shall I dare to say to you in written words that I have been going through a sort of crisis—. . . . To risk brevity I will strike at the center of the disturbance and say that I have been facing the almost intolerable and painful question, whether the Ethical Movement, as such, any longer commands my heart. . . . You know that this is no sudden eruption. You and the others have endured my expressions of uneasiness for many years. I have been a trying dissenter and I should like to quit that role. . . . Let time help. . . . The perspective may alter. . . . I will put the thing by for a while.[21]

The frustration of those who could not accept with philosophic equanimity the slow painful tempo that Adler regarded as necessary and even desirable was reinforced by seeing groups appear and disappear, seeing potential colleagues arrive with great enthusiasm only to vanish in a few years into other fields of work, seeing the societies struggle for survival year after year. The "negative side" was abundantly in evidence, the problems and defeats much more obvious

[20] Letter, to Elliott, August 31, 1931.
[21] November 14, 1932.

than the successes. From time to time reports of new groups would be heard, but all were short-lived.

In January, 1920, *The Standard* reported a group in Wilmington, Delaware; one or two brief reports were its entire history. Somewhat more extensive but equally abortive were efforts to develop a Society in Detroit with Dr. Daniel Roy Freeman as its Leader and in Milwaukee. It was formally organized in March, 1919, with forty subscribers, but Dr. Adler reported in 1925:

> You all know the history of the Detroit Society. It was started with great enthusiasm, and with backing financially and then went to pieces. . . . Some of our most promising prospects have been destroyed by the actions of Societies in choosing their own leaders without the advice of other people in the Movement. . . . There never was a better opportunity for the Ethical Movement—I mean the Milwaukee Society . . . [its] president said we are perfectly able to manage this Society without any . . . advice from the East. . . . For a Leader they chose a lawyer who was something of a student, and gave rather respectable lectures. He died, and then . . . they bet on the wrong horse, on a horse that no horse dealer would have bet on. The result was a scandal, and the Society had a black eye and it perished and we lost one of our best chances.[22]

In Wilmington, Detroit, Milwaukee, Grand Rapids, and Pittsburgh, societies flared briefly. The Pittsburgh experience encountered yet another difficulty. Organized by Professor Max Schoen of Carnegie Tech, the group consisted largely of prominent Jews who had had some experience with the New York Society. With the rise of Hitlerism two years after its founding in 1931 the Pittsburgh group vanished as its members returned to Jewish organizations as part of a "united front" movement within Jewry. Ethical Culture was tried for a second time in Boston. A small group organized in 1920 with Daniel Crandon as President, Clarence Kingsley as Chairman of the Executive Committee, and Harold K. Estabrook as Executive Secretary. Martin had helped the group start and indeed had been visiting Boston regularly since 1918 to lecture on Ethical Culture. By 1925 the Boston Society had nearly 200 members, and by 1927 it was looking

[22] Philadelphia Conference, AEU Records, May, 1925, pp. 258–59.

for a larger meeting room. Martin continued to travel from New York but it became obvious that permanent Leadership was needed. In 1931 Frank Swift, from St. Louis and trained in New York, was named to the Boston post. At the annual meetings of the AEU in the fall, before embarking on his work in Boston, Swift was critical of his older colleagues:

> . . . (Mr. Swift) introduced a critical note . . . by asking whether we were in the face of the unprecedented conditions of the times, making our due contributions as leaders in ethical and religious thought. The world was . . . moving fast; furthermore it was moving in our direction . . . [but] we were not keeping pace with contemporary movements, much less keeping ahead of them. Our ideas and ideals were excellent, . . . but our effectiveness quite inadequate . . . [he] spoke of the need for a consciousness of the movement as a whole. . . . We must be a movement and not a loose aggregation of separate units.[23]

Swift's brashness did not go unremarked. Elliott wrote to Chubb of Swift's ". . . unending self-confidence . . . [which is] I think almost pathological. . . . " The Boston Society seemed well on its way to becoming a full participant in the movement. In the fall of 1933, Swift became assistant to the aging S. Burns Weston in the Philadelphia Society. Returning from a Leaders' meeting in New York that December, Frank Swift was killed in an accident, and the movement lost a promising young critic. Failure to find a replacement for Swift coupled with depression and international crisis which turned people's minds elsewhere sounded the end of the Boston Society.

In 1924 a group of about fifteen families, members of the New York Society who lived in Westchester County north of the city, began to meet. David Muzzey, who lived in Yonkers, agreed to serve as its Leader, and the group convened regularly at the New Rochelle Public Library. Troubled by failures in Detroit, Wilmington, Grand Rapids, and Milwaukee, Adler insisted that every officer and board member of the Westchester Ethical Group be a member of the New York Society. By 1930 the group was ready to apply for independent status, and in 1931 the Westchester Ethical Society was admitted into the AEU. The Society emphasized informal adult organization and

---

23 St. Louis, AEU Meeting, October, 1931, pp. 392–93.

Sunday school in a pattern that was to predominate in the period after the Second World War. But in the twenties Westchester (and suburbia) were unique in Ethical Culture.

In 1929 Philadelphia moved into its new meeting house on Rittenhouse Square. In Chicago Dr. Bridges and Clarence Darrow debated the question: "Is Man a Mechanism?" The women of the St. Louis Society were cooperating with the Board of Religious Organizations in social and civic welfare. In 1922 the Brooklyn Ethical Culture School opened with an enrollment of twenty-four, half of whom were on scholarships. The next year the enrollment doubled. Julie Neumann, a graduate of the New York School, was giving her services voluntarily as principal—and as guide and goad. By 1925 the school was housed in its own quarters on Prospect Park West, in part made possible by a $10,000 gift from Ralph Jonas. The struggle to found the school was complicated by the depression. Money was always a problem for Brooklyn.

The American Ethical Union continuing under George O'Dell's part-time supervision was restricted to periodic conventions and minor publications. In 1930 the AEU reported thirty-three hundred members in seven societies (Boston, 195; Brooklyn, 350; Chicago, 435; New York, 1,350; Philadelphia, 525; St. Louis, 417; Westchester, 123). Repeated efforts to strengthen a national movement came to naught. Though Martha Fishel of St. Louis called for scholarships and increased training funds for the AEU in 1928 and Chubb in 1931 for a field secretary as well, it was obvious that little would be done. This was due, in part, to the fact that the New York Society performed many of the functions of a national movement—and without cost to the other societies. It provided fellowships, trained Leaders, encouraged its Leaders to serve as ethical missionaries. The smaller societies feared that transfer of authority to a national movement would only mean legitimizing and perpetuating New York's control.

Internationally, there were a few signs of vitality. The British movement under Snell's presidency was recovering; Boerner was helping the Vienna Society come back to life and even the German movement could report that it still have some three– to four–hundred members. Snell and Jean Wagner were appointed Foreign Corresponding Secretaries with small stipends, thus provided with an income while they gave help to the British and Swiss movements respectively. Adler spoke at Oxford on "The Spiritual Message of the Ethical Movement" and was invited to return to deliver the Hibbert Lectures in 1923. By 1923 Boerner reported attendance in excess of 800 at Vienna's Sunday meetings, and a Czechoslovakian Ethical Society was announced. The founding society in New York was experiencing its own crisis. Attendance was not keeping up at Sunday meetings; a report in 1924 indicated an average attendance of 500. "The attendance at meetings when Dr. Adler spoke had declined slightly, that of the other meetings increased slightly." The problem of the Platform was put before the Board:

> Dr. Elliott speaking for the Leaders said he was conscious of the crisis through which the Society was passing. The Sunday Platform was for fifty years a Felix Adler platform and is now passing into a platform of a group.[24]

Elliott suggested that the Society examine the possibilities of radio broadcasting. A month later the Platform was discussed again with Muzzey referring to ". . . the double criticism, namely the need for more inspirational material in the Sunday addresses and for defining more clearly the ideals of the Society." [25]

New York had instituted a series of Sunday evening meetings with Alfred Martin on the great religious traditions, the higher criticism, and the relation of Ethical Culture to contemporary religious trends. The Sunday evening forums drew a large, appreciative, and regular audience for more than fourteen years, though very few new members for the Society.

The program expanded over the period, but difficulties of coherence multiplied too. Alfred Martin had been developing ideas on spiritualism, and in 1924 Adler discussed the relationship between the Ethical movement and spiritualism:

> . . . does the ethical life depend on immortality? I answer with an absolute no . . . we meet with the inverted argument that belief in immortality arises out of ethical experience. . . .

[24] New York Board of Trustees, Minutes, February, 1929.
[25] *Ibid.*, March, 1929.

Are we then veering toward spiritualism? Can an ethical leader combine spititualistic teaching with ethical teaching, as Bridges has thought to combine Unitarianism with ethical leadership? Now mark well the point of distinction. We say ethical experience . . . is our business as ethical leaders. Whether out of this arise the starry ideas of Eternality and Insunderable Relation between spirits is a matter of private belief which may fairly be presented to the Societies but by no means as fundamental to [them].[26]

Near the fiftieth anniversary of the Movement, Adler said,

. . . that it was time to get on top of some high building and look at the future . . . great changes are preparing. The city is going to be decentralized. The town itself will be surrounded by a corona of residential suburbs, . . . and the Society . . . will probably be dispersed in a number of suburban centers.

. . . the sanctity is going out of Sunday and the question is whether or not these meetings can be kept up. . . . It has been the ambition of my life to get beyond the philanthropies, the social service, to that ultimate interest, to turn men's attention from the preliminaries to the thing that counts supremely. . . . The spiritual interest is ebbing and they say the Society is ebbing with it.[27]

In 1926, restating the "purpose of the Ethical Movement," Adler emphasized the need to keep the field of ethical exploration open and to avoid dogmatic certitude as a defense against frustration. He concluded: "The Ethical Movement seeks to preserve the ethical ideal from petrifying. . . . it must ever be a growing ideal. . . . " With a wry and satiric humor, yet with an underlying sadness, Adler revealed his uncertainty:

Dr. Adler . . . discussed the use of the word, "Platform" . . . and concluded that perhaps the word, "scaffold" might be closer to the truth. . . . [Defined as] a temporary structure on which workmen stand while they are building, still, scaffold, is also . . . associated with . . . a place for the execution of criminals. So I am at a loss what to suggest and will suggest nothing at all. . . .

[26] "The Ethical Movement and Spiritualism," 1924.
[27] New York Board of Trustees, Minutes, November, 1924.

"My whole course of years . . . has been determined by one fundamental motive. . . . If I may compare my state of mind it is the same as that . . . [of] a very close physician friend when he was asked why he was so absorbed and apparently so troubled. He said that he had a very difficult patient on his mind, that he was trying to probe the nature of the disease, and his whole heart was in it, and he found it very difficult to be sure of the remedy. . . .

"Well, friends, I think that I am not departing from the line of truth if I say that from the outset the motive was to see if it were possible to remove, at least to alleviate the terrible ethical and spiritual sickness of mankind. . . . I have been all my life . . . trying to get light." [28]

Adler knew he was dying. And mortality struck Ethical Culture like a machine gun; in the early thirties death took Golding, Swift, Salter, Adler. The Depression was growing worse. Many of the basic questions about Ethical Culture were still unanswered. The ambivalences which had been tolerable grew as Adler and his early followers left the scene. The problems multiplied, calling for the reconstruction of a philosophy able to deal with them in the new environment of the twentieth century, calling for a Leadership that would attend these questions. But before these demands could be met, the movement had to weather the shock of death within and of crisis in the nation and the world without.

[28] New York Annual Meeting, Board of Trustees, Minutes, November, 1930.

CHAPTER XX

The Lengthened
Shadow of a Man

In the summer of 1931 Chubb wrote from St. Louis
to Elliott in New York:

> Your equanimity is beyond me. No doubt, your more roseate view of
> things is safer than mine, certainly it is more comforting. I was too early
> corrupted by the prophets. And then my lot falls in a smug community.
> The spiritual anemia and intellectual inertia of this city-parish are exas-
> perating. And the present state of the nation and the world is hard to
> bear.[1]

Elliott contradicted the twilight mood in Chubb's words:

> In regard to the general indifference, there is a change. . . . I had
> thought that the talk with the young people in our later gathering would
> be just jolly but, not at all. They wanted to talk about God and immor-
> tality. . . . The radical sex excitement undoubtedly had died down.
> . . . If the depression hasn't done anything else, it's driven sex off the
> front page. With us in New York, [Norman] Thomas is quite a hero. As

[1] August 30, 1931.

242

an educational influence I don't believe there is anything better. . . .
For the first time, the Communists are figuring in New York. We had our
first Communist meeting here at the Guild the other night which, although it wasn't very well attended, marked the coming in of this group
into our Catholic, Tammany district. Of course, the talk was wild . . .
but there was a human almost brotherhood note in it that made people
listen.[2]

Whether it was change or decay could be argued, but it was an
unhappy time. Ethical Culture's claim to be for its followers what
other faiths were for theirs was now put to the test. Could a movement
without the security of creed and rite provide support for people in
crises? On all sides people were turning to those who promised salvation—political or religious. In Ethical Culture, "religious" themes
drew more people to the Sunday meeting than did questions of social
ethics. If Adler had drawn a line between what was "religious" and
what "ethical," most members did not; they wished to satisfy, as did
so many others, their religious needs. Elliott wrote:

. . . I wouldn't know now whether one should make exceptions of art
and God as the permanent things one can hold on to in desperation. I
should say that many people had found their way to peace laying hold of
freedom and country as well as God and art. That is, there seem to be
many roads worth travelling. Of course, this isn't a new idea but hasn't it
stood the test of experience? [3]

Whether moral religion could stand the test remained an open and
aggravating question.

The generation of founders was passing from the scene, and with
them a perception of the world that had been nurtured in the tempo
of nineteenth-century enlightenment, manners, and vitality. In 1931
news came of the death of William Salter after a long, lingering
struggle with cancer. One of Adler's earliest colleagues, his death had
dramatic meaning for a movement built around personality.

In writing to Horace Bridges of Golding's death, Elliott reported:
"I have never known Adler to be so deeply affected emotionally by
any event." [4] Recalling the earlier days of free religion, news came of

[2] Letter, John Elliott to Chubb, November 4, 1931.
[3] Letter to Mrs. Alexander M. Bing.
[4] January 17, 1931.

Anna Garlin Spencer's death in the same year. Though she had left the Leadership and moved into professional social work for a while and then into liberal Unitarian circles, she had been a fellow pioneer on the religious frontier. In 1932, Alfred Martin died. In a tribute, John Haynes Holmes said:

> His work as a teacher and a preacher is a part of the noblest record of the liberal ministry of the last generation. More than any other man of our time, he led the way in the reconciliation of religious faiths and the true fellowship of man.[5]

Each death was a blow and a reminder that the founder was also of that earlier generation, also a silent sufferer of terminal illness.

Adler was aware of the problem created by any strong founder. From time to time, and as early as the turn of the century, he had raised the question of the movement's survival without him. As his life drew to a close and the pain of his cancer increased, he reflected more and more on his work and its meaning. At the beginning of the 1929–1930 season Adler spoke to his Board:

> I wish to come into contact with the Trustees after the absence of last year. I have wanted to be with you as I have for fifty–four years. . . . I will be well . . . to ask ourselves what exactly this faith is, what exactly the purpose of the Ethical Movement is . . . , especially as the times . . . and surroundings change, and new tendencies come up of which we did not dream in 1876. . . . There is utter chaos in . . moral relations. . . . I do not need to tell you that I stand against the skeptics, the behaviorists and the pragmatists. There is such a thing a truth, although our expressions of it need constant correction. . . There is such a thing as right although our moral codes are being shat tered because they are more or less corrupt. . . .
>
> Some people had an idea that the Ethical Movement was going to sweep over the world like a prairie fire. That is foolish. . . . Ideas grow slowl in the lives of men. I have started on my seventy-ninth year. I think of my successors. . . .
>
> It takes a long time for an idea to be put over. . . . They say that a [with] Genevieve, the patroness of Paris, the wind sometimes blew ou

[5] Ethical Culture Archive.

her lamp, but such was the luminousness of it that it ever rekindled itself. So I think that the lamp which we lit in the darkness of the storm may in future centuries be obscured and plunged into darkness and be again rekindled.[6]

In these last years Adler did not often speak from the Platform. When he did, he gave his attention to first and last things. As he had done at the beginning, he reviewed the religious scene—commenting on the businessman's Christ, on the attempts to develop a "life of Jesus" in the absence of genuine biographical information. In much of Judaism he found decay as well: "Jewishness has taken the place of Judaism. Its emphasis is race, not religion." As for his movement, Adler was looking inward, speaking of love and friendship, of their centrality in human nature though the pilgrimage be long and painful. In a way, Adler had withdrawn from the bustle of the social arena toward more contemplative themes. He was, in these last years, writing a spiritual testament, seeking to separate what was permanent in his thought from topical responses to passing events. A few days before his death he noted in what was his last manuscript:

> In the future I can only see the transformation of human relationships as a dawning glory. If I could convert my abstractions into living images, I could begin to accomplish what seems to me the most august aim of which I am aware, that of drawing the circle of spiritual comradeship about myself and others.[7]

The dialectic which had created Adler's ethical philosophy—the pull between future and past, between actual and ideal, between intimate and public—remained with him to the last.

In 1931 Adler's illness required a series of operations. They were unsuccessful and the man suffered painfully for the remaining months of his life. But, true to his sense of himself, the pain had to be conquered, its presence not admitted. In the summer of 1932, Elliott wrote:

> Although Adler has only been out of the hospital something like four months, when I was with him in the mountains he was clambering over

---

[6] New York Board of Trustees, Minutes, October 1929.
[7] *The Standard*, XX (1933), 44.

rocks and taking walks in a way that, I think, astounded even him and more than satisfied the rest of us.[8]

The evidence of physical recovery was illusory. As Muzzey reported, ". . . his unimpaired mental and moral vigor fought courageously against the visibly failing body. . . ." Adler died on April 24, 1933, in his eighty-second year. Algernon Black recalled the last meeting of the seminar with Adler present:

> He had on his frock coat. . . . It was a late afternoon in the autumn . . . ; the golden sunlight from the west came into the room and shone on the beautiful rug and on him. He started [to read]. . . . He got about 2 sentences into his paper and he got lost. . . . He started over again and got about 3 or 4 sentences and got lost again. Very slowly and deliberately he took out his watch . . . , a gold watch, and he pressed a little button and opened it. Then he said, "I guess my time is up." Slowly, he closed it and walked out. . . .[9]

Adler continued to read, to write, to see people, to keep track of what was happening in his movement. Scarcely ten days before his death, he met with Dr. Thayer:

> My last interview with Dr. Adler will long remain with me. It was the evening of April 13. I had received word . . . that the . . . foundation to which the school had applied . . . had granted our request and that the way was now open to develop amply the work of the pre-professional courses at Fieldston. . . . I hastened to Dr. Adler's home. . . . I was told by Mrs. Adler that he was exhausted from the effects of an unusually strenuous day. We both hesitated to intrude upon his rest. Evidently, however, he had heard my voice and perhaps suspecting the purpose of my call entered the room. . . .
>
> I . . . delivered my message. Somewhat to my surprise, he received it calmly. . . . But the questions which he at once put to me regarding the conditions of the financial grant . . . revealed to me both the extent of his vision into the future and that rare capacity . . . to combine boldness and novelty of thought with sane and well considered methods of procedure.
>
> In a short time he gave evidence of fatigue . . . and considerable physical discomfort. But he discouraged all reference to his physical

[8] Letter to Lord Snell, August 1, 1932.
[9] Interview, 1963.

condition. . . . Finally, as I was about to leave he remarked, "It is difficult to understand the desire to communicate . . . even with the dead."

"Of whom are you thinking?"

"Of Alfred," he replied with a smile. "When I first heard the good news, I said to myself, 'I must tell Alfred Wolff.' " [10]

It was the spring of 1933 and Felix Adler was dead. To the public he had represented Ethical Culture for more than fifty years. To his followers he had been almost a god, austere, distant, powerful, and supportive. To those few with whom he worked very closely there were memories of humor and a twinkling eye. Over the years he had become a man of some fame in education, in city and state government, in the academy. His combination of intelligence and practical skill had provided the motive energy for the movement and its works. His death, long prepared for, still came as a shock.

Naturally, immediate attention was given to the ceremonial rites attending death—even in a relatively unadorned moral faith. The memorial meeting included President Butler of Columbia and Stephen Wise of the Free Synagogue. Messages came from around the world. John Haynes Holmes spoke of Adler as a "religious statesman of a high order . . . as a formidable person. . . . " At the meeting Stephen Wise said:

> Never shall I forget that moment . . . in the midst of an unreserved and precious conversation, he turned to me and said, "When I was asked to be Rabbi at Emanuel I might have recited the 'Hear O Israel,' but if I had done so it would have meant so much more to me than to them that I could not—I could not say it," and an ineffable wistfulness not untouched by tender remembrance lighted up his face.

In *The New York Times,* Wise was quoted as saying, "Though he spelt the name of God other than we do, he was a great religionist. Adler was one of the truest of modern mystics. . . ." [11] Some months later, Mrs. Adler received this letter:

[10] Interview, 1963.
[11] *The New York Times,* April 26, 1933.

I hope you will understand these conditions [official work] and will forgive me for not writing you sooner to express my deep sympathy in the passing of your distinguished husband, Felix Adler. Those of us who were privileged to know him in life have lost a true friend and valued advisor. The nation mourns the passing of a profound philosopher, a cultural leader of spiritual force, a philanthropist and a beloved citizen. There is no doubt but that his teachings will continue to be a tremendous influence for the good of many generations to come.

FRANKLIN DELANO ROOSEVELT [12]

But ceremonies end and the fine words and warm feelings that draw men together at times of death give way to facing life anew. A light had gone out; could another light be kindled? Adler's death had not been surrounded by the mysteries of sacrifice attendant on religious founders of legend. In a secularized world, the event was mundane not magical. The comfort of mythological death which had carried earlier ventures in faith past the point of immediate loss was not available to Ethical Culture. And because philosophically and temperamentally these were people of the world, the romance of ritual which might have helped build a bridge between past and future was not available.

Through the late spring and summer there was much talk about the future of the movement. While skepticism was expressed privately, there were efforts publicly to bolster a failing morale. That fall, the Leadership met at the Hudson Guild Farm. David Muzzey sounded an optimistic note. "It was in a way a memorial meeting for Dr. Adler and yet I think it would be fair to say that quite apart from any feeling of responsibility of carrying on his work for his sake, there was a decided feeling that the work for the work's sake would be carried on." [13] The centrality of the Ethical Platform was emphasized and plans for strengthening it discussed. The time was "ripe for real missionary effort." The Leadership reaffirming its faith in the validity of an "ethical point of view" committed itself to go on.

Even as the words of dedication were uttered, practical problems had to be faced. Caught in a cataclysm of events, wedded to a viewpoint quite out of step with the dominant themes of the day, and now

[12] January 6, 1934.
[13] New York Board of Trustees, Minutes, October, 1933.

without the strength of its founder, the movement was committed to a many-sided battle for survival. Problems ranged from inability to pay the bills to the need for succession. Much in the minds of the Leadership was the issue of the distinctiveness of the Ethical movement; in fact four of seven sessions at the Hudson Guild that fall were devoted to that question. Adler had maintained the value of an "implicit" religion, but, with his death, the pressure mounted to make things explicit. A subtle drive to write down moral religion threatened, at its very root, its genius.

Much as members and Leaders alike had complained about the authority of Adler, they regretted its absence. Despite relative inactivity during his latter years, he had been for all of them a point of security. Few remained who could assert with Adler's sureness that there was truth, there was right. The effort to reestablish such sureness was to become the theme of the next period in the movement's development—on its success or failure rested the question of whether Ethical Culture was but the "lengthened shadow of a man" or a continuing contribution to human history.

The programs, meetings, good works continued as before, while the process of self-doubt and self-examination went on. An ancient poet might have read in the succession of fatalities from Golding to Swift a kind of vengeful drama. A religion more romantic and primitive in temperament might well have created saving, heroic epics. The more naturalistic and down-to-earth movement saw in death, whether by accident or illness, only the ordinary painful processes of nature.

Over the years Ethical Culture had evolved both an attitude toward mortality and a style of marking it. Illustrative was a letter from Adler to Elliott on Roger Elliott's death in 1931:

I surmise that you, who have had such large experience in consolation, will make some discoveries in your own loss. There are so many shades of bereavement—that of Roger's wife at a distance and then when she returns, that of the children and friends. And then there is your own intimate experience. You say that your relation to a brother nine years younger was like that of a father to a son, the fraternal and paternal feelings mingling. The thought in my mind is, "the heart knows its own bitterness," and even insists on going apart from all the others into its private corner and holding fast to its own painful treasures.

And yet, paradoxical as it may seem, we never feel the need and the balm of communion with our kind so strongly as in such moments—communion with those who belong to our closer group, and beyond that with all the sufferers of the world. It is a paradox—how do you explain it (perhaps it is nothing else than that which is at the bottom of all art and all ethics, the vivid bloom of the universal in the particular, an intimate personal experience which has such value that it might be shared by all).[14]

An attitude toward death—focusing on the naturalness of the event, on the need for acceptance, on the relationships which had created life, and on the need to renew attention to life and its demands—was held commonly throughout the movement. Never a ceremonious people, the celebration of death rested on a sublime faith in the powers and meanings of natural life. Without the promises of orthodoxy, Ethical Culture had developed its own style, honest, direct, without expectations. At a personal level, this attitude and its expression were successful, even positive for many people, as Elliott shows in his response to the above letter:

> I have found that there is peace even in tragedy but there are many things to disturb that peace. One of them was the Episcopalian service that was read. It brought in the element of travesty. Aside from the kindness of a great many people, your letter was the one help that brought understanding of the situation.[15]

It remained to be seen whether the philosophy of mortality which had served individuals and families in times of sadness and loss would serve more generally to enable the movement to renew its dedication to its own life.

[14] September 1, 1931.
[15] Letter to Felix Adler, September 8, 1931.

CHAPTER XXI

Reform
without
Philosophy

America was in the midst of the Great Depression. In Germany, Hitler was coming to power; in Italy, Mussolini made the trains run on time and was looking for new worlds to conquer. Thousands of miles away imperial Japan was extending its hegemony over Asia. If the shock of the First World War had traumatized the liberals, it was mere prelude to the shocks now being felt. The death of Felix Adler at just this time seemed calculated by a fickle destiny to force the question of the movement's relevance when it was least able to respond. Could it recapture the spirit that had filled its deliberations with excitement, or would it cherish memories of a brief golden age?

The New Deal was building a more subtle crisis for the reformers. After decades of reform as a private and local effort, the hopes for social democracy became national law. It was a famous victory, but as attention turned to Washington, reformers questioned their role. Nurtured in protest and resistance, could reform survive the shock of acceptability? More to the point, could reformers turn from long-established cares to newer needs not yet eligible for the attentions of legislators and bureaucrats?

Unable to comprehend all that was demanded of it, the tiny Ethical Culture movement sought to regain its balance. First a successor to Dr. Adler had to be named. Herbert Wolff recalled:

> . . . many felt that the Society could not survive. Who was to become the senior leader? There were some who felt that Dr. Elliott was the logical one. Others favored Dr. Muzzey. As a matter of fact, Dr. Muzzey . . . sincerely and strongly favored his good friend, Dr. Elliott. I recall speaking to Dr. Elliott just about that time that it was decided that he was to be the Senior Leader. He was 63 years old or thereabouts and he told me that he felt he had ten years of service ahead of him . . . and as a matter of fact that's just about what he did have.[1]

In May, 1933, New York named Elliott its Senior Leader. The Board was at pains to point out that "the Leadership of the Society should henceforth be the joint leadership which Dr. Adler had always planned for it." In naming a successor, they also made clear that no one could succeed Felix Adler. Elliott expressed the same feeling to Chubb:

> The spell of Keene Valley [where the Leaders had gathered for many years] for me is somewhat departed. . . . There is a sense of familiarity, the look of the mountains, and each year they seem to say, "As on the first day," but the special magic is no longer there. On the other hand, there is something new that comes out of the thought of the work since Adler left, and that joins on with what he did and accomplished. I don't feel particularly at home in Keene Valley, but neither did I anywhere else.[2]

Then in his sixties, Elliott brought to the Senior Leadership the habits of a lifetime. Ill at ease in the academic tradition and more likely to respond to a concrete human need than an abstract idea, Elliott commanded in ways quite different from his predecessor. His style and ability were far more personal than philosophic. Elliott enjoyed the arena of social ethics but seldom removed himself from the battle long enough to develop a perspective that could be communi-

---

[1] Interview, 1963.
[2] Letter from Elliott to Chubb, August 15, 1939.

cated beyond the range of personal influence. Drawn by the Hudson Guild, he could not bring himself to devote his attention solely to the movement. Responsive to the crisis through which the country was passing, he could not limit himself (nor could the others) to a narrow attention to institutional needs.

In 1933 George O'Dell addressed a letter to Elliott outlining a fourteen-point plan for the Ethical movement. He wished to develop membership and a movement instead of "half a dozen isolated Societies which have a common likeness only because of the impetus given at their foundation by the early leadership." A concern of that document as well as of others that followed was to institutionalize the functions that had been carried symbolically by Adler, but it was a nice question whether an institution could replace a living personality. Nor was O'Dell without humor:

P.S. Out of sheer wickedness and in order to get up your monkey, I *will* add a Fifteenth Point. The Humanist ministers are experimenting with simple liturgical forms such as any of our Societies might profitably use. But why not experiment with our own? Are our members all so Quakerish that they are convinced Beauty is somehow of the Devil? [3]

Institutional building, long neglected in the Ethical societies, now received verbal attention, but more often than not the result was another committee. A year after O'Dell's letter, Horace Friess in a note to Elliott reviewed the calendar from October through June, indicating how Adler had focused the life of the Society through the Ethical Platform. Some of the pattern was retained—a Children's Festival in December, Muzzey's annual address on Lincoln, a welcoming of rebirth at the coming of spring—but the unity Adler had given to the pattern was missing.

From a third colleague, Elliott heard:

Now you are the head of the Movement. And *this* is your chief problem. I suggest that you should cut yourself loose from all details of Guild and School . . . and devote the next four years to securing and preparing at least a dozen men, to provide for the succession in the existing societies and found half a dozen new ones. For, unless this is done, the present

---

[3] Letter, O'Dell to Elliott, June 13, 1933.

societies will perish in a few decades; and the schools and settlements will either die or pass wholly out of the control of people animated by the spirit and principles of those who founded them.[4]

Elliott knew that the image of Adler lingered and that his shadow remained. The movement's ambivalence about its founder was nowhere more clearly illustrated than in its failure to produce a suitable biography. Suspicion of reinforcing a "cult of personality" prevented laying the ghost to rest. A further complication was the protective attitude of the Adler family, which was concerned that nothing derogatory or critical appear. Attempts were made to honor Dr. Adler's memory. O'Dell regularly included one or another of Adler's manuscripts in *The Standard*. On the occasion of the sixtieth anniversary of the schools, the first of a series of annual Felix Adler Lectures was delivered by John Dewey, who spoke on "Democracy and Education in the World Today." But the biography was not forthcoming.

Elliott had to establish his own priorities and these, in a sense, precluded building a movement out from a founding personality. As successor to Adler, Elliott continued the personal style he had developed during the early days of the Hudson Guild. Paradoxically, Elliott's personalism, precisely because of its unevenness of likes and dislikes, served less adequately than Adler's austerity and distance to unify the membership and the Leadership.

Elliott was particularly troubled by the victims of the Depression. When rumors reached him in the spring of 1934 that the city might be forced to discontinue some of its prenatal clinics, he immediately wrote to an old friend and member of the Board of Health, Dr. S. S. Goldwater:

> Of all of those who come to the Hudson Guild . . . the expectant mothers make the strongest appeal to one's sympathies. . . . There are regularly 120 women coming to the clinic twice a week. . . . The predominant nationalities are Irish-American and Puerto Rican. . . . It is probable that no others are in greater financial difficulty. It is of great value to these women because of their poverty and their condition to be able to walk to a nearby clinic instead of being obliged to go a distance to a hospital.[5]

[4] Letter from Horace Bridges to John Elliott, June 2, 1936.
[5] April 24, 1934.

In the summer of 1934, Elliott served on the Mayor's Relief Commission (administering public welfare), but he found that "somehow I couldn't be part of what was going on." [6] A more personal approach was necessary for Elliott.

Perhaps one of the most important of [the] relationships he [Elliott] developed . . . was with the Roosevelts, when they were in Albany. He was constantly up there testifying [and] . . . appealing for clemency. . . . He had a similar relationship with LaGuardia in the City. . . . He, Rabbi Wise, and John Haynes Holmes started the City Affairs Committee—Paul Blanchard was the Executive Secretary.[7]

Elliott was consulted on a number of social welfare problems and saw Mark McCloskey play a major role in the National Youth Administration. Elliott wrote to B. Edmond David:

She [Mrs. Roosevelt] happens to be an enthusiasm of mine, and incidentally one of Mark McCloskey's strong backers. . . . Two things stand out in my mind. One is that Mark is persona grata in Washington and he holds quite an important place in New York public life as well. The first time I ever ate a "meal of vittles" in the White House, my invitation was brought by a Chelsea boy who, while the Ethical Meeting House was being built, used to bring the family baby carriage to what is now 2 West 64 Street in order to break up wood and take it home to his mother. If you think that that picture of democracy doesn't please me, you have to guess again. . . . I never left Washington with so satisfied a feeling. . . . I never saw so many efficient capable looking people working so hard in so many offices at any time in my life. There is honest work being done in our capital as at few times in my history anyway.[8]

Elliott's local political interests continued too. In 1937 he wrote to Bishop Robert Paddock, Chairman of the Non-partisan Citizens Committee to elect Stanley Isaacs as Borough President, inquiring whether Isaacs was a man worth supporting. Reassured, Elliott did what he could to support him as he also supported LaGuardia for Mayor and Dewey for Governor. His interest was in defeating Tammany.

[6] Letter to Linda Langer, December 24, 1934.
[7] Dr. and Mrs. Ormsby Robinson, interview, 1963.
[8] March 23, 1937.

Washington, Albany, City Hall, Hudson Guild, and the Senior Leadership—these were more than enough to befuddle a younger man. Elliott not only kept up with them all, but continued his interest in people in trouble. A sampling of letters suggests the range of his efforts. From a letter of Edward Tighe, Voluntary Defenders Committee, from John Elliott, April 27, 1936:

> I learned by accident the other day that the friends of James C—had not only scraped together and gotten him out on bail but that . . . they had gotten him a lawyer. . . . This puts me in an embarrassing position, that of having asked the Voluntary Defenders to take action . . . and then having someone else come into the situation.

A letter to John Elliott from Robert F. D———, January 9, 1937.

> I got a small raise . . . so here's a check for $50 which . . . finally makes up the full $250 that many years ago you loaned to me without my ever even asking for it. That was in 1919, nearly twenty years ago.

Memorandum for Mrs. Roosevelt from John Elliott, referring to a polio victim and suggesting assistance in 1939.

> The boy is completely paralyzed in all limbs. . . . He has been home for nine months. . . . The mother is now ill (cardiac case) and unable to care for him any longer.

From a letter from C. Parker R——— to John Elliott, November 30, 1939:

> . . . since that day I first talked to you—a few days after my release from Trenton [state prison]. Last Spring I had made so many worthwhile contacts I felt it possible to open an office of my own. . . . I met with extremely great success [and] am now doing work for a number of the biggest firms in the country, making a very good living. . . . You may not know it, but that five dollars you gave me as "advance payment on work to be done in the future" coupled with your wise advice, meant much more than words can ever tell you.

In a letter from John Elliott to Gertrude Marx, December 28, 1939:

The last time I went to call on Mrs. Roosevelt. . . . I found her . . . in Greenwich Village, three flights up in the rear, and she spoke of the place as her hideout. I share Barbara's enthusiasm for the First Lady. The only habit that she has that I don't care for is that when she gets a particularly stiff case of a refugee she has a way of sending it to me, and I'm sure that I can't crack any nuts that she can't.

Elliott was also reminded that the years were fast claiming his fellow innovators in social work. The family of Lillian D. Wald sent word that she had asked for Elliott to speak at her funeral: "I would like my old friend, John Elliott to be spokesman for me . . . , and I will have the assurance of knowing that he will mention only that my message is of the worthwhileness of love and fellowship and mutual respect for each other—the world over." [9]

Letters from the Vienna Society reminded Elliott and the Americans that the Depression's effect was as devastating in Europe and made more difficult by political unrest. Efforts to raise money for the European movement continued. The need to save victims of Nazi persecution from imprisonment and death became primary. In 1936 Elliott tried to bring Friedrich W. Foerster here to teach and lecture. Foerster, living on the Swiss border in France without books or money, was no longer close to Ethical Culture and indeed seemed to be moving toward Roman Catholicism. Nevertheless, Elliott in a letter to Muzzey promised that the Ethical societies would help if a suitable teaching post could be found.

Word came that Drs. Boerner and Eckstein had been arrested by the Nazis in Austria and imprisoned. Elliott immediately arranged to go to Berlin and then, on advice of the U.S. Consul and a high Nazi official, to Vienna. In Vienna he waited with the wives of the imprisoned men for the decision from Berlin. Elliott reported his dismay at the thousands of people looking for ways of leaving their country.

It is a maddening experience . . . to witness the nervous tension and strain that is prevailing. What is difficult to understand is that here is no law—yet perfect order. We are accustomed to associate law with order —when we find order we think there must be law. But in Austria and Germany, there is neither law nor right.[10]

[9] Transmitted to John Elliott in July, 1939.
[10] New York Board of Trustees, Minutes, June, 1938.

Fortunately, both Boerner and Eckstein were released and came with their wives to the United States. The New York Society provided hospitality and work. The experience with Boerner and Eckstein made the refugee problem real to Ethical Culture, and the movement undertook to aid victims by an extensive program of work with refugees in the United States.

James J. Hart was responsible for that program. Born in England, Hart was for a time minister of the Unitarian Church in Madison, Wisconsin, and on the faculty of Alexander Meikeljohn's Experimental College at the University of Wisconsin. In 1931 he accepted a fellowship offered by the Ethical Culture schools. Chubb urged Elliott that Hart be trained for Leadership, but attitudes toward Hart by leading movement figures prevented it. As Algernon Black recalled,

> He said what he believed and it was pretty straight humanism. He was critical of transcendentalism or anything that had any repressive moral preachment in it . . . when he was here just a short time he cut loose in this way, and Adler couldn't take it and was sort of through with him almost immediately. Dr. Elliott had an awful time accepting . . . the brutal intellectual statement.[11]

Scholar, critic, and humanist, Hart was a quiet and warm human being. Hart kept in the background for a time as assistant to Dr. Ellliott, reviewing the latest literature for him and reading to him each morning. He had an acute mind and spoke it; some of his younger colleagues like Jerome Nathanson recalled with gratitude the help he gave them in clarifying their ideas and expression. On the fringes of the movement, Hart never demanded much for himself. As the refugee problem became acute and the question of Ethical Culture's response to it was raised, Hart was asked to head up the work.

Following Elliott's return from Vienna, an advisory committee on refugee problems was formed in the New York Society. Opposition to immigration and isolationist propaganda ran counter to the increasing number of displaced people. In January, 1939, Elliott proposed on behalf of the committee that a center for refugees be established which would combine general education, vocational guidance, and

---

[11] Interview, 1963.

living facilities. The Board was favorable to the idea but appalled at its potential costs, especially in the light of the depression-induced deficit. After some hesitation and modification, a program was developed under Hart's direction. By November, Elliott reported that nearly 600 people each week "have had the opportunity of hearing experts in American history, politics, and business affairs, and of discussing their problems with experts."[12] As of April, 1940, more than 200 people were coming daily to the Meeting House for English lessons; more than fifty people were giving individual instruction in their own homes; the children of refugees were being brought in three times a week for special education. The Society also helped distribute food and clothing, counseled on jobs, and conducted social programs each Friday evening.

The movement tried to interpret the problem to the rest of the American community. A conference called in May, 1939, on "The Emigré and the Community" aimed at examining ways of meeting this "challenge to American idealism and intelligence." Among its sponsors were Dr. Everett Clinchy, Harry Emerson Fosdick, Stanley M. Isaacs, Clarence E. Pickett, Paul Tillich, Roger Strauss, and Ethel H. Wise. To broaden support for the program The Good Neighbor Association was formed with Eleanor Roosevelt as honorary chairman, John Elliott as chairman, and James Hart as executive.

> I remember the meeting at Hyde Park with 150 people concerned about the refugees. Mrs. Roosevelt not only invited them all up there . . . but she served the food herself. . . . John Elliott, by the way, was very critical of the Christians who would not help the refugees. And actually, more Christian refugees were saved by Jewish money and Jewish generosity than anybody knows. At one time he was so mad that he said, "if we don't get more money for refugees from the Christians, I'm going to change my name to Elliofsky. And that, he said, "will make the German Jews as mad as the Christians."[13]

The Good Neighbor Association was designed as a nationwide effort to aid refugees. By October, 1941, the program was well on its way to being launched. Within three months, however, the United States entered the war and all other matters faded into the back-

[12] Letter to Llewellyn Parsons, November 20, 1939.
[13] A. D. Black, interview, 1963.

ground. In any case, Elliott, under orders from his doctor to take a long rest, was unable to provide the energetic leadership the program would have required. Hart, at the war's end without a specific task within the movement, left New York to spend the remaining years of his life in Florida growing citrus fruit.

There was no dirth of program or activity. Indeed, the thoughts that the movement would end with Adler's death seemed foolish. A succession of young men were being drawn into the orbit of Ethical Culture, though in most instances the association was temporary. Late in 1930 Adler had reported that Stanton Coit had recommended a young Scotsman, J. Hutton Hynd, as successor to Chubb in St. Louis. In July, 1931, he was offered a fellowship with the New York Society. A graduate in philosophy from the University of Perth, Hynd was an excellent scholar and lecturer with a somewhat distant and rather crackling personality. While giving little attention to organizational effort, he was deeply committed to the fellowship structure of the American movement. On his return to England following the war, he fought, unsuccessfully, to keep the British movement within that framework. For some twenty-five years he served the St. Louis Society, following in the traditions of Sheldon and Chubb.

A group of young men who later went on to successful careers elsewhere worked for a time with the movement. Among them was Saul Bernstein, who moved to the School of Social Work in Boston. Unable to secure Elliott's support he was not named to the Leadership. Dr. Harold Buschman, brought by Adler from the University of Chicago to develop adult education programs, worked briefly before returning to academic life as Chairman of Philosophy at the University of Kansas. Ormsbee Robinson, whose grandmother had listened to Adler at Chickering Hall and whose mother was a lifelong member of the Brooklyn Society, worked with the Society until the Second World War. He resigned from New York City's public school system to accept responsibility in adult education and in the Ethics Department of the schools. For a time, he and his wife, Janet, helped develop the work camp program at Camp Felicia. He left to accept an executive position with IBM. A former Baptist minister, Elliott Shirk, was briefly involved, as was Ralph Habas from Chicago and Tom Galt in New York. But none of them developed extended professional relationships with the movement.

In Philadelphia, a successor to Weston was found in an Englishman, W. Edwin Collier. Coming to the United States in 1934, Collier had originally prepared for the Episcopal ministry. He never quite lost his interest in ritualism or his sense of formality. A sensitive and intelligent man, his presence in a Philadelphia Society accustomed to the unassuming yet strong role of Weston was not uniformly accepted, and he had difficulty there from the beginning. He remained, however, for some twenty years before resigning to work with a publishing house. In New York, efforts were made to name Horace Friess to Leadership as a philosophic successor to his father-in-law, Felix Adler. Friess continued his work in Columbia's philosophy department but accepted reluctantly a special assignment for the training of candidates and the developing of philosophic and educational materials. In a related effort to strengthen the Leadership, the New York Board named Dr. Thayer a Leader in order to emphasize the integral relationship between the Ethical Culture schools and the movement. As Elliott expressed it:

> . . . the direction that the School takes is very important and unless it is along the line of the Ethical Movement, we shall miss a very great opportunity. . . . I am sure that Thayer is our best connection. I would like to see him more closely with us and this association had best come through Leadership.[14]

With Friess and Thayer, the movement continued Adler's tradition of broadening the Leadership in order to avoid developing a mere parish ministry. Moreover, Friess' personal relationship with Adler was significant for continuity. A painstakingly careful scholar, never prolific, Horace Friess provided some balance to the emphasis on activity that seemed so pertinent for the thirties. He did bring to the Leadership a philosophic authority which it sorely needed. Unfortunately, the demands of his work at the university and his personal reticence prevented him from playing a major role. The host of worthy yet disparate efforts still needed a coherent and relevant intellectual basis.

Among the young men brought to the work of the movement in the thirties was Jerome Nathanson. An honors graduate in English at

[14] Letter to David Muzzey, June 29, 1937.

Cornell University, he did graduate work in history and philosophy at Columbia. Nathanson was for a time a journalist and then briefly managed his father's business. He recalled his introduction to Ethical Culture:

> . . . in my senior year . . . one of my close friends [Saul Bernstein] was invited to New York to be interviewed by Felix Adler and John Elliott. . . . He was granted a fellowship, . . . so in January 1928, I . . . became acquainted with . . . the Ethical Movement. . . . I got to know Dr. Elliott and then Al Black and a few others. . . . In 1930, I started to lead one of the teen age groups though I wasn't then a member of the Society. . . . When the first refugee groups began coming here very early in the Hitler period [1934], Dr. Elliott asked me if I'd lead a group acquainting them with American Government and culture, which I gladly did since there were very few things that I wouldn't have done for Dr. Elliott, whom I revered.[15]

In the fall of 1937 Elliott proposed a fellowship for Nathanson and it was granted. To his work with teen-agers and refugees, Nathanson now added leadership in developing a program for college people to meet the intellectual and political turmoil of the period. Nathanson's decision to work with the movement was not quickly made. The demands of his father's business coupled with a genuine scholarly interest and ability conflicted with the attraction of Elliott and the Ethical movement's practical idealism. Elliott finally tipped the scales. Aware of Nathanson's intellectual abilities, Elliott saw in him a man who could provide a balance to the more active social role Black was developing.

As Nathanson matured he managed to conceal a certain shyness behind a forceful voice and presence. He developed a Platform style that combined philosophic analysis with deep emotional commitment. In connection with some of the social reform efforts during the late thirties, Nathanson met and became friendly with John Dewey. Guided by Elliott within Ethical Culture and Dewey outside it, Nathanson arrived at a philosophic and moral approach to democracy as an interpretation of Ethical Culture. He seemed, for a time, to be working out Elliott's democratic translation of the movement's idea.

[15] Interview, 1962.

With Elliott's death and with the demands of the war and postwar periods, he didn't find the time and energy to complete a rounded philosophy of ethical democracy. Nevertheless, in organizing the Conferences on Science and Democracy, in helping found the Americans for Democratic Action (ADA), and in his efforts to secure federal aid to public schools, Nathanson demonstrated a consistent commitment to his interpretation of Ethical Culture. As Chairman of the Fraternity of Ethical Leaders, in his efforts to train younger men for Leadership, and from the Platform, Nathanson helped lead the movement out of its Victorian mold and toward its second century. His work with the New York Committee to Abolish Capital Punishment, the Church-State Committee of the Civil Liberties Union, and the Sex Information Council continued long-standing traditions of social ethics within the movement. A philosophic naturalist, he represented a viewpoint quite different from the transcendentalism and Kantian idealism of the founding group. In the fall of 1940, Elliott recommended his election to New York's Board of Leaders and that December, at the Society's annual meeting, this recommendation was favorably acted upon.

As the Second World War neared and the depression dragged on, the movement was stimulated to great activity, but at the same time deeply troubled. Blunt, as usual, Chubb wrote,

. . . seeking one's forty days in the summer wilderness. One must recover from the excessive tensions of "civilization,"—too much strained thinking and perverted feeling; the too constant battle with frustrations. . . . One loses one's innocence of heart and mind or tries to conquer by sheer intellectual violence. So we become superficial, thin and ineffectual. That's what's the matter with us.[16]

The problem of morale was complicated by the disappearance of the men who had been greeted with such hope during the thirties. Elliott was growing older. Black's radical critique of society, however valuable, was dividing the membership. Friess and Gutmann were developing their academic careers. David Muzzey was having more honors heaped upon him, in which the Society could take pride but from which it could gain little in the way of solving its problems.

[16] Letter to John Elliott, July 31, 1940.

Nathanson was still in his formative years. The other societies and their leaders were struggling just to stay alive. In England, Coit sought and found a successor in Harold Blackham. Henry Neumann, continuing his heroic efforts in a depression-ridden Brooklyn, was honored by the Alumni Association of City College. Robert Kohn was named architect for the New York World's Fair in 1939–40. He had served for a brief time as Director of Housing in the Emergency Public Works Administration and on Governor Lehman's committee to expedite loans in New York State. Kohn was elected to Leadership and served also as President of the New York society. Good works and responses to social needs grew steadily despite the movement's lack of internal shape and direction. The honors, the calls from Albany and Washington served to underscore the weaknesses within.

The founding group had been conservative reformers with a vision of a better society, but unsympathetic to the revolutionaries on the left. But in the thirties the left could not be ignored and liberals were flirting with a united front. In Ethical Culture, Algernon Black was perhaps the most sympathetic supporter of socialist democracy. For him and those who followed him, deed before creed now included a basic reform of the state. Deeply troubled by injustice, Black on the Sunday Platform called attention to the problems of labor and labor organization, to the rise of fascism and Nazism, to the danger of American isolationism. Black drew a large and regular audience on Sunday mornings. Characteristic was his commentary on the Spanish Civil War:

> The revolt has meant not only the deaths of hundreds of thousands of innocent people, not only the death of the cream of Spanish life, but the death of democracy and liberty. If anyone is left to rule and be ruled, the result will be dictatorship. . . .

> We cannot maintain a moral neutrality. Liberals and progressives have failed to meet the issue in almost every major crisis of ethical values since the World War. The Spanish tragedy may well become a world tragedy. If there is love of right as against might, if we believe in the solidarity of all men and women in making a better world, we must help the legitimate and recognized government of the Spanish people. . . . We must insist that no other regime be recognized and make heard our protest

against this revolt with far greater effectiveness than we did in the case of Manchuria and Ethiopia and other examples of Fascist aggression.[17]

Efforts to secure movement-wide support for Spain at the meetings in St. Louis in the fall of 1936 failed. The conservative mood of many of Ethical Culture's older members blocked consensus on the issue; others regarded any attempt at taking a position, even when they agreed with it, as a violation of the noncreedal character of the movement. In New York, the Society's public affairs committee recommended aid to the war's victims, "the desperate needs of the civilian population of Spain, especially the women and children for food, clothing, and medical aid. . . ." A campaign for contributions was coordinated with the Association to Save the Children of Spain and The Committee on Medical Aid of the American Friends of Spanish Democracy, whose chairman was John Dewey. But a stand on the issues of the war itself was not taken. The old problem of when and how Ethical Culture should put itself on record, still unresolved, plagued the movement.

Voices from the left were not restricted to the Platform. The gentlemen reformers were challenged within the movement by the organization of a Worker's Fellowship "to study ways and means of promoting a more ethical society than is possible under the profit system." Criticism came almost immediately, and Black moved to defend the action:

As I permitted the mailing to our members of the circular [announcing a program of the Worker's Fellowship] to which you take exception, I must try to justify my action.

A group of members of the Society . . . formed a Worker's Fellowship. . . . They probably realized that the Society as such would not take action . . . but thought that there were quite a number of its members who might wish to join [together]. . . . Groups are constantly formed and go their way within the Society. For many years we have taken the position that hospitality is accorded to groups of our own members for meetings of a serious character on problems of the day. . . .

I hope you will agree that we should not refuse to members of our own

[17] *The Standard,* XXIII (December, 1936), 76–77.

Society the privilege of inviting other members to join with them in the study and consideration of any topic, social, economic, or political.[18]

Members of the New York Board of Trustees expressed their distrust of the program and were concerned about the "unfavorable comment on the Society as a whole" which the Fellowship's activity might produce. However, when the Worker's Fellowship requested formal recognition and representation on the Society's Council, it was granted despite serious misgivings. It was pointed out that though its members shared a "collectivist" view, there was great variety within the Fellowship as to the specific course of social reform. The problem of the group's right to issue public statements was not resolved and doubt was expressed whether control was possible. This was compounded by the news, some two years after its organization, that the Workers' Fellowship was beneficiary of a legacy of some $30,000, originally bequeathed to the Society.

Audiences of a hundred and more people came to hear the Fellowship's discussions of technology, of socialism, of industrial planning. While primarily "middle class" in membership, the Worker's Fellowship tried to develop a relevant relationship with the labor movement. They tried to carry into a new era the central ethical idea of helping people help themselves. The Fellowship developed almost independent of the Society. In the late forties there was some suspicion that the group had been infiltrated by Communists. An extended and painful effort to dissolve it was not successful until the early fifties, and the feelings of hostility engendered led to loss of membership and of morale for Ethical Culture in New York. Some felt the Society had surrendered to red-baiting and McCarthyite hysteria; others that the Society had been overly scrupulous and patient with a program that had long since lost its claim to ethical validity. However evaluated, the nearly twenty-year course of the Fellowship revealed once again the shift from an earlier day. It showed also the almost anarchic character of Ethical Culture in a period when action was unguided by a commonly held philosophy. The middle ground between dogma and chaos, which Adler had plotted under the guiding notion of an "implicit" religion, had not been reconstructed.

The problems of war and peace were met on the Platform, in con-

18 Letter, A. D. Black to Albert Stieglitz, March 29, 1935.

ferences, in public forums. The Jewish question became increasingly troublesome as questions of Jewish identity were forced by Hitler's anti-Semitism. Many who once had thought little of giving up nominal loyalty to a faith they had long since left, now felt guilty at denying it. Racial tensions, too, were building, and at the AEU Assembly of 1933 Dr. Elliott called for the organization of a second international races congress—but the call went unheeded. A plan to hold the International Congress on Moral Education in Berlin in 1936 was protested vigorously as an evident travesty. Numerous educational ventures included a course on moral education at New York's City College with lectures by Black, Elliott, Neumann, and Muzzey. To celebrate the sixtieth anniversary of the movement a series of institutes were organized on peace and the chief ethical and social problems of the arts and professions. Henry Wallace and Mrs. Roosevelt spoke at those institutes. The continuing problem of child labor motivated a new resolution in support of the child-labor amendment in 1937. The proposed "boycott" of Japan and support for the war in Spain mingled with perennial concerns. So many issues, by their very nature, brought to the fore again the question of how Ethical Culture should make its position known, which led to the formation of a national Public Affairs Committee. Established hesitantly, and hedged by numerous caveats, explicit institutional devices were again substituted for more personal styles. The problems to which such devices were addressed were not solved; the real issue was the searching out of common ground, not the development of paraphernalia.

Programs multiplied. Arrangements were made to broadcast the Sunday meetings of the New York Society over WQXR. The Sunday schools and youth work continued and grew. Membership increased slowly, but it was not a membership that could provide financial resources. The Societies experienced continuing fiscal trouble. Requests for help continued from individuals and organizations that had been related to the movement. Typical were words from Madison House and from Camp Felicia of serious deficits. The Summer Play School went on. The Ethical Culture schools, hard hit by the depression, were experiencing great difficulty.

. . . a number of the parents of full tuition pupils who had been in the school a long time came and said they needed scholarships. They had lost practically all their money. Others withdrew and around July or August in the middle of the 30's—I think it was—there was an indicated deficit of over $100,000. . . . I recall meeting after meeting during that summer with B. Edmund David who was ailing at the time. . . . Also at these meetings . . . were Robert D. Kohn, Dr. V. T. Thayer. . . . We had to keep very quiet because if it were known that there was even a possibility that the school would not be able to open its doors in September . . . the withdrawals probably would have pyramided.[19]

With Thayer taking the lead, the faculty agreed to a voluntary program of salary reduction and to additional work in order to reduce the number of faculty members needed. The economic crisis together with the requirements of a four-year program forced the closing in 1939 of the teacher education department of the schools. More to the point, the need to meet the crisis made all thought of educational experiment and challenge to the educational "establishment" quixotic.

In the societies around the country the Depression and the death or resignation of the older generation of Leaders and members were producing their own changes and problems. By 1934, Weston, more and more feeble, was unable to lead the Philadelphia Society. The Society managed to survive with Collier, though its efforts as publishing house for the movement ceased. In 1937 Chicago celebrated its fiftieth anniversary and the twenty-fifth anniversary of Horace Bridge's leadership. Henry Herman reported:

> . . . I think . . . the Chicago Society had passed its zenith by that time [the mid-30's]. Bridges was older and pretty much had a personal following that was highly literary. . . . With Bridges it was a small group . . . much less dynamic . . . in terms of social causes.[20]

The Boston Society was disappearing despite efforts to reorganize after Swift left. New groups were reported in South Orange, New Jersey, in Flushing and Far Rockaway, New York, but these came to naught. The Westchester group had been led briefly by Elliott Shirk, but personal difficulties forced his resignation and Muzzey returned as part-time advisor. The picture was not a happy one, despite the

[19] Interview, Herbert A Wolff, 1963.
[20] Interview, 1962.

range of activity spearheaded from New York and the continuing stability in St. Louis.

Many of the Movement's members were growing restive. Mrs. Edna Gellhorn of St. Louis suggested these themes for discussion at the forthcoming national meetings:

1) Purpose of AEU besides publishing *The Standard*

2) Why the Annual Assembly

3) Reasons for stagnation of the Ethical Movement

4) Why after 55 years no societies outside the seven in existence

5) Any intention to take aggressive measures to recruit new leaders and plant "colonies" in Kansas City, Denver, etc.[21]

A year later, the Fraternity of Leaders was addressing itself to similiar themes. Underlying the discussion was dissatisfaction with the lack of institutional and numerical growth and a latent awareness that a genuinely national movement did not exist. The census of 1937 revealed how tiny the movement was, reporting some 2600 members with 1100 in New York and fifty in Boston.

Ideologically, the movement was at sea too. From the left new voices were heard in 1932 in a Humanist Manifesto, a rallying point for nontheistic, and often antireligious, liberals. The Leadership tried to give voice to the ethical idea but found itself unable to speak in unison. Opposing the utterly secular thrust of the humanists, the movement was troubled on the other side by demands for security and absolutism. Acknowledging its roots in the liberal tradition, the Leadership recognized that liberalism seemed discredited by the economic crisis and its implications. Troubled by a reawakened religious orthodoxy, the movement was troubled too by its apparent inability to make affirmative, alternate statements. Elliott tried once again to draw the relationship between religion and democracy:

Our fellowship is not demonstrative. . . . We have always been part of a small group. The roots of democracy were always in small groups of people. . . . When you get to deal with a vast group, you lose hope.

[21] AEU Records, August, 1933, p. 432.

The small group can believe in change. . . . Faith in people comes out of face to face meetings. They are the essence of religion as well as democracy.[22]

The appeal to the small group may have been satisfying, but it failed to have relevance to the problem of mass movements in the thirties. Moreover, democracy stood as an undefined hortatory term in a day when it needed more than ever to be expressed clearly and convincingly. The shadows of fascism and communism had darkened the spiritual horizon, and the brave words lacked power to move people. From England Coit, still the gadfly, reviewed the spreading totalitarianism and the possibility that the democracies themselves might "become sufficiently totalitarian to curtail full freedom of thought and assembly." Speaking of the tyrannical possibilities of public opinion even if police and law were not repressive, Coit chastised the movement:

> To believe that an institution will grow and develop into a great world power for good merely by virtue of its inherent moral and spiritual worth is the most foolish and paralyzing of ethical superstitions. . . . A movement may begin poor . . . but if it remains poor . . . it is doomed either to extinction or to a worse fate—that of becoming a mutual admiration society.
>
> Unfortunately, some of my Ethical colleagues are still inclined to glorify poverty and to believe that if the Ethical Movement increases in prestige and wealth it will become corrupt and worldly. . . . My judgment is that, if our Movement were to fall away from grace because it succeeded in becoming a world-wide influence, the sooner it falls the better both for us and for the communities we had hoped to enlighten and ennoble.[23]

Elliott, Nathanson, and Black had hold of an idea which might have transformed Adler's religion of duty and transcendental idealism into a relevant response to the changing scene. A religion of social justice, prophetic criticism, democratic relationship, and naturalistic confidence would have been both meaningful and valuable in a world

[22] New York Board of Trustees, Minutes, November, 1939.
[23] "Ourselves and the Great Religions of the World," February, 1940. Ethical Culture Archive.

of power, anonymity, and degradation. But the overwhelming demands for pragmatic activity and the shadow of Adler prevented the development of the necessary new synthesis. Reform continued without a life-giving philosophy, while over everything loomed the fearful horror of total war.

CHAPTER XXII

Can Democracy Survive?

At the outbreak of the Second World War, the forces of light seemed arrayed in final battle against the forces of darkness. In fact "moral crusade" was a less than accurate description. Hitler's Germany and its allies were clearly wrong, but it required a certain blindness to ignore the exploitative and acquisitive characteristics of the Western allies and their friends to the east. The "wave of the future" was mass man—well fed, perhaps, but also well led.

Against the background of the time, the struggle of the few souls constituting Ethical Culture seemed unimportant and Emerson's moral religion but a museum piece. The Protestants had rediscovered sin; the Jews, a loyalty tragically reinforced by murder and horror. Like others, Ethical Culture concerned itself with problems of isolationism and war. Algernon Black wrote:

> . . . the world seems to be drifting rapidly toward war. . . . I am so utterly against [it] . . . but . . . I think I am realistic when I say that any peace in the world will have to be based on the recognition of the unity of the human race and the interdependence of the nations of the

272

world. . . . It . . . means that the isolation policy is both an unethical ideal and an unrealistic approach to keeping America at peace. . . . Isolation is an illusion and collective security means taking the risks of war.[1]

The communist scare increased as war drew near. A letter to John Elliott expressed dismay at a "member of the Fieldston Faculty who was actually a Muscovite agent." The writer withdrew financial support. Joseph Jablonower, a leading member of the movement and an honored educator in New York City, was accused of left-wing sympathies on his nomination to the City's Board of Examiners, and this too drew fire upon the Society. In vain, Elliott sought to quiet the fears and to demand fact in place of rumor. But the panic was not to be met with reason and many of the wealthier supporters of the New York Society continued to leave.

The question of pacifism also arose. Elliott and Neumann, both pacifists in the First World War, felt that the situation was different now. Elliott in particular expressed puzzlement about his own attitudes and shared his doubts with Dr. Neumann, who did not yield his position. So fearful were the times that when the announcement was made that the 1941 AEU meetings in Philadelphia would include joint sessions with the Quakers on "The Basis of Our Faith in a Moral Order in the World," many Board members demurred. The public might be misled into thinking of Ethical Culture as a pacifist movement, and it was recommended that a formal statement of neutrality on this issue be circulated. At the same time efforts were made to secure recognition for "the Ethical Culture Movement and other minority religions" in the armed services so that young men drafted into service would not be classified only as Protestant, Catholic, or Jewish.

With the coming of the Second World War, the many Englishmen who had joined the American movement were deeply affected. As Elliott put it:

I had a long letter from Hynd. . . . It had more of the fraternal feeling than any word I have had from him so far. Of course, like the other English-born persons in our Movement, he is terribly anxious about the situation in Europe. It is astonishing how men like O'Dell and Hart keep

[1] Letter to Bessie Stillman, April 24, 1939.

a perfectly smooth face when they have some of their closest relatives and friends in England. It is as fine a thing as I have ever seen.[2]

War hysteria was mounting and again everything German was seen as evil. Elliott was deeply troubled by the blindness that so readily created villains. Hopelessly, he suggested the need for a book publicizing the contributions of Germans to world culture:

If it isn't brought to public consciousness (and it would be very difficult, perhaps impossible to do so) we will have another Versailles or possibly something worse. I am constantly haunted by the spectre of a third World War. I'm afraid you can't consider this a cheerful communication.[3]

During the war dances and a canteen for servicemen were conducted in New York and elsewhere. Conscientious objectors were counseled. The Play Schools expanded as "mothers are out of the home more and children are on the streets." The New York Society organized its recreation program for servicemen "without discrimination as to race, color or nationality and purely on a first come first served basis." Resistance to integration came from both Negro and white; the good intentions came to naught.

With increasing frequency news came of the deaths of the last of the founding group and their immediate successors. In 1939 the New York Board recorded the death of Edwin R.A. Seligman; in 1940, of B. Edmund David and Mrs. Lionel Sutro; in 1943, of Jennie Fels; in 1944, of Abraham Gutmann; in 1945, of Moses Newborg. By 1940 nearly all of the societies in England, France, Germany, Austria, and Italy had disappeared; the international movement had ceased to exist.

In 1941 Horace Bridges was seriously ill. A letter to Elliott from Chubb said:

I'm just back from Chicago; spoke there yesterday to meet an emergency. I had better be silent as to what I found. . . . It was trying—

[2] Letter to Henry Neumann, August 7, 1940.
[3] Letter to Horace Friess, March 7, 1942.

that small sprinkled, distant and stolid audience! Today, I'm trying to get over it. We need vitality, elan! [4]

More hopefully, Westchester reported work on a child guidance center and, in 1945, the purchase of its own meeting house. Brooklyn, too, began to meet its financial problems and purchased property on Prospect Park West in 1943. Muzzey, returning from a series of speaking engagements for the movement in 1944, reported that despite its difficulties, Chicago still survived. St. Louis, he said, was "flourishing, with good audiences of about 550 people at Sunday Services." He told, too, of meeting with a group of more than fifty people in Newark, New Jersey. This latter group finally formed itself as the Essex County Society.

The war brought many people to the nation's capital, among them Sidney Scheuer, a leading member of the New York Society. This active and successful businessman worked during the war as Executive Director of the Foreign Economic Administration. Influenced early in his career by Felix Adler, Scheuer brought together a group of about thirty people in 1943 to meet with Algernon Black in order to form a Washington, D.C., Ethical Society. Unlike a similar effort in the First World War, this one succeeded and survived beyond the war. Scheuer was one of the few remaining active in the movement who was similar in motivation and achievement to the group of early followers of Dr. Adler. Interpreting business as "vocation," in Adler's sense of the term, Sidney Scheuer demonstrated an active interest in an ethical politics as a founder and later Chairman of the National Committee for an Effective Congress. His work in international trade took him beyond the cash nexus. He served as a member of the United States Delegation to the Inter-American Conference on Problems of War and Peace in Mexico City (1945), visited Germany at the request of the Secretary of War to survey its textile industry, and was a member of the Economic Mission asked to report on the position and prospects of Japan and Korea at the end of the war. At the same time Arthur E. Briggs, an attorney and former student of Felix Adler, started a small group in Los Angeles.

[4] January 31, 1942.

News of the deaths of Nathaniel Schmidt in 1939 and of Gustav Spiller in 1940 continued to remind Ethical Culture of the problem of a succession of prophets. In 1944 word came of Stanton Coit's death as well, and the last of the founding generation was gone. The war made the task of finding young men even more difficult. Nevertheless, in 1942 Muzzey reported that three young men had been found who should be granted fellowships. The three "H's," as they came to be known, were William Hammond, James F. Hornback, and Henry B. Herman. Hammond remained for a training period but moved on to the Unitarian ministry. Hornback began his work, then entered the military service as a noncombatant, and returned after the war to complete his training. Herman, who had attended the Ethical Culture schools, the New York Society's Sunday school, and its youth clubs, remained with the New York Society on fellowship and later as one of its Leaders. A graduate of the University of Wisconsin who worked for a time with the National Youth Administration, Henry Herman brought to the Leadership a social work orientation more professional in character than Elliott's but quite similar in temperament. At one time or other Herman taught ethics in the schools, conducted the youth work in New York, helped Algernon Black to develop the Encampment for Citizenship, advised numerous smaller fellowships, and administered the New York Society. As he said in an interview:

> Sometimes there are moments when there is more to do than you can do and . . . you wonder whether this really the most effective way to use your energies and your life. The problem is focus. . . . The demands on you are very great from the outside as well as the inside. . . . I think it's a job in which you can't ever really know enough to be adequate for it, which is both challenging and frustrating.[5]

In the late fifties Herman served for four years as Leader of the Westchester Society before returning to New York's Leadership. In 1965 he resigned to become Director of Program at the Student Union of the University of Wisconsin.

Hornback, completing his apprenticeship after the war in New York and in Brooklyn, served as Leader of the Westchester Society from 1947 to 1951 and then went to St. Louis to succeed Hynd. A

[5] Interview, 1963.

Midwesterner, Hornback was educated at a small denominational college. Early in life he developed an anticlerical attitude and was one of the first of the Leadership to adopt a straightforward Humanist position. For a time, he served as a board member of the American Humanist Association. Concerned with issues of conscience, he worked actively with the Missouri Civil Liberties Union and for the absolute separation of church and state. An idealist and a very quiet man, Hornback's bent was philosophic, but the demands of the St. Louis Society often militated against extensive philosophic effort. Ironically, for one so anticlerical, he served a Society which from Sheldon onward had developed most explicitly the image of an Ethical Society as a religious institution.

As these three young men set out on careers that were to turn out so differently, belated recognition was granted George O'Dell, who in 1944, at age seventy, was finally elected an Associate Leader of the New York Society in honor of thirty years of service to the movement. Robert Kohn, rounding out twenty years as President in New York, was also elected to Leadership. Wilhelm Boerner was similarly recognized by the American Ethical Union in 1942. But these honorary elections did not meet the evident problems. Since the turn of the century the movement had struggled to develop a meaningful training program for a task which seemed by nature to evade preparation. Fortunate in its personalities, Ethical Culture was still caught up in the weakness of such dependence—its future was to be determined by the accidental availability of this or that strong and competent individual.

Elliott was nearing the end of the "ten years of useful work" which he had forecast to Herbert Wolff. Active almost to the day of his death, much of his correspondence nevertheless took on a rather nostalgic character.

In recent years two of my brothers have passed on and they have left a lonesome place along the sky, but I am very happy in the fact that memory plays such a living part in my life. Felix Adler, for instance, is actually a living person. It sounds superstitious but it's not. I admire him more than I ever did and depend on him . . ., but I also differ with him more than I ever did and that makes it very human. I wouldn't know how to make a wish for a friend that would mean any more than that they might in an entirely natural and wholesome way live with memories. And it's fortunate, too, because at my age certainly a great number of those whom I have loved are not here.[6]

On more than one occasion he expressed gratitude that he would not live long enough to be forced to make judgments as a pacifist about what was going on in the world. He wrote to Chubb that he agreed with the importance of "beauty, festivals, and everything that makes for the joy of life." Apologetically he quoted Kipling's comment that the American's idea of fun is work. Still responsive to human need, Elliott went to Montreal in the fall of 1941 to seek the release from an internment camp of William Hecksher, grandson of Friedrich Wilhelm Foerster. He reported that the release would probably be forthcoming but that a U.S. visa would be difficult if not impossible to obtain.

Ill and tired, Elliott spent his last days in the hospital and died in April of 1942. Stephen Wise had written years earlier:

> What a chance I missed to say what is in my heart about you when the Chairman called on you or me to invoke the benediction, and I might have said exactly what I believe, "I can do no more than *ask* the benediction. Dr. Elliott *is* one.[7]

This time the mourners gathered from Chelsea and Hyde Park, from Fifth Avenue and Sing Sing, from the Mayor's mansion and Harlem. If Adler had in death evoked the respect granted a man of brilliance and forcefulness, Elliott called forth the warmth of love and the deep sadness of parting friendship.

For the second time within a decade Ethical Culture was in need of a Senior Leader for New York and hence for the movement. In June, 1942, a special committee of the New York Board met with the Leadership to seek an answer. The Leadership reported:

> We realize that no one of us should now attempt to fulfill all the manifold functions that John Elliott as Senior Leader and Rector of the School was able to cover, and as Felix Adler in his way had done before him. We hope that these titles would not be bestowed now upon any one

[6] Letter to Mabel Goodlander, October 24, 1940.
[7] Letter to John Elliott, December 8, 1932.

of us. But this decision . . . accentuates our intention to move on constructively to fulfill these and other essential functions as a cooperating group.[8]

The report detailed a series of specialized responsibilities: Muzzey was to act as Chairman of a Board of Leaders; Algernon Black, to serve as Executive Leader; and Jerome Nathanson, as Administrator. Adler had envisioned Leadership as a corporate task, a fellowship of equals, and now, for the first time, the New York Leadership gave this idea a try. It was motivated in part by a genuine sense of equality, in part by an inability to decide among various legitimate claimants. The decision to leave the Senior Leadership and the School Rectorship vacant was symbolic of the special place both Adler and Elliott had held in the movement. Dr. Neumann, who was the eldest of the active Leaders, might have been named to the post, but he still served the Brooklyn Society as well as New York. Moreover, his pacifism in the midst of war seemed ill calculated to provide the rallying strength which a new Senior Leader needed. Hurt by this, Neumann continued to serve, accepting the challenge to build a Board of Leaders.

To honor the memory of Dr. Elliott, the New York Society established its John L. Elliott Institute for Human Relations in the fall of 1942. At the annual meeting in 1941, shortly before his death, Elliott had spoken of the schools as the "first story" in an educational edifice. The time had come, he said, to build the "second story" in the field of adult education. Over and over again, Elliott had advised, "get yourself a skill." The Institute was created "to further in the community at large a practical yet expert dealing with problems in Ethical terms" and in the hope of building a program for adults to the same level of comprehensiveness as the Ethical Culture Schools were for children. Responsibility for the Institute was vested in a committee of the Board with Thayer as Chairman, and Mrs. S.S. Goldwater, Mrs. Joseph Jablonower, James Hart, Alegernon Black, and Jerome Nathanson as members. Nathanson, who had discussed the idea with Elliott many times, accepted responsibility for the project. As with the earlier attempt to establish an Ethical College, the Insitute encountered too many difficulties to achieve the vision of its founders.

[8] New York Board of Trustees, Minutes, June, 1942.

The School for Printer's Apprentices dedicated a tablet in Elliott's memory. A small booklet of his more trenchant paragraphs was published under the title *John Elliott, Unconquerable Spirit*. Lawrence S. Mayers, an active trustee of the New York Society, suggested in a letter to Mrs. Roosevelt that a "Victory" ship be named in his honor and this was done. In Chelsea at the close of the war one of New York City's major housing developments was appropriately named the John L. Elliott Houses. Adult education and housing, brief sayings and bronze plaques were testimony to the variegate career of John Elliott. If, as he so often complained, he could not explain what he was doing in rounded philosophic prose, his activity and presence had embodied a philosophy of human relationship. For a movement that needed to carry that philosophy beyond the limits of personality, its implicitness was a stumbling block; but for the man it had been an inspiring life's guide.

In the late twenties Elliott had commented that the Ethical Platform which had been Adler's alone was passing into the hands of a group. Adler had pointed out the fact that the "sanctity" seemed to be going out of Sunday. During the thirties the Ethical Platform continued, though attendance was greatly diminished. Leading figures in soical ethics and in the active work of the world were brought to it. In 1940 Professor Hans Kohn of Smith College spoke. The next week, the Chinese Ambassador to the U.S. addressed the Society on "Social Immorality." Jerry Voorhis, liberal Congressman from California, was invited. Despite these efforts to make the Platform relevant to contemporary life, its audiences were not only decreasing in number but changing in character. Even the leading members of the Society seldom attended, which drew comment from Elliott:

> Dr. Elliott stated that one could not be in touch with the function of the Ethical Society unless he attended the Sunday morning meetings. He expressed the belief that these Sunday meetings were a particular responsibility of the Trustees as the meetings represent the most significant and typical function the Society performs.[9]

A year later Nathanson bluntly asked the Trustees why they did not attend Sunday morning meetings and urged that they write the

[9] New York Board of Trustees, Minutes, March 3, 1941.

Leaders giving their reasons. Perhaps changing styles of living in the urban center more than anything else accounted for the changing response to the Platform. It was not merely the death of Adler, for even in the twenties diminution of attendance had begun. As early as 1929, Elliott, Black, and others had suggested radio broadcasts. In 1936 at the urging of Black and on the occasion of the start of WQXR as a station devoted to fine music, the New York Board agreed to sponsor a regular Sunday broadcast of its Platform. Arrangements were made with Elliott Sanger, manager of the station, whose wife was a graduate of the schools and a member of the Society. The committee named to develop Ethical Culture's first major venture with the mass media was headed by Frank Karelsen III, graduate of the schools, attorney, and member of the New York Board. By 1941 the Sunday morning program was well established and other broadcasting ventures were tried. Black emerged as an effective radio personality and for many years broadcast under the title *Ethical Issues in the News*. From 1944–46 Nathanson also developed a weekly forum, broadcast over station WEVD. In the early forties both programs took up the topics of isolationism, the America First movement, morale in the military camps, minority problems, and civil rights. The programs received numerous awards as well as much criticism from extremists who accused the Movement of left-wing sympathies and from those who did not agree with Black's more radical stance. Nevertheless, the Society recorded that,

. . . for this year [1941] it was decided that the Saturday evening broadcasts [Black's] would be recognized as a Society broadcast, with the understanding, however, that the announcement which is now given, that the views expressed are not necessarily those of the Society, be continued.[10]

Much later, when the world was caught up in cold war and iron curtain, the Society's support was withdrawn, and Black's views became a center of controversy for the Trustees and for his colleagues. During the early forties, however, the criticism and angry letters were greeted as signs that important ethical ideas and attitudes were being expressed under an Ethical Culture banner. Thus, when WQXR indi-

[10] New York Board of Trustees, Minutes, December, 1941.

cated it might have to cancel "Ethical Issues" after complaints were received from *The Tablet* (a right-wing Roman Catholic newspaper published in Brooklyn), the Board

> . . . charged [Mr. Karelsen] with writing to the radio station, thanking them for the use of their facilities, pointing out . . . that the work Mr. Black is doing is of great importance, and expressing the hope that they will find it possible to continue the Thursday night broadcasts next fall.[11]

Over the years Ethical Culture had taken a prophetic position on critical issues. For example, three scripts which had been kept off the air were concerned with the Wagner Labor Relations Act (before its adoption), with racial segregation of blood in Red Cross Blood Banks, and with the "attempt of a Catholic named Moran in Boston to start a pro-fascist riot in the Irish American association." Board discussions of these and other matters were a constant reminder that by its very nature Ethical Culture attacked superstition, sectarianism, and dogma.

After WQXR dropped the broadcasts, another station, WMCA, took them over in 1946 on Sunday evenings. In St. Louis, over Station KMOX, Hynd was conducting "The St. Louis Society on the Air." New York, however, led the way in employing the new medium to reach beyond the meeting house. Caught in the lecture habit of the nineteenth century and still modeled in part after the church service, the Platform of Sunday mornings continued too for the dwindling number in the pews.

Whatever the form of communication, issues for ethical explication increased in variety and complexity. Pacifism and war presented new faces in the light of total warfare, bombing of civilian populations, racial murder. Sectarianism and a reawakened orthodoxy began to divide the American public into three major religious categories— Protestant, Catholic, Jew—leaving the minority voices outside of acceptable Americanism. One consequence was reflected in the following letter:

> . . . one of our younger Brooklyn members . . . is having difficulty about getting a child for adoption. His wife is Protestant while he him-

[11] New York Board of Trustees, Minutes, 1943.

self had a Protestant mother and a Jewish father. Mrs. Wise will not hear of giving them a Jewish child. Therefore they must turn to the Protestant agency.[12]

Social welfare problems in the wake of the New Deal continued to command attention. Thus the Chelsea Neighborhood Association begun by Elliott and the Guild continued to press for more and better housing. In Chicago, Horace Bridges criticized the growing professionalism of social work:

> The fact that our "settlements" *are* needed is the greatest burden on my conscience as an American and a democrat. And, to my horror, I find developing here among "social workers" an outrageous trade-union temper that seeks to multiply jobs for themselves, to exclude from them all who aren't "initiated" according to the pet theories of the "organized" —laying down standards that if applied earlier would quite certainly have shut out Jane Addams, Barnett, Coit, and yourself.[13]

The city continued to fascinate Ethical Culture. A group of younger members of the New York Society under Nathanson's Leadership began to work in the San Juan Hill area of New York, an area of massive Puerto Rican settlement on New York's West Side. A major effort of the project was a film portraying the problems of Puerto Rican migrants for use in community education and propaganda. The volunteers were struggling to find a role for themselves between the jealous proprieties of governmental investment and professional interest.

The problem of racial justice began to assume a more pressing character, to which Algernon Black responded first in New York and then nationally. The meetings of the Citizen's Committee on Harlem were held at the New York meeting house; the organization of the New York State Committee Against Discrimination in Housing took place in Black's study.

Issues alone were more than enough to occupy a movement many times the size and strength of Ethical Culture. Fortunately the habit of seeking allies in the wider society and of avoiding a narrowly conceived sectarian approach to reform prepared Ethical Culture to ac-

[12] Letter to John Elliott from Henry Neumann, May 16, 1940.
[13] Letter to John Elliott, April 2, 1941.

cept leadership or initiative, but certainly in all instances to depend upon a larger community of concern than was to be found within the societies themselves. The nascent civil-rights movement, the developing alliance on the question of church and state separation, the growing awareness on the part of the more acute social workers of the need to include in valid ways the amateur—all of these were illustrative of such a community. Ethical Culture took its place, did its work, established its position. The Leadership sought to interpret this wider community as a "larger ethical movement," recognizing that an ethical culture could not be the prerogative of any one institution. This open alliance, which demanded more energy and thought than the institution itself, failed to contribute institutional strength to the struggling movement and its societies. Even as more people came to share the common desire for reform and social criticism, the Ethical Culture movement weakened.

The movement began a series of experiments with young people which, less formal than the schools, seemed more promising. In New York, always the center for innovation, a series of "youth courses" were organized by Black in the early forties. The first of these (in 1941) was called "The Faiths Men Hold," and speakers included Horace Friess and Ruth Benedict. In 1942 the theme was "Frontiers of Freedom," and the final lecture was given by Eleanor Roosevelt. The third and last program in the spring of 1943 was called "The Challenge of Victory" with Quincy Howe, A. Phillip Randolph, Henry Steele Commager, J. Raymond Walsh, Morris Ernst, and Mrs. Roosevelt as the speakers. Following the formal speeches, the hundreds of upper high school and young college students who attended were divided into discussion groups for further investigation. The idea of the program was that the young would be responsible for the postwar world and the belief that a relevant liberalism would emerge from intensive exploration. It was, of course, the old liberal confidence in the process of education.

Complementary to this program was the development of Work Camps for Democracy (later Work Camps for America) in 1939, 1940, and 1941, in cooperation with the Hudson Guild, the Progressive Education Association, and the Ethical Culture schools. Their purposes were:

To create a loyalty to American Democracy and a will to serve the
country

To train young Americans for citizenship

To develop a strong and healthy youth, capable of hard work and responsibility

To make clearer the methods and problems and meaning of democracy
through the sharing of work and social living and study

To develop leaders who have a clearer sense of those problems which
have to be solved if democracy is to survive or move forward in
the world.[14]

Sparked by Black with Ormsby Robinson's help, the program hoped
to provide for college students practical and educational experience
with a democratic community and an opportunity to be of genuine
service. In 1941 a brief experiment with more mature high school
students, Junior Work Camps for Democracy, was tried. Robinson
described one camp:

> The American campers study art, language, etc. in the mornings under
> the tutelage of refugee instructors, and the refugees learn about Ameri-
> cans through their informal contacts with the campers and the local
> townspeople rather than by any formal instruction. The work activities
> find all sharing equally.
>
> The group is . . . somewhat better balanced "racially." . . . The lat-
> ter aspect has been very helpful for some of our Fieldston students.[15]

By 1940 four camps were in operation with much of the support coming from the New York Society and with staff and campers coming
from as many as fifteen states of the union and from abroad. Black's
hopes for the experiment were high:

> I hope . . . that the camps will become so important to the youth and
> to the adults interested in citizenship training and especially organiza-
> tions who wish to develop their own youth leaders (Unions, coopera-
> tives, employers, etc.) that they will excuse farm youth and even worker
> youth on a scholarship opportunity. . . . Concerning the idea of an all-

[14] Quoted by Algernon D. Black, *The Young Citizens*, p. 31.
[15] Letter to John Elliott from Green Mountain Camp, Goddard College, Plain-
field, Vermont, July 31, 1939.

year round camp, may I say that this has been in our minds. . . . If the need grows this will be quite possible. The point is, of course, that these would be *non-governmental* volunteer work camps with an emphasis on the educational program.[16]

Forerunners in spirit and ideal to the Encampment for Citizenship founded after the war, both the youth courses and the work camps reflected an unarticulated faith in educational exposure and work as means of resolving the democratic crisis. Robert Lynd, the Columbia sociologist, raised the question, "There seemed to be a kind of mystical reverence for 'working together.' It *is* good, but working together for what?"[17] Lynd went on to comment that the program seemed to him too "social worky" and "respectable." He suggested that a meaningful democratic program needed more definition and to be "mobilized to take the offensive against this bumbling world we older people have tolerated." Prophetically, Lynd concluded,

> I think we're entering a time of real danger to people who urge "more radical" action upon respectable organizations. . . . But there seems to me no use in shouting abroad one's doubts about the liberal type of organization. It's a bitter period we're entering and those of us who believe large changes are inevitable are in for trouble. It's tougher to carry a bit of the courage of Felix Adler into the Ethical Culture sphere than it is to carry it into the more general moral sphere!

The problems of liberal reconstruction and a more relevant democratic ideology appeared in a different way in the Conference on the Scientific Spirit and the Democratic Faith, organized by Jerome Nathanson in the early forties. The first program was held in the spring of 1943 at the New York meeting house. The public sessions of the Conference were addressed to "Science and Morality" and "The Authoritarian Assault on Democracy." Smaller, private sessions discussed the problems of democratic responsibility in religion, philosophy, education, and government. Nathanson, speaking at the Conference, said,

> We say that modern society, especially a democracy, must be pluralistic. . . . We go even further and say . . . that it is desirable, we *ought* to

[16] Letter to Sidney Blumenthal, December 30, 1940.
[17] Letter to A. D. Black, November 6, 1940.

have it . . . without the principle of pluralism no decent democratic society can exist . . . there is, or ought to be a common stress on the promotion of those potentialities of human beings which release [them] in ourselves and others. . . . Let us recognize that once we adopt this sense of a working religious leadership dedicated to a pluralism of religious values, then we see that some traditional religious manifestations are, from a democratic point of view, not only anti-democratic but antireligious and must courageously be labelled such.[18]

John Dewey served as Honorary President, and John Herman Randall, Jr., as Chairman. Among participants and sponsors were Max Otto, Arthur Morgan, Brand Blanchard, Horace Kallen, William Hurd Kilpatrick, and Edward C. Lindeman. Speakers at the Conference included philosophers and anthropologists, physicists and psychiatrists, educators and businessmen. Bringing together liberals from many different fields, the Conference was attended by more than 500 participants and succeeded in opening up anew a number of issues. Plans were made to continue the program and to publish the contributions to the discussions.

A second Conference, arranged in the spring of 1944, was even better attended. The program focused on "Education in a Democracy," and more than thirty speakers affirmed the values of "democratic experimentalism, the free play of modern science and unhampered philosophic speculation, . . . the search for progressive experience."

In 1945 "the bomb" forced attention to the problems of atomic energy. The third Conference spoke to the themes of "Science in the National Economy" and "The Challenge of Science to Social Thinking." In addition to those who had participated earlier, contributions to the program were received from Felix S. Cohen, Gerald Wendt, Robert Lynd, Ernest Nagel, and F. C. S. Northrop. In the spring of 1946 a much more modest effort was organized, presenting William O. Douglas of the U.S. Supreme Court speaking on "Law as an Instrument of Democratic Justice."

For four years the Conference on Science and Democracy ex-

---

[18] "The Democratic Responsibility of Religious Leadership" in *The Scientific Spirit and Democratic Faith* (papers from the Conference in New York, May, 1943), pp. 69–73 passim.

amined questions that were to plague democracy in the postwar decades. One useful consequence was bringing together a group of people who could join forces as new issues arose. When federal aid to education was debated in 1948, Dale DeWitt of the American Unitarian Association and Nathanson, using a small fund left over from the Conference, organized the National Committee for Federal Aid to Public Education. With additional support received from the Southern Baptists and others committed to Church-State separation, Leo Pfeffer, an attorney of the American Jewish Committee, helped draft a bill for presentation to the Congress by Representative Graham Barden. The policy of wider alliance again was in evidence. The informal, yet important, effects of the Conference were felt for many years.

Conferences and institutes, courses and work camps were undertaken while the United States fought in the largest and most costly war in history. If the spiritual ideal had not been reconstructed, Nathanson, Black, and others were continuing in the tradition of Ethical Culture to penetrate the issues with deeper perceptions and meanings. Caught up in the distractions of issues and in the problems of institutional viability, they nevertheless sought to transcend the momentary response. If they were unsuccessful—and in a sense they were—they shared that frustration with the rest of the liberal community. At the very least, they were unsuccessful in the right cause and they were asking the relevant questions.

CHAPTER XXIII

The Institutional Game

Another war was over. Roosevelt was dead. In the White House, Harry Truman gave promise of the "uncommon ability of the common man." A speech by Mr. Churchill at Fulton, Missouri, added "iron curtain" to the lexicon of the twentieth century. The alliance against Nazism was breaking apart. Veterans were returning from Europe and the Pacific, entering schools, beginning new families. Briefly, the crusaders put aside their moral armor, stretched their legs, and wriggled their toes in unaccustomed freedom.

A new chapter was opening on suburbia and McCarthyism, atomic weaponry and cold war. Popular literature began to speak of other-directedness and status, of security and organization men. The common man yielded the stage to the mass man. It was also the time of the red scare, Alger Hiss, and the Rosenbergs. A few short years after the guns grew silent they spoke again on a little known Asian peninsula called Korea. On the East River in New York City and at Lake Success on Long Island, a new attempt at world order called the United Nations was created. Soon—all too soon—the Russian *"nyet"* was to irritate the American public which did not really understand how anyone could doubt its good will.

A Europe ruined by war was being helped to help itself with the Marshall Plan. China was completing its revolution; India, winning its independence from Great Britain. Strangely-called young men were making small wars in the name of freedom in Africa. The old empires were dying and new power blocs being formed.

It was a time of transition—still uncompleted—before which human intelligence stood baffled. New schools of philosophic, religious, and psychological thought seemed to capture the confusion and anxiety as "existential" became a word to conjure with. Talk of abundance was appearing in the work of social commentators and critics. The dispossessed, here and abroad, were stirring with new-found purposes and desires. The diet of change was, perhaps, too rich in too short a time—and coupled with the frustrations of disappointed moral crusaders, led both to defensive apathy and aggressive stereotyping. If things were wrong, then there must be villains who made them so. If life was overly complex, then there must be formulae that would simplify, like "peace of mind" and "positive thinking." If this world was not manageable, at least the next world might be—so back to the churches and temples.

Ethical Culture still waited to define its role and to reestablish a moral religion responsive to the vast currents of transition. The movement's anniversaries had traditionally been occasions for self-examination. Thus, it was appropriate to use the seventieth anniversary in 1946 as a time for looking forward.

Led by Algernon Black, whose intuitive style informed the occasion, a three-fold plan for the future evolved. Herbert Wolff, then New York Society President, recalled:

> We took on the responsibility of raising a fund of about $200,000, the proceeds of which were to be used. . . .
>
> 1. to build up finances of the New York Society
>
> 2. to vitalize the AEU which for years had been merely a paper organization . . .
>
> 3. to make a contribution to the community in general by establishing the Encampment for Citizenship.[1]

[1] Interview, 1962.

Special programs were scheduled throughout the year to reinvigorate the Platform with a roster of speakers including Judge Jerome Frank, Carey McWilliams, and Frances Perkins. New societies in New Jersey and Washington, D.C., seemed to promise an expansion which had halted with the founding of the Westchester Society decades earlier. By May, 1946, it was clear that most of the fund would be raised (about $150,000 was finally contributed), and on the anniversary date, May 15, greetings were received from such notables as Mrs. Roosevelt and Henry Wallace. Led by Wolff, Lawrence Mayers, Hannah Sherman, and Mrs. Alice K. Politzer, that first step in reconstruction was accomplished.

About one-third of the Seventieth Anniversary Fund was pledged by New York to building a national movement, with the other Societies agreeing to collectively match that sum over a five-year period. Sidney Scheuer from New York and Walston Chubb, son of Percival Chubb, from St. Louis, agreed to serve as .AEU vice presidents in order to give some organizational stability to the program. A full-time field secretary, Cornelius Cochran, was found to succeed Mr. O'Dell in early 1948. Florence Wolff Klaber, a long-time member and ethics teacher, agreed to develop a program and literature for the religious education of children. National membership was reported at about 4,000 with the New York Society contributing half that number. Much talk was heard of new directions, new publications, and movement. Mid the flurry of activity between the seventieth and seventy-fifth years new patterns began to emerge as the institution became more conscious of itself.

Characteristic of this self-consciousness was attention to organizational instruments. A debate in 1947 settled that Leaders would be added to the national Board of Directors. (Scarcely anyone seemed aware that the very need for debate on the issue marked a change.) The old dream of a publishing house was recalled, but without success. However, Muzzey, Neumann, and Nathanson each produced books by 1951. Numerous national committees were created, each seeming to have a purpose. Tax exemption on religious ground was granted by federal tax authorities. Increasingly the paraphernalia of institution took the center of the stage; the countless implicit and informal arrangements gave way to what could only be identified as a bureaucratic style.

Further evidence of this trend was appearing in the sudden increase in the number of smaller fellowships. The New York Society devised a "unit plan," the purpose of which was to break the Society membership down into small groups in the hope that people would get to know each other better and their needs be taken care of more adequately than in the past.[2] Under New York's tutelage a unit was built in Essex County, New Jersey, under the chairmanship of Joseph Lebrecht. Similarly in Nassau County, Long Island, Rebecca Goldblum led in forming a unit. In Pleasantville, New York, and Fairfield, Connecticut, similar ventures were undertaken. In the Riverdale area, under the chairmanship of Leo Rosen, a Riverdale-Yonkers Fellowship began its first meetings in the Nathanson apartment there. A common concern for each unit was the need for religious education, for an acceptable equivalent to the more traditional Sunday school.

In Cleveland, Stephen and Jean Kaufman started a fellowship whose first major venture was a Sunday school enrolling seven children in two classes. From Baltimore came news of a similar project. In Washington, D.C., the wartime group formally organized itself with Dr. George Beauchamp as part-time Leader and L. D. MacIntyre as President. And in Los Angeles, Arthur E. Briggs continued his effort to build Ethical Culture in California. In nearly every instance the founding group of the new fellowships included men and women from one of the older societies. Thus, the charter membership in Los Angeles included Charles Ellis, formerly of the Chicago Society, Milward Pick of the Brooklyn Society, and Louise Scherpe of the St. Louis Society.

The active professional Leadership took a major role. Nathanson, Herman, and Black frequently visited the various fledgling groups. Eustace Haydon, retired from the University of Chicago and serving as Leader of the Chicago Society, was the first speaker at Cleveland's opening public meeting. James Hornback while serving the Westchester Society worked also with the group in Connecticut. The style was reminiscent of the old Methodist circuit rider. The earlier Leadership had seldom thought in parish or congregational terms. It had rarely engaged in the extensive organizational work which now became part of the accepted role of Ethical Leadership. Unlike other

---

[2] New York Board of Trustees, Minutes, June 16, 1943.

institutions, no separate missionary staff was developed; instead the responsibilities of the existing professional group expanded. The American Ethical Union was headed by an administrator (Cochrane was succeeded in 1951 by a young man named Judson Chrisney) who by the very nature of his assignment could do no more than routine institutional tasks.

This shift in the vision of Leadership had unforeseen consequences. Inevitably, as the Leadership gave increased service to leaderless groups, the level of organizational busyness increased. In an earlier day much of the travel had been for spreading a message, not necessarily to an internal audience. Now travel was tied to parochial needs. Inevitably too, lacking a clear institutional plan, a good deal of effort was wasted and some contradictions made as men with differing temperaments and concerns were asked for and gave conflicting advice to the newcomers. Yet, this individualism fostered an experiment which to some degree countered the conformist trends at work in American culture.

The vast population shift of the postwar period which created new suburbs and a preponderance of young families was the primary motive for the newer Ethical fellowships. Philadelphia reported in a series of radio recordings on the religious and moral education of the child. Washington announced that its Leader was moderating a regular broadcast on the theme "The Character Education of the Child." Moral education of children now subtly veered to "religious" education in response to cultural pressures for recognizable forms. By a kind of inversion of priorities, Ethical Culture turned from seeking a "consecrating influence in our own lives and the lives of our children" to serving the children's "needs." Adult activity was almost an afterthought. Comparative religion and Bible study, defensiveness toward more orthodox neighbors, were justified for "the sake of the children."

Certainly no one intended this inversion. Florence Klaber, who directed the program, and Algernon Black as its advisor tried to maintain an affirmative educational direction. But working against them was the child-centered anxiety of the young postwar families and the manifest institutional success of those societies such as Long Island's and Bergen County's which devoted resource and attention to Sunday school. Changes were made in the work with young people of high school and college age. The New York Society's Sunday Evening

Clubs took the radical steps of admitting girls and scheduling the program for Fridays. Teen-agers from the New York metropolitan area with "greater diversity of background than ever before" attended. Still maintaining the movement's nonsectarian stance, little effort was made to encourage identification with Ethical Culture, although concern was expressed about the failure to attract young people into formal membership.

With the advent of newer societies the problem of finding Leadership became even more acute. With the addition of Herman in New York, Hornback in Westchester and later in St. Louis, Beauchamp in Washington, and in 1951 Sheldon Ackley in Long Island, the problem seemed on its way to solution. However, some of the new societies survived without Leadership for extended periods of time. Assistance for these groups was met by adding to the burden of the Leadership and by the use of volunteers. But the practice of Leadership had created expectations which volunteers could not ordinarily meet— competence as a speaker, prophetic idealism, confidential and competent ethical counsel. Frustration was often expressed in hostility toward the Leadership (a latent anticlericalism) and by overly critical attitudes toward the institutional procedures that were evolving.

New York, meanwhile, was experimenting with its own Leadership patterns. In 1948 it named to its Board of Leaders the well-known social psychologist Lawrence K. Frank to assume specialized responsibilities in education and to provide counsel for the children's and youth programs. He attempted to adapt his professionalism to the more fluid conditions of the Ethical Society, but after several years both he and the Society had to admit failure and he left. Adler had visualized an orchestration of interests by the membership and the Leadership, but the renaissance tradition of Leadership—the Leader as amateur and generalist—created expectations that specialization by nature could not meet. The meaning of Leadership became another unresolved question for the movement.

As the seventy-fifth anniversary approached, the need to clarify the image of Leadership as well as to provide for the future became pressing. Repeatedly Horace Friess called for ways to make "Leadership appealing and challenging." A particular urgency was given by the resignation of V. T. Thayer from the New York Leadership and the Ethical Culture schools, the retirement of David Muzzey, and the news that Hutton Hynd was resigning to return to England. Many realized that while the movement was managing to replace Leaders as occasion arose, little was being done to anticipate future requirements. The ringing of change was accented by the deaths in 1948 of Sidney Blumenthal, who had joined the New York Society in 1878, and Mrs. Felix Adler.

Drained of some of its earlier energies and required to devote many of its resources to carrying on the programs initiated in an earlier day, Ethical Culture nevertheless felt the need to respond in some special fashion to the problems of the postwar world. One response was the Encampment for Citizenship, a way of coming to grips with the problems of democratic life. In its conception, the Encampment had all the earmarks of Ethical Culture: it was open and nonsectarian, it saw reform in educational terms, it was committed to a conception of liberal democracy, and it was responsive to a specific social need. Many returning veterans had been educated to the realities of world politics, to new forms of human relationships (this was particularly true of returning Negro veterans), and to a more sceptical view of American political and social organization.

Sensitive to this and mindful of the experience with the Work Camps for Democracy, Algernon Black posed the idea of the Encampment. Herbert Wolff described it:

He [Black] came forth with the idea in the early Fall of 1945. . . . There was, of course, no organization, . . . site, . . . faculty, . . . students and, except in the most general way, no curriculum. There was not much more than a glint in Al Black's eye. . . . I would listen to Mr. Black address audiences gathered together in connection with the 70th Anniversary. . . . He was inspiring and at each meeting he waxed more eloquent. . . . But as the weeks and months rolled by, I became worried that the time was too short, and there was too much to do.[3]

Inspiration overcame the obstacles, and the summer of 1946 saw the first Encampment underway. Black was Educational Director, Henry Herman accepted administrative responsibility, "Nanny" Politzer led a Board of Trustees, and a distinguished staff included historians Henry David and Bert James Lowenberg. Lola Cross, a public

---

[3] Interview, 1963.

school dietician, volunteered to establish the food services for the program. Supported by Wolff and the Seventieth Anniversary Fund, enough money was raised to ensure the project in its first years.

To recruit campers, the staff traveled throughout the country, speaking to citizen's groups, young people's organizations, and youth leaders. As a result, 128 students from twenty-seven states attended. They were sponsored by groups as diverse as the Farmer's Union and the Federation of Women's Clubs. Of great significance in providing support and public acceptance of the Encampment was the willingness of Mrs. Roosevelt to lend her name and prestige to it, to invite the campers to Hyde Park each summer, and to visit the Fieldston School. The purposes of the Encampment were set down in its prospectus:

> The Encampment program is based upon the assumption that to learn to be a citizen the individual must have an actual experience in democratic living and citizenship in a democratic community. The Encampment must afford the individual an exemplification of democratic living. It is not enough to learn the principles and ideals of democracy. It is not enough to be trained in the techniques of democratic action. We learn democracy by living it. We learn citizenship by practicing the role of being a citizen.

The Encampments brought together youngsters from the ages of eighteen to twenty-five and from greatly varying religious, racial, and social backgrounds. They studied the idea of democracy, economic issues, problems of minorities, and international relations. Gradually, the program came to include workshops, extensive field trips, and a long and distinguished list of guest lecturers. Communal participation became its style and, as later evaluation showed, the combination of didactic and social experience was successful in training thousands for community leadership. By the time of its seventh year, in 1951, the Encampment was strong enough to employ a full-time director, and William V. Shannon was named to replace Henry Herman, who had been giving part time to the project. Black continued as Educational Director and Mrs. Politzer continued to provide inspiring voluntary leadership.

The vision of the seventieth anniversary was gaining substance. The American Ethical Union had an executive and an embryonic program, the New York Society seemed to be rebuilding its Leadership and expanding its work, the Encampment existed. In 1950, with the seventy-fifth anniversary approaching, a sum of more than $175,000 was raised for carrying on the program initiated earlier and for a more adequate program of training for future Leadership.

As anticommunism became a popular theme in American life, the movement took up the issue as well. The storm centered on Algernon Black, a confirmed social democrat. Outsiders seemed almost happy to pounce on another "villain," and some inside the movement used the issue, perhaps unconsciously, to evade the more frustrating problems of building Ethical Culture. Never a reticent man, Black responded in kind. At a meeting of the New York Board in 1947 he "expressed anxiety that the present red hysteria would force the Society to retreat from a militant position." In 1948, he was publicly attacked and sought advice on whether to sue for libel from Max Grossman, attorney and President of the Society.

> . . . the very fact that a charge of Communism is made these days is sufficient to raise doubts in some people. . . . To bring a liberal action is out of the question. . . . Imagine a court room scene. Mr. Black, Executive Leader of the Ethical Society having testified is now being cross-examined by a clever attorney. "Were you a member of this organization, were you a sponsor of this, that, and the other?" "Did you say this about Russia?" "Are you the Leader representative of the Worker's Fellowship?—were you present at this, that, or the other meeting that followed the communist line?" Calling you a fellow traveler is not libelous —some of the Trustees might enjoy seeing you squirm on the witness stand.[4]

Black tried to hold back. He refused to serve on the Seabury Fusion Committee on the grounds that he could not become "political beyond a certain point." Yet a man of his temperament could not remain silent on the drift toward hostility, blind hysteria, and political reaction. Many in the movement and the wider community regarded Black's criticisms as islands of sanity expressing a courageous and necessary point of view in a world which heard few such independent voices.

[4] Letter from Max Grossman to Algernon Black, July 26, 1948.

While Black was the storm center, he was not alone in his vulnerability during this period. In 1951 Mr. Nathanson reported to the Board in New York on an unsuccessful effort to deny Henry Neumann the right to deliver two addresses in Los Angeles. The local Chamber of Commerce, acting on information from the U.S. Chamber of Commerce, justified this because Dr. Neumann was on an "undesirable list" for the reasons that:

> 1) in 1931–32, Dr. Neumann was on a Committee pressing for the recognition of the Soviet Union; 2) he was a member of a committee seeking to raise funds to send food to Soviet children; 3) he is a declared pacifist; 4) as late as 1950 he is known to have been associated with Mr. Black[*sic*].[5]

The last charge suggested one of the difficulties for the Leadership as well as the membership. Everyone was tarred indiscriminately with the attitudes, actions, or words of one or another of his associates. Nathanson, for example, never a Marxist and in a liberal rather than a socialist tradition, was identified with his more radical colleague. Tension between them was thus increased by a problem over which neither could exercise control. However, the freedom of the Platform and the respect for the individual integrity which permitted—indeed required—giving voice to conscience without regard to consequence was not seriously threatened by the hysteria. It is to the credit of the movement that despite serious disagreements and in the face of loss of support, the voices of Black, Neumann, Nathanson, and others continued to be heard without censorship.

A voice for freedom remained one of the major contributions of Ethical Culture. Repressive government behavior was attacked from the Ethical Platform, on radio programs, and in the movement's publications. For example, Nathanson spoke for open and frequent social criticism in a radio broadcast:

> The threats to freedom which appear in the Mundt-Nixon bill, the House UnAmerican Activities Committee and other movements in the United States are instances of a widespread temper of repression. . . . Neither the Soviet Union nor any similar state can tolerate organized

[5] New York Board of Trustees, Minutes, February, 1951.

protest today. . . . A democratic society should not only tolerate but encourage such [protest] movements. It needs them for its health.[6]

When McCarthyism was at its height, the New York Platform was one of the few places where public criticism was heard. Black voiced his protest from the left, others sounded a similar note from a more traditional liberalism. Nathanson said:

> The unspeakable Senator McCarthy becomes a person of influence through the most vicious rabble rousing and demagogic techniques. . . . And he becomes a power not to be ignored, how? By the wheelhorses of politics? Oh no! By Mr. Taft, the soul of integrity. What has happened to us? . . . Is the man's ambition to be President so great that there is no compromise that is not too much to make?
>
> But increasingly we don't try people in court. . . . We have trials by publicity. . . . There is something completely cockeyed about a people who can . . . make publicity stunts . . . out of the whole democratic process . . . that pillories . . . not simply the individual but the lifeblood of the democratic way of life.[7]

From the Platform, in resolutions, and in community organization, the Movement moved rapidly into the area of civil rights and civil liberties. Black led the work on fair housing. The Washington Society in 1947 supported legal action to overturn restrictive covenants. Fair Housing Committees were led in many communities by Ethical societies, for example, in Cleveland, in Bergen County, on Long Island.

Civil rights was first on the moral agenda, but was joined by the problems of freedom of conscience and the relationship between church and state. American secular politics had seldom gone without attack. In the postwar period the attack on the "godless" state was mounted primarily by the hierachy of the Roman Catholic Church led by Cardinal Spellman and focused on the demand for public funds for parochial education. No doubt this was partially motivated by fear that without tax support parochial schools could not survive.

---

[6] "The Role of Protest in a Democracy," Ethical Issues in the News, WMCA, June 20, 1948.

[7] "Personal Responsibility in an Age of Anxiety" and "Mobilization and the Threats to Civil Liberties", The Ethical Platform, broadcast over WQXR February 25, and March 11, 1951.

A counter-campaign organized hostility to Romanism and challenged the loyalties of American Catholics and the integrity of their faith. Ethical Culture, though it had its quota of the prejudiced, argued more affirmatively that public education needed federal support and safeguarding from sectarian influence. Leading the way was Jerome Nathanson, who developed a community-wide committee in support of federal aid to public education.

> . . . the religious reactionaries and their co-rightists on the one side and the communists and their fellow travellers on the other confront each other in mortal combat, each willing to ride roughshod over those who stand between them. I say a plague on both their houses. . . . I think the case against communist teachers is a strong one. . . . I also think that the same arguments hold true against teachers who embrace any authoritarian or dogmatic point of view. . . . [But] . . . the question is not what you do or do not do with communist teachers. The question is what you do with teachers and for teachers. The brute fact is that we shy away from the problem . . . through the old scapegoat technique. . . . The poison spreads. . . . We will never get democratic education until the citizens of a democracy create an atmosphere for [it]. . . . The schools of a democracy must grant the existence of controversy. . . . To shy away . . . is betrayal of the democratic process.[8]

A campaign was organized to secure support for a policy of aid to the public schools and for legislation in the Congress embodying it (HR 7610, the Barden Bill). The committee's platform included the requirement that there be adequate safeguards against discriminatory treatment of Negroes and other minorities.

The question of tax funds for parochial education represented one front in the continuing struggle for separation of church and state. Another developed on the questions of prayer in the public schools and the use of their facilities for religious education. If the tax question was a Catholic issue, the prayer question was primarily Protestant. The New York Board of Regents stated in 1951 that they favored the opening of each school day with public prayer. Opposing their action, the New York Society's Board of Leaders issued a statement to the press and sought to join with others in securing a reversal of the

[8] "The Fight for Democratic Education," Platform and WQXR broadcast, March 27, 1949.

Regents' policy. Public sentiment, however, favored the Regents' position. Few legislators and few voters wanted to be "against God."

In consequence, the issue of sectarian practice in public education was taken to the courts, and the postwar period records a long and brilliant series of cases in which the issue was judicially resolved. The beginning of this new page in American history was the McCullum Case (1946) challenging the state of Illinois for permitting school children to attend religious instruction on school time (the released time program.) When the case reached the Supreme Court, the movement filed a Brief *Amicus Curiae*. The Court in its ruling issued a landmark decision affirming the independence of public education from sectarianism.

The experience with the McCullum Case opened a new avenue for Ethical Culture, a program of legal intervention where cases seemed to have a particular relevance to the movement's philosophy and program. Herbert Wolff, whose law firm Greenbaum, Wolff and Ernst numbered among its partners Leo Rosen and Harriet Pilpel (both active members of the movement), led that program. Mr. Rosen, accepting assignment to develop a National Law Committee, undertook the work in the courts in addition to meeting more routine legal needs of the movement. Serving as volunteers, Messrs. Wolff and Rosen evolved through court cases a significant means of social reform scarcely explored by Ethical Culture in an earlier day. In 1957 the movement successfully brought to the courts the Washington Tax Case on the right of Ethical Culture to be treated as a religion for tax purposes. Ethical Culture intervened in the Torcaso Case in 1960 on the right to hold public office without religious test; the Regents' Prayer Case for the elimination of prayer as a regular exercise in public schools in 1961; the Murray and Schempp Cases involving the elimination of Bible reading as a religious exercise in the public schools in 1962.

In 1919 the American Ethical Union had called for a general amnesty for conscientious objectors. In 1948 a similar position was taken and representation made to President Truman. Unlike the first postwar period, after the second war debate on universal military training arose and continued. A draft law stayed on the books, and after a brief respite the draft was resumed. In consequence, the issue of conscientious objection did not die down, and, particularly for Ethical

Culture, the rights of nontheists had to be fought for. Debated in 1951 by the American Ethical Union Board, the strategy agreed upon was to build an alliance of interested groups—with, for example, the American Humanist Association and the Unitarians—and seek change in the law. When the issue came before the Congress, official testimony was given by representatives of Ethical Culture. As with the question of sectarianism in public education, the issue was finally settled in the courts; the Seeger Case in 1965 affirmed the rights of nontheists.

As these dramatic efforts engaged the movement's attention, old concerns brought new challenges. The Hudson Guild found itself serving a different population; as Negro families moved in to replace the Irish and Italians it had to deal with inter-group tensions. Ethical Culture came to support more liberal divorce laws in the interests of maintaining the integrity of the family and its members. Much later, in the late 1950s, the movement supported removal of religious requirements for adoption, and in the early 1960s it was to concern itself with the problem of a "humane abortion" law as well. Symbolic of the changes with which the reforming idealism of Ethical Culture had to contend was the change in title of the National Committee Against Child Labor, which Dr. Adler had helped to found, to the National Committee on the Employment of Youth when Henry Herman was serving as its chairman in the 1960s.

The last references carry beyond the boundaries of our story in order to illustrate the transition through which the human community was passing, the fact that no part of human life was untouched by rapid and bewildering change. Ethical Culture often found an up-to-date position on a given issue, yet remained adrift on larger questions. As early as 1949 Lawrence Frank proposed to the AEU that Commissions of Inquiry bring together an interdisciplinary group to face social problems which "no single profession or academic discipline can deal with." Approved in principle, the proposal was never acted upon. In 1951 the Fraternity of Leaders sought a procedure for arriving at consensus on issues, but again success eluded them. Adler's dream of diversity in the creed, unanimity in the deed, was cruel reality in the postwar period.

The myriad institutional activities, the numerous issues, the elusive problem of consensus—all this and more posed the question of Ethical Culture's viability. Hints of regressive trends appeared as Philadelphia reported a ceremonial use of meditation and silence both in its adult meeting and its children's assembly. In Chicago several members requested a "spoken meditation," and this was prepared from a text by Robert Louis Stevenson. New York and Brooklyn continued to mark Easter Sunday as the ceremony of greeting new lives. As the fifties dawned there was a genuine possibility that the movement might enter too comfortably into the religious cultus of the period, participating in the so-called religious revival.

Inevitably, this led to questions about the nature of Ethical Culture and its validity in a new world. Repeatedly the question of the distinctive role and place of Ethical Culture was asked. From the right the religious revival seemed to threaten the success of Ethical Culture; from the left organized humanism was challenging it on deeper philosophic grounds. Proposals came from Los Angeles and from a newly formed group in Long Beach, Long Island, to name themselves "ethical humanist" societies; within the movement a significant number was prepared to yield Adler's metaphysical neutrality for an unequivocal naturalism and humanism. At the American Ethical Union Assembly in Chicago (1950) a discussion of the Ethical movement's relationship to the American Humanist Association concluded that "neither Humanism nor any other philosophy can be made the creed of the Ethical Movement."

But the issue would not and could not rest there. From Europe and England came word that a nascent Humanist Movement was growing out of the ashes of the war. The American group, desirous of rebuilding the International Ethical Union, agreed to delay its effort in hopes of developing a more inclusive program with groups in the Netherlands, France, the Scandinavian countries, Belgium, and England. As discussions of a new International proceeded it became clear that the American Ethical Movement stood nearly alone in its focus on the autonomy and centrality of ethics. Blackham, successor to Coit in England, felt that the British movement must turn away from Coit's communal emphasis to a more modern scientific naturalism and secularism. The Dutch, led by J. P. Van Praag, were explicitly humanist though organizationally rather like the American Ethical Movement. In India, led by the left-wing socialist M. N. Roy, the Indian Radical Humanist Movement had both a definitive social platform and a philosophic view.

Ethical Culture faced the choice of going it alone with distinctive voice but in isolation from kindred spirits around the world or seeking a common position which, while not entirely its own, would be continuous with its prior history. After lengthy discussion and debate, the Leadership recommended that, "the AEU be committed to cooperation with the Amsterdam Congress of Humanists in 1952 and that the AEU take active part in planning the agenda for that Conference and for designating representatives to it." [9] Acting on this recommendation the American Ethical Union agreed to participate in this first International Congress on condition that the ethical interest would be given recognition along with that of humanism.

By the seventy-fifth anniversary of the movement another step had been taken in the evolution of moral religion, the consequences of which were unforeseeable. The road from the challenging years of the 1870s to the anxious 1950s had been traversed. To the surprise of many, the movement had survived with its integrity and character intact. True, many questions remained open—whether ethical leadership could be a profession, whether self-conscious institution building could escape the trap of self-serving institutionalism, whether philosophic eclecticism and metaphysical indifferentism could survive demands for ideological clarity, whether a new and convincing voice could be found to stir a membership. What came to be called a "crisis of meaning" afflicted Ethical Culture, too; it was seen most clearly in the fruitful pragmatic successes joined with a lack of coherent overall policy and philosophy. Implicitness in religion depended on explicit strong personalities, but the new era was antiheroic and contemporary personality styles almost demanded coolness of temperament.

The agenda of unresolved questions was long and growing as the movement faced its seventy-fifth year. Yet it had come through world war, cold war, the death of its mythic figures, and depression. It still existed though its world was no longer the manageable environment in which it had been created. Responsive since its founding to the trends of the day in science, in urbanization, in popular revolu-

[9] Leaders' meeting, AEU Records, May 16, 1951.

tion, it was perhaps better placed than earlier faiths in not needing to purge itself to outworn symbols and historic accretions. For all its disadvantage, therefore, it had at least the advantage of currency and potential relevance built into its very character. This promised greater possibility for meeting the unresolved questions than was evident on preliminary examination or clear to those caught up in the immediacy of operation. Whether the promise would be fulfilled awaited the test of generations. But that it could be fulfilled was clear from the record. As with so much that confronts impatient mankind, the issue and its outcome requires the perspective of time; the present, any present, still requires an act of faith.

Chronology
of the Ethical
Culture Movement,
1876–1968

1876   The organization meeting of the Society for Ethical Culture
        in New York City, May 15; incorporation, February 21,
        1877; Felix Adler, founding Leader.
1877   Establishment of the first free kindergartens in New York
        and San Francisco; first session, January 2, 1878.
        Establishment of the District Nursing Service which grew
        into the Visiting Nurse Service. This was the first social
        service that did no missionary work for organized religion.
        Establishment of the Tenement House Building Company.
        The first model home was completed at this time to ac-
        commodate 100 families, and Shaefer and Avery Homes,
        family homes for orphaned children, were built.
        New York Society establishes classes for member children.
1878   Felix Adler is elected President of the Free Religious Associ-
        ation.
1879   Incorporation of the United Relief Works of the New York
        Society: a consolidation of the Society's social welfare
        work into one organization.

1880　Founding of the Workingman's School.

Stanton Coit becomes associated with the Ethical movement.

1882　Founding of the Chicago Ethical Society.

Felix Adler is the organizer and member of the Governor's Tenement House Commission in New York State.

Felix Adler resigns as President of the Free Religious Association protesting the lack of the association's commitment to social welfare activities.

1883　Felix Adler, with Edmond Kelly, founds the Good Government Club, now known as the City Club, to oppose political corruption in New York City.

William Macintire Salter becomes Leader of the Chicago Ethical Society.

1885　Founding of the Philadelphia Ethical Society; S. Burns Weston, Lecturer

1886　Founding of the St. Louis Society; Walter L. Sheldon, Leader

Stanton Coit founds the Neighborhood Guild in New York City, the first settlement house in the United States and today known as the University Settlement.

1887　William M. Salter and Henry D. Lloyd circulate a petition for a fair trial for the anarchists in the Haymarket affair, Chicago.

The Working Boys Club of the Philadelphia Society develops into the Neighborhood Guild with S. Burns Weston as headworker.

Founding of the South Place Ethical Society (London). Stanton Coit, Percival Chubb, and the philosophers Muirhead and Bosanquet are associated with it.

St. Louis starts its Sunday school.

1888　New York Society starts the Mothers' Society to Study Child Nature, later the Child Study Association.

Chicago Society organizes The Bureau of Justice, the organization that precedes The Legal Aid Society.

Walter Sheldon and the St. Louis Society, pioneering in adult education, establish the Self-Culture Halls Association.

The Ethical Record, a quarterly journal, is started.

1889 New York Society starts the Visiting and Teaching Guild for Crippled Children.

The American Ethical Union is founded, a federation of Ethical Culture societies and fellowships in the United States.

1890 The AEU begins publication of *The International Journal of Ethics*, replacing *The Ethical Record*.

1891 Felix Adler, with Crawford Howell Toy of Harvard and Henry Carter Adams of the University of Michigan, is founder of The School of Ethics at Plymouth, Massachusetts; such people as William James, Jane Addams, and Josiah Royce were associated with it.

1892 Founding of the West London Ethical Society with Stanton Coit as Leader. Later called the Ethical Church, it succeeded a nonconformist church founded toward the end of the eighteenth century. Among its ministers had been Winchester, Fox, and Conway.

Berlin Society for Ethical Culture is organized; F. W. Foerster, well-known astronomer and head of the Royal Observatory, Leader.

M. M. Mangasarian becomes Leader of the Chicago Society.

1893 Chicago Society participates in the founding of The World Congress of Religion.

Founding of the International Ethical Movement with its first meeting at Eisenach in Germany.

St. Louis Society incorporates The Self-Culture Halls Association separately.

The Women's Conference of the New York Society is organized.

1894 John Lovejoy Elliott becomes associated with the Ethical movement as a Leader in the New York Society.

Frederick Jodl founds the Vienna Ethical Society.

Felix Adler joins with Rev. Edgar Gardner Murphy and others in the formation of the National Child Labor Committee.

1895 The Workingman's School becomes The Ethical Culture School.

John L. Elliott organizes The Hurly Burlies in the Chelsea area of New York City.

American Ethical Union begins publication of *The Ethical Addresses,* which appear annually for twenty years.

Milwaukee Ethical Society is founded.

1896   Founding of The English Ethical Union, a federation of English Ethical societies.

The International Union of Ethical Societies is organized, with headquarters in Zurich and F. W. Foerster as Secretary.

New York Society organizes the Sunday Evening Clubs, young peoples' groups.

1897   The Hurly Burlies incorporate as The Hudson Guild.

Rudolph Penzig is appointed Lecturer to the Berlin Society.

William M. Salter returns to the Chicago Society as its Leader on the resignation of M. M. Mangasarian.

1898   Founding the Down-Town Ethical Society in New York City, which later becomes known as Madison House; Henry Moskowitz an active organizer.

Chicago Society founds the Henry Booth Settlement House.

The Ethical Culture High School is started in New York.

David S. Muzzey becomes associated with the Ethical movement.

1900   Nathaniel Schmidt becomes associated with the Chicago Society and is in residence at Henry Booth House.

The Ethical Record resumes publication with Percival Chubb as Editor.

1901   New York Society starts Camp Felicia, known today as Madison-Felicia.

St. Louis Society establishes the Colored Peoples Self-Improvement Federation.

1902   The Women's Conference of the New York Society starts the Manhattan Trade School for Girls, now a part of the New York City public school system.

New York Mayor Seth Low lays the cornerstone of the Mid-Town Ethical Culture School.

Wilhelm Boerner is appointed Leader to the Vienna Society.

Felix Adler becomes Professor of Political and Social Ethics at Columbia University.

1903 Felix Adler is a founding member of the Committee of Fifteen for the ending of political misrule in New York City.

Anna Garlin Spencer is appointed Associate Leader in New York Society.

George O'Dell becomes assistant to Stanton Coit in the West London Society.

1904 Morris Raphael Cohen starts the Harvard Ethical Society.

Blythedale, a summer home for crippled children, is founded at Hawthorne, New York, by the New York Society.

Felix Adler leads in founding The National Child Labor Commission and serves as chairman for seventeen years.

Felix Adler establishes The Philosophy Club of Faculty at Columbia University and Union Theological Seminary, which now includes faculty from Johns Hopkins, Princeton, and Yale.

1905 In Chicago The Bureau of Justice merges with the Women's and Children's Protective Agency to become The Legal Aid Society.

1906 Philadelphia Society starts The Southwark Neighborhood House.

Brooklyn Ethical Culture Society is organized with Leslie W. Sprague as Leader.

1907 Alfred W. Martin is appointed Associate Leader in New York Society.

Summer Conference on Ethical Studies is held at Glenmore, New Jersey.

Henry Moskowitz is named to the Leadership in New York Society.

Walter L. Sheldon dies.

1908 American Ethical Union organizes the Summer School of Ethics at Madison, Wisconsin, with courses in moral education, ethics, the Ethical movement, ethics of great religions; Anna Garlin Spencer, Director.

Felix Adler is appointed Theodore Roosevelt Exchange Professor at the University of Berlin.

Felix Adler and Gustav Spiller of the English movement organize the International Congress on Moral Education, the first in a series held at four-year intervals under inde-

pendent sponsorship. Representatives come from governments in thirteen countries including the United States,
France, Italy, Great Britain, Russia, Spain, Japan.

Hudson Guild Settlement moves into its own building.

1909   Dr. Henry Moskowitz and the writers Mary Ovington White
and William English Walling hold an informal meeting to
discuss "the spirit of the abolitionists." At this meeting,
organization of the National Association for the Advancement of Colored Peoples is started, with active participation by John Lovejoy Elliott, Anna Garlin Spencer, William M. Salter, and Dr. Moskowitz of Ethical Culture.

1910   Felix Adler is appointed Chairman of the Arbitration Committee of the Garment Industry.

Dedication of New York Society's meeting house.

Leslie Sprague resigns as Leader of the Brooklyn Society.

1911   Felix Adler convenes the International Races Congress in
London.

Percival Chubb becomes Leader of the St. Louis Society.

Henry Neumann is appointed Leader of the Brooklyn
Society.

1912   New York Society and the Hudson Guild found the Cooperative Printing School for Apprentices.

1913   Horace J. Bridges comes from England to become Leader to
the Chicago Society.

Anna Garlin Spencer leaves Ethical Leadership to become
Assistant Director of the New York School of Philanthropy, now Columbia Graduate School of Social Work.

George O'Dell becomes Field Secretary to the American
Ethical Union. Newark Society is started with his help.

1914   AEU starts publication of *The Standard* with George O'Dell
as Editor.

Philadelphia Society dedicates its new meeting house.

1915   Wilmington, Delaware, Society is started.

1916   Hudson Guild sponsors the Chelsea Model Tenement
Houses.

1917   John L. Elliott serves with Norman Thomas, Roger Baldwin,
John Haynes Holmes, and others on the Civil Liberties
Bureau, which expands to the American Civil Liberties
Union after First World War.

Chicago Society joins in founding the Chicago Urban League.

Brooklyn Society purchases a meeting house.

1917–   Founding of societies in Grand Rapids and Detroit, Mich-
1918   igan, and Scranton, Pennsylvania.

1918   New York Society and Mid-Town Ethical Culture School join in starting the summer play school.

1919   John L. Elliott is elected President of the National Federation of Settlements.

Horace J. Bridges becomes President of the Urban League in Chicago after helping with its organization.

1920   Boston Ethical Society is founded.

1921   Hudson Guild Farm is established to continue pioneer work in family camping.

1922   Brooklyn Society starts the Brooklyn Ethical Culture School.

Harry Snell of the English Ethical Union is elected to Parliament as a Labour Party member.

Roy Franklin Dewey is appointed Associate Leader of the Chicago Society.

John Elliott arbitrates a labor dispute in the printing trades.

1923   Algernon D. Black joins the New York Society staff.

Ethical Culture School Camp is started at Cooperstown, New York.

Henry J. Golding comes from England to work as Leader in the New York Society.

1924   Felix Adler is appointed Hibbert Lecturer at Oxford University.

Chicago Society appoints a committee on narcotics.

David S. Muzzey becomes Leader to the Westchester Ethical Society.

1925   Philadelphia Society purchases farmland for a summer camp for Southwark Neighborhood House.

1926   Mrs. Martha Fischel of St. Louis Society is elected President of the American Ethical Union.

1927   The cornerstone is laid for Fieldston School.

1928   V. T. Thayer is appointed Director of the Ethical Culture schools and elected to membership in the Fraternity of Leaders.

Frank Swift is appointed Leader of the Boston Society.

1929   Felix Adler is given the honorary degree of Doctor of Letters by Columbia University.

Harry Snell is appointed to the commission sent to Palestine to investigate hostility between Arabs and Jews.

1931   Antioch College confers the honorary degree of Doctor of Humane Letters on S. Burns Weston.

Harry Snell is raised to peerage in England and becomes Lord Snell of Plimpton.

William M. Salter dies.

Henry J. Golding dies.

Pedro G. Salom is elected President of the AEU to succeed Mrs. Fischel.

1932   Algernon D. Black is appointed Leader of the New York Society.

Percival Chubb retires as Leader of the St. Louis Society.

Alfred W. Martin dies.

Stanton Coit goes into semi-retirement working with Harold J. Blackham as assistant.

1933   Felix Adler dies.

J. Hutton Hynd becomes Leader of the St. Louis Society.

John Lovejoy Elliott becomes Chairman of the Fraternity of Leaders, Rector to the Ethical Culture schools, and Senior Leader of New York Society.

Henry Neumann becomes a member of the Board of Leaders of the New York Society.

Frank Swift dies.

1934   W. Edwin Collier is appointed to Leadership in the Philadelphia Society.

Percival Chubb is elected President of the AEU to succeed Pedro Salom.

Lord Snell becomes Chairman of the London County Town Council.

1936   S. Burns Weston dies.

1937   Jerome Nathanson is appointed to Fellowship with the New York Society.

1938   John Elliott starts the Good Neighbor Committee, a cooperative effort to assist refugees.

The Felix Adler Annual Lecture Series is begun in New

York; John Dewey, H. J. Randall, Jr., A. A. Berle, and Gerald Wendt are lecturers.

John Elliott goes to Germany to secure the release of his colleagues Wilhelm Boerner and Walter Eckstein, Leaders of the Vienna Society who have been imprisoned by the Nazis.

New York Society and Hudson Guild start a work camp, which leads to the Associated Junior Work Camps and Work Camps for Democracy.

1939   The Good Neighbor Committee for helping refugees introduces economic assistance, language and work training classes. This cooperative effort with various other agencies centers its work in the New York Society Meeting House under the directorship of James Hart of the Society staff.

Nathaniel Schmidt dies.

1940   Jerome Nathanson becomes Leader in New York Society. Robert D. Kohn is elected President of the AEU to succeed Percival Chubb.

1941   Good Neighbor Committee National Conference at Hyde Park; Mrs. Eleanor Roosevelt becomes an active participant.

Youth education courses are started by New York Society in such areas as comparative religion, citizenship, education, and economics.

1942   John Lovejoy Elliott dies.

John Lovejoy Elliott Institute for Adult Education is started in New York.

Horace L. Friess and Robert D. Kohn are elected to Leadership in the American Ethical Union and to membership in the Fraternity of Leaders.

1943   Conference on Science and Democracy is held in New York with Jerome Nathanson as Chairman, also in 1944 and 1945.

1944   Washington, D.C., Ethical Society is started.

Los Angeles Ethical Society is founded with Dr. Arthur E. Briggs as Leader.

Stanton Coit dies.

Harold J. Blackham succeeds Stanton Coit in The Ethical Church after fifteen years with the British Ethical Union.

Lord Snell dies.

1945   Essex County, New Jersey, Ethical Society is founded.

New York Housing Authority begins the building of the John L. Elliott Houses in the Chelsea area.

A. Eustace Haydon becomes Leader of the Chicago Society.

1946   Establishment of the Encampment for Citizenship under the Directorship and Leadership of Algernon D. Black and Henry B. Herman of the New York Society; Mrs. Alice K. Politzer active in its founding.

American Ethical Union submits *amicus curiae* brief in the Illinois Released Time Case (McCullum Case), the first of the religious freedom cases.

Henry B. Herman is appointed Leader of the New York Society.

1947   The National Women's Conference of the American Ethical Union is accredited to the Department of Public Information of the United Nations.

The American Ethical Union is incorporated in New York State.

V. T. Thayer retires as Director of the Ethical Culture School.

George Beauchamp becomes Leader of the Washington Society.

James G. White is elected President of the AEU to succeed Robert D. Kohn.

James F. Hornback is appointed Leader of the Westchester Society.

George O'Dell retires and returns to England.

1948   New York Society summer play school joins with Riverside Neighborhood Center to form Riverside Community Center.

1949   Wilhelm Boerner returns to Europe to rebuild the Vienna Society.

1950   Long Island Society is founded with Dr. Sheldon Ackley as Leader.

Baltimore Ethical Society is founded.

J. Hutton Hynd retires as Leader of the St. Louis Society and returns to England to become Secretary to the South Place Ethical Society and semi-retirement.

Dr. Horace L. Friess becomes a member of the Board of Leaders of the New York Society.

AEU begins its Member-at-Large program.

Riverdale-Yonkers, [New York] Society is organized.

Ethical Culture Society of Northern Westchester is founded.

Dr. Alexander S. Langsdorf becomes Acting Leader of the St. Louis Society and Member of the Fraternity of Leaders.

1951 American Ethical Union becomes a member of the National Civil Liberties Clearing House.

David S. Muzzey becomes Leader Emeritus in New York Society.

James F. Hornback leaves Leadership in Westchester Society to become Leader to the St. Louis Society.

L. D. MacIntyre is elected President of the AEU to succeed James White.

1952 Cleveland Ethical Society is organized.

Pittsburgh Society is founded.

Miami, Florida, Society is started.

W. Edwin Collier resigns as Leader of the Philadelphia Society; R. Lester Mondale replaces him.

Jerome Nathanson becomes a Member of the Board of Directors of the International Humanist and Ethical Union (IHEU).

Walter Pedersen is appointed Leader of the Westchester Society.

IHEU has its first congress in Amsterdam; participating are the United States, Great Britian, India, Holland, Austria, Norway; groups from France, Belgium, Germany, Israel, Japan, Italy, Ceylon, Yugoslavia, New Zealand, Canada. Active in congress are H. J. Blackham, Julian Huxley, Lord Boyd Orr of England; M. N. Roy of India; J. P. Van Praag of Holland; Karl Roretz of Austria; H. J. Muller of the United States.

AEU Foundation is established.

1953   Bergen County, New Jersey, Society for Ethical Culture is founded.

Vineland, N.J. Fellowship is organized.

Matthew Ies Spetter is appointed Associate Leader of the Brooklyn Society.

1954   Henry Austin is appointed Leader of the Essex Society.

American Ethical Union founds the National Ethical Youth Organization (NEYO).

1955   Southern Connecticut Society is founded.

Boston Ethical Society is reactivated since dissolution in the 1930s.

Foothill, California, Society is started.

Suburban Philadelphia Society is founded.

Walter Pedersen becomes Leader of the Cleveland Society on resigning as Leader of the Westchester Society.

Metropolitan Council of Leaders is organized.

Henry Herman becomes Leader of the Westchester Society on resigning Leadership in New York.

Benjamin Miller becomes Leader of the New York Society.

Dr. Matthew Spetter becomes Leader of the Riverdale-Yonkers Society.

1956   Howard B. Radest is appointed Leader to the Bergen Society, New Jersey.

Joseph L. Blau is elected to Ethical Leadership and membership in the Fraternity of Leaders.

AEU becomes a member of the National Committee Against Discrimination in Housing.

The Standard becomes *The Ethical Outlook.*

AEU publishes *We Sing of Life,* a song book.

1957   Washington Society Tax Case; the Court of Appeals upholds the position of the Washington Society as a religious body.

Walter Pedersen resigns from Leadership of the Cleveland Society.

Rockland County Ethical Fellowship is organized.

George O'Dell dies in England.

Henry Neumann becomes Leader Emeritus of the Brooklyn Society.

IHEU holds its Second Congress in London.

Henry Austin leaves the Leadership of Essex Society to become Leader of the Brooklyn Society.

George Beauchamp retires as Leader of the Washington Society.

1958 West Los Angeles, California, Society is founded.

Walter Lawton is appointed Leader of the Northern Westchester Society.

Second Encampment for Citizenship at Berkeley, California.

Douglas Frazier becomes Leader to the West Los Angeles and Foothill Societies.

Santa Barbara, California, Ethical Fellowship is founded.

Kissimmee, Florida, Fellowship is started with Dr. George Beauchamp as Leader.

David Norton is appointed Associate Leader in the St. Louis Society.

West Coast Council for Ethical Culture is organized for the West Los Angeles, Foothill, Los Angeles, and Santa Barbara societies.

Walter Pedersen dies.

1959 The Fraternity of Leaders of the American Ethical Union holds the First Institute for Ethical Leadership under the direction of Horace L. Friess at Columbia University.

Delaware Valley Fellowship is started.

Fellowship of Ethical Pacifists is organized.

Sheldon Ackley leaves Leadership of the Long Island Society to teach at New York University.

Henry Austin leaves Leadership of the Brooklyn Society to become Leader of the Long Island Society.

Edward L. Ericson becomes Leader of the Washington Ethical Society.

Leo Goldsmith, Jr., is elected President of the AEU to succeed L. D. MacIntyre.

Princeton Ethical Fellowship is founded.

Queens Ethical Fellowship is started.

R. Lester Mondale retires from Leadership with the Philadelphia Society.

New York Society's Women's Conference helps develop the Planned Parenthood Clinic in Manhattan's Upper West Side.

National Women's Conference publishes report on *The Religious Factor in Child Adoption*.

Foothill Society purchases a meeting house.

Bergen Society purchases a meeting house.

1960   Barbara Raines is appointed Associate Leader to the West Coast Council for Ethical Culture.

Percival Chubb dies.

Henry Herman resigns Leadership of the Westchester Society to return to Leadership of the New York Society.

Ethical Culture Fellowship of Monmouth County is started.

Howard Box is appointed Leader to the Brooklyn Society.

AEU submits a brief as *amicus curiae* before the Supreme Court in the Torcaso Case challenging the Maryland state law requiring an oath to hold public office.

Second Institute for Ethical Leadership is held at Columbia.

Encampment for Citizenship undertakes another experimental program in Puerto Rico.

Bay Area (California) Ethical Fellowship is founded.

New York Society starts the Institute for Ethical Studies under the direction of Joseph L. Blau.

The Hudson-Delaware Council for Ethical Culture is organized for Bergen, Essex, Monmouth, Princeton, and Rockland Societies.

1961   Valley Ethical Society (California) is founded.

Jerome Nathanson is elected Chairman of the Fraternity of Leaders to succeed Dr. Neumann.

Walter Lawton becomes part-time Leader-Advisor to the Queens Society.

AEU submits a brief as *amicus curiae* before the Supreme Court in the New York Regents Prayer Case.

1962   Harold J. Quigley is appointed Leader of the Cleveland Society.

Peninsula (California) Fellowship for Ethical Culture is started.

IHEU holds its third congress in Oslo, Norway.

Jerome Nathanson becomes Director of the Institute for Ethical Leadership.

Kenneth J. Smith becomes Leader to the Philadelphia Society.

Howard B. Radest and Bergen Ethical Society start Camp Elliott, a work camp for teen-agers.

AEU participates as *amicus curiae* before the Supreme Court in The Murray-Schempp Case, another of the religious freedom cases.

David Norton becomes Leader to the Boston Society after four years as Associate Leader in St. Louis.

Walter Lawton becomes Leader-at-Large to the AEU.

1963   American Ethical Union organizes the Commission on Race and Equality, a program of education for racial integration.

Arnold E. Sylvester is elected President of the AEU to succeed Leo Goldsmith, Jr.

Ernest H. Sommerfeld is appointed Leader of the Westchester Society.

1964   Dale H. Drews is appointed Leader of the Queens Society.

Walter Lawton resigns as Leader-at-Large of the AEU to take up Leadership of the Chicago Society.

Howard B. Radest is appointed first Executive Director of the AEU, resigning Leadership of the Bergen Society.

Douglas Frazier leaves Leadership of the California Society to become Leader of the Bergen Society.

Jerome Nathanson is reelected Chairman of the Fraternity of Leaders.

Encampment for Citizenship creates the Center for Education in Democracy for youths aged 15–18.

Ethical Culture Fellowship of Greater Hartford, Connecticut, is founded.

The Eastern Branch of the Long Island Society becomes the Ethical Fellowship of Commack.

AEU Commission on Race and Equality carries out its four-point program in education for integration in Birmingham, Alabama.

American Ethical Union starts the monthly newsletter, *Ethical Culture Today* with Frieda Moss as Editor.

Max Grossman is elected to Leadership and to membership in the Fraternity of Leaders.

John Moore becomes Fellow-in-Training with the St. Louis Society.

1965   AEU organizes the Social Service Commission to coordinate the social service activities of the societies and to initiate new projects.

The North American Commission of the IHEU holds its first meeting with participants from the American Humanist Association and the American Ethical Union and with guests from Canada.

North Shore (Chicago) Ethical Humanist Society is formed.

Lakeland (New Jersey) Fellowship for Ethical Culture is started.

Algernon D. Black is named Senior Leader by the New York Society.

AEU starts publication of *The Ethical Forum* to focus attention on recent thought on the moral problems of the day.

William Rogers, Jr., becomes Leader to the Essex Society.

Henry Herman resigns Leadership in New York Society and joins the staff of the University of Wisconsin.

St. Louis Society dedicates its new meeting house in suburban LaDue.

Riverdale-Yonkers Society builds a meeting house.

Ross A. Weston joins the Ethical movement as Leader of the Long Island Society.

AEU submits a brief as *amicus curiae* before the Supreme Court in the Andrew Seeger Case, supporting nontheistic grounds for conscientious objection.

M. Michael Grupp is appointed Leader of the Southern Connecticut Society.

Peninsula, Foothill, and West Los Angeles societies unify in Los Angeles Society.

Richard Gambino becomes Associate Leader of the New York Society.

Leonard Mandelbaum is appointed Associate Leader of the New York Society.

David S. Muzzey dies.

Robert Kopka becomes Assistant Executive Director of the AEU.

1966 Harold J. Quigley leaves Leadership with the Cleveland Society to become Leader to the new Los Angeles Society and Leader-Advisor to the Bay Area and Peninsula Societies.

IHEU holds its fourth congress in Paris.

AEU begins publication of *Ethical Impact*, a periodical for college-age youth.

Henry Neumann dies.

Washington Society dedicates its meeting house.

AEU establishes the Board of Ethical Lecturers to examine the moral dilemmas in a changing society and intended as a platform for people noted for their creative participation in the mainstream of American life. Heading the Board as Honorary Chairman of the Advisory Committee is Herbert M. Rothschild, member of the New York Society, and serving with him are Harrison Brown, Jerome D. Frank, Horace L. Friess, Sidonie M. Gruenberg, Michael Heidelberger, Robert M. Hutchins, Saul K. Padover, Harriet Pilpel, Sidney H. Scheuer, Earl Ubell, and Gerald Wendt. The first lecturers are Robert Heilbroner, Senator Eugene J. McCarthy, Saul K. Padover.

Paul Weston becomes Fellow-in-Training to the New York Society.

1967 AEU creates a Peace Commission.

Arthur Dobrin is made a Fellow-in-Training with the New York Society.

Howard Lischeron becomes Fellow-in-Training to the AEU.

Richard Gambino becomes Leader of the New York Society.

Warner Klugman is elected President of the AEU to succeed Arnold Sylvester.

Chicago Society and North Shore Ethical Humanist Fellowship merge to create a larger Chicago Ethical Society.

Werner Klugman, Northern Westchester, is elected President of the AEU, succeeding Arnold Sylvester.

The 60th AEU Assembly in Philadelphia is a joint meeting with the American Humanist Association seeking to explore areas of common ground.

The Fellowship of Religious Humanists becomes an affiliate member of the AEU.

1968   AEU and the AHA jointly sponsor the Council on Humanist and Ethical Concerns (CHEC) to represent an ethical/humanist point of view in Washington, D.C. and to alert the membership to critical public issues.

AEU is recipient of a large acreage in northern New Jersey from the Metropolitan Recreation Association. The AEU Conference Center is opened on that site.

Khoren Arisian leaves the Leadership in Boston to join the Board of Leaders of the New York Society.

AEU files an *amicus curiae* brief in the case before the U.S. Supreme Court protesting the exclusion of people from jury service who do not believe in capital punishment.

David Evans is appointed first Henry Neumann Fellow.

M. Michael Grupp is named Leader in Queens.

John H. Moore is named Leader in Essex County succeeding William Rogers.

Ethical Culture Fellowship of Monmouth County becomes an Associate Society.

Robert Kopka, Associate AEU Director, is elected to the Fraternity of Leaders.

John H. Kendrick is named part-time Leader in Boston.

Douglas Frazier becomes Leader-in-Residence at the AEU Conference Center and resigns from Leadership in Bergen County.

Arthur Dobrin becomes Acting Leader in Long Island succeeding Ross A. Weston, who resigned because of ill health.

Paul Weston is named Acting Leader in Baltimore.

Howard Lischeron is named Acting Leader in Cleveland.

Bibliography

Addams, Jane. *Twenty Years at Hull House*. New York, 1914.

Addams, Jane and Robert A. Woods. *Philanthropy and Social Progress*. New York and Boston, 1892.

Adler, Felix. *Creed and Deed*. New York, 1886.

————. *An Ethical Philosophy of Life*. New York and London, 1918, 1946.

————. *Incompatibility in Marriage*. New York and London, 1930.

————. *Life and Destiny*. Selections by Mrs. Felix Adler. 1903. Reissued with an introduction by Horace L. Friess. New York, 1956.

————. *Marriage and Divorce*. New York and London, 1923.

————. *Our Part in This World*. Selections by Horace L. Friess. New York, 1946.

————. *The Moral Instruction of Children*. New York, 1898.

————. *The Reconstruction of the Spiritual Ideal*. New York, 1929. (The Hibbert Lectures of 1923.)

————. *The Religion of Duty*. New York, 1905.

————. *The World Crisis and Its Meaning*. New York, 1916.

Adler, Felix and Octavius B. Frothingham. *The Radical Pulpit*. New York, 1878.

Bacon, Samuel F. *An Evaluation of the Philosophy and Pedagogy of Ethical Culture*. Washington, D.C., 1933.

Barrett, William, *Irrational Man: A Study in Existentialist Philosophy.* New York, 1958.

Birmingham, Stephen. *Our Crowd: The Great Jewish Families of New York.* New York, 1967.

Black, Algernon D. *The First Book of Ethics.* New York, 1965.

——. *The Young Citizens: The Story of the Encampment for Citizenship.* New York, 1962.

Blackham, Harold J. *The Human Tradition.* London, 1954.

——. *Stanton Coit, 1857–1944: Selections from His Writings with a Prefatory Memoir.* London, 1944.

——. *Six Existentialist Thinkers.* New York, 1959.

Blau, Joseph L. *Cornerstones of Religious Freedom in America.* Boston, 1949.

Bliss, W. D. P. *Encyclopedia of Social Reform.* New York, 1897.

Boette, Cecelia R. *Children's Songs in Use by the Ethical Societies.* St. Louis, 1924.

Bridges, Horace J. *As I Was Saying.* Boston, 1923.

——, ed. *Aspects of Ethical Religion: Essays in Honor of Adler.* New York, 1926.

——. *Criticisms of Life.* Boston and New York, 1915.

——. *The Emerging Faith.* New York, 1937.

——, ed. *The Ethical Movement: Its Principles and Aims.* London, 1911.

——. *The Fine Art of Marriage.* Chicago, 1930.

——. *The God of Fundamentalism.* Chicago, 1925.

——. *Humanity on Trial.* New York, 1941.

——. *On Becoming an American.* Boston, 1919.

——. *The Religion of Experience.* New York, 1916.

——. *Signs of the Times in Religion.* Chicago, 1936.

——. *Taking the Name of Science in Vain.* New York, 1928.

Brown, Dee. *The Year of the Century: 1876.* New York, 1966.

Burns, C. DeLisle. *After War—Peace?* London, 1941.

——. *Challenge to Democracy.* New York, 1935.

——. *Civilization: The Next Step.* London, 1938.

——. *Contact Between Minds.* New York, 1923.

——. *Democracy.* London, 1935.

——. *Democracy: Its Defects and Advantages.* New York, 1929.

——. *First Europe: A study of the Establishment of Medieval Christendom.* New York, 1948.

——. *Government and Industry.* London, 1921.

——. *Greek Ideals.* New York, 1917.

——. *Growth of Modern Philosophy.* New York, n.d.

Burns, C. DeLisle. *Horizon of Experience: A Philosophy of Modern Man.* New York, 1934.

―――. *Horizon of Experience: A Study of Modern Mind.* London, 1933.

―――. *Industry and Civilization.* New York, 1925.

―――. *Introduction to the Social Sciences.* London, 1930.

―――. *Modern Civilization on Trial.* New York, 1931.

―――. *Modern Theories and Forms of International Organization.* London, n. d.

―――. *Morality of Nations.* New York, 1916.

―――. *1918–1928, A Short History of the World.* New York, 1928.

―――. *Old Creeds and the New Faith.* London, 1911.

―――. *Philosophy of Labor.* London, 1925.

―――. *Political Ideals.* London, 1919, 1926, 1931.

―――. *Principles of Revolution.* London, 1920.

―――. *Short History of International Intercourse.* London, 1924.

―――. *War and a Changing Civilization.* London, 1934.

―――. *Whitehall.* London, 1921. (World of Today series.)

Burr, Nelson R. *A Critical Bibliography of Religion in America* in *Religion in American Life,* vol. IV, pts. 1–5. Princeton, N.J., 1961. (Princeton Studies in American Civilization, no. 5.)

Chubb, Percival. *Festivals and Plays.* New York and London, Harper and Bros., 1912.

―――. *On the Religious Frontier.* New York, 1931.

―――, ed. *Selections from Addresses, Inaugurals, and Letters of Abraham Lincoln.* New York, 1930.

―――, ed. *Selections from Emerson.* New York, 1930.

―――. *The Teaching of English.* New York, 1924.

―――. *The Teaching of English in the Elementary and Secondary Schools.* New York, 1922.

Cohen, Julius Henry. *They Builded Better than They Knew.* New York, 1946.

Coit, Stanton, ed. *Ethical Democracy: Essays in Social Dynamics.* London, 1900. (Edited for the Society of Ethical Propagandists.)

―――, trans. *Ethics,* by Nicolai Hartmann. New York, 1932.

―――. *Is Civilization a Disease?* New York, 1917.

―――. *The Message of Man.* London, 1895.

―――. *National Idealism and the Book of Common Prayer.* London, 1908.

―――. *National Idealism and a State Church.* London, 1907.

―――. *Neighborhood Guilds.* London, 1891.

―――. *The One Sure Foundation for Democracy.* London, 1937.

―――. *Social Worship.* New York, 1913.

Coit, Stanton, ed. *The Soul of America.* New York, 1914.

————. *The Spiritual Nature of Man.* London, 1910.

————. *Woman in Church and State.* London, 1910.

Columbia Associates in Philosophy. *An Introduction to Reflective Thinking.* Boston, 1923.

Conway, Moncure D. *Addresses and Reprints, 1850–1907.* Boston, 1909.

————. *Autobiography: Memories and Experiences.* Boston, 1904.

————. *Idols and Ideals, with an Essay on Christianity.* New York, 1877.

————. *Lectures.* London, 1864.

————. *Lessons for the Day, Discourses.* 2 vols. London, n. d.

————. *My Pilgrimage to the Wise Men of the East.* Boston, 1906.

————. *The Sacred Anthology (Oriental), A Book of Ethical Scriptures.* New York, 1899.

————. *Tracts for Today.* Cincinnati, 1857.

Crapsey, Algernon Sidney. *The Last of the Heretics.* New York, 1924.

David, Henry. *The History of the Haymarket Affair.* New York, 1958.

Dewey John. *A Common Faith.* New Haven, Conn., 1934. (The Terry Lectures.)

Dombrowski, James. *The Early Days of Christian Socialism.* New York, 1936.

Ethical Hymn Book, compiled and edited for the Union of Ethical Societies. 4th ed. London, 1905.

Ethical Songs with Music. London, 1892.

Ferm, V., ed. *Religion in the Twentieth Century.* New York, 1948.

The Fiftieth Anniversary of the Ethical Movement. New York and London, 1926.

The Fiftieth Anniversary of the Ethical Movement, 1876–1926. New York, 1926.

Flower, Benjamin O. *Progressive Men, Women and Movements of the Past Twenty Years.* Boston, 1914.

Frank, Lawrence K. *Nature and Human Nature.* New Brunswick, N.J., 1951.

Frankel, Charles. *The Case for Modern Man.* Boston, 1959.

Frankfurter, Felix. *Felix Frankfurter Reminisces.* New York, 1960.

Freeman, Daniel Roy. *God and War.* Boston, 1915.

Friess, Horace L. *Our Part in This World: Selections from the Writings of Felix Adler.* New York, 1946.

Friess, Horace L. and H.W. Schneider. *Religion in Various Cultures.* New York, 1932.

Frothingham, Octavius B. *Recollections and Impressions, 1882–1895.* New York.

————. *Transcendentalism in New England.* New York, 1876.

Goblet d'Aloiella, Count. *The Contemporary Evaluation of Religious Thought*. New York, 1886.

Goldman, Eric F. *Rendezvous with Destiny*. New York, 1956.

Gompers, Samuel. *Seventy Years of Life and Labor*. New York, 1925.

Goodlander, Mabel. *An Historical Sketch of the Ethical Culture Schools*. New York, 1939.

Gould, Frederick J. *Brave Citizens*. London, 1911.

————. *Bright Lamps of History and Daily Life*. London, n. d.

————. *A Catechism of Religion and the Social Life*. London, 1908.

————. *Children's Book of Moral Lessons*. London, 1909–1915.

————. *Common Sense Thoughts on a Life Beyond*. London, 1919.

————. *Funeral Services without Theology*. London, 1906.

————. *Pioneers of Hearts and Minds*. London, 1912.

————. *Pioneers of Johnson's Court*. London, 1929.

————. *Stories for Young Hearts and Minds*. London, 1912.

————. *Stories of Moral Instruction*. London, 1909.

————. *Young People's Bible Book*. London, 1931.

Hawton, Hector, ed. *Reason in Action*. London, 1956.

Haydon, A. Eustace. *Biography of the Gods*. New York, 1941; reissued New York, 1967.

————. *Man's Search for the Good Life*. New York, 1938.

————. *Quest of the Ages*. New York, 1929.

Hohoff, Tay. *A Ministry to Man: The Life of John Lovejoy Elliott*. New York, 1959.

Holmes, John Haynes. *I Speak for Myself*. New York, 1959.

Hopkins, Charles Howard. *The Rise of the Social Gospel in American Protestantism, 1865–1915*. New Haven, Conn., 1940.

Hunter, Nancy. "Felix Adler and Morris R. Cohen, Two Generations of Jewish Liberal Thought." Unpublished thesis, January, 1955.

Huxley, Julian. *Religion without Revelation*. New York, 1958.

Hyman, Herbert, Charles R. Wright, and Terence K. Hopkins. *Studies in Evaluation: A Case History of Research on the Encampment for Citizenship*. Berkeley, California, 1962.

Jacobs, Leo. *Three Types of Practical Ethical Movements of the Past Half Century*. New York, 1922.

Johnson, Emily Cooper, ed., for the Women's International League for Peace and Freedom. *Jane Addams, Centennial Reader*. New York, 1960.

Lamont, Corliss. *The Philosophy of Humanism*. 4th ed. New York, 1957.

Lloyd, Caro. *Henry Demarest Lloyd*. New York and London, 1912.

Lyttle, Charles H. *Freedom Moves West: A History of the Western Unitarian Conference, 1852–1952*. Boston, 1952.

Mackenzie, John S. *Cosmic Philosophy*. New York, 1931.

Mackenzie, John S. *Elements of Constructive Philosophy.* New York, n. d.
———. *Fundamental Problems of Life.* New York, 1928.
———. *Manual of Ethics: Designed for the Use of Students.* London, 1925.
———. *Outlines of Metaphysics.* New York, 1929.
———. *Outlines of Social Philosophy.* New York, 1918.
———. *Ultimate Values in the Light of Contemporary Thought.* London, 1924.
Malone, Dumas, ed. *Dictionary of American Biography.* New York, 1935.
Mangasarian, M. M. *A New Catechism.* Chicago, 1902.
Mann, Arthur. *Yankee Reformers in the Urban Age.* Cambridge, Mass., 1954.
Martin, Alfred W. *Character and Love.* Boston, 1890.
———. *Comparative Religion and the Religion of the Future.* New York and London, 1926.
———. *Consolations.* New York and London, 1931.
———. *The Dawn of Christianity.* New York and London, 1914.
———. *Faith in a Future Life.* New York and London, 1916.
———. *The Fellowship of Faiths.* New York, 1925.
———. *Great Moral Leaders.* New York, 1933.
———. *Great Religious Teachers of the Past.* New York, 1911.
———. *Ideals of Life.* New York, 1895.
———. *The Life of Jesus in the Light of the Higher Criticism.* New York and London, 1913.
———. *The Message of Man: A Book of Ethical Scriptures Gathered from Many Sources.* London, 1895.
———. *The Modern Ideal of Marriage.* New York, n.d.
———. *A Philosophy of Life and Its Spiritual Values.* New York and London, 1923.
———. *Sixty Years of Christian Science: An Appreciation and a Critique.*
———. *The World's Great Religions.* Seattle, 1906.
———. *The World's Great Religions and the Religion of the Future.* New York and London, 1921.
Martineau, Harriet. *How to Observe Morals and Manners.* London, 1838.
———. *Positive Philosophy and Religion Explanatory of the Society of Humanity.* 3rd ed. New York, 1877.
May, Henry F. *Protestant Churches and Industrial America.* New York, 1949.
Meyerhardt, M. W. "The Movement for Ethical Culture at Home and Abroad," *American Journal of Religious Psychology and Education,* vol. III, no. 1 (May, 1908).
Mezes, S. E. *Ethics, Descriptive and Explanatory.* London, 1901.

Mondale, Lester. *The Unitarian Way of Life*. Boston, 1947.
———. *Values in World Religions*. Boston, 1959.
Morgenthau, Henry. *All in a Life-Time*. New York, 1922.
Muzzey, David S. *American Adventure*. 2 vols. New York, 1927.
———. *American History*. New York, 1925.
———. *American History for Colleges*. New York, 1943.
———. *Ethics as a Religion*. New York, 1951; reissued New York, 1967.
———. *History of the American People*. New York, 1929.
———. *A History of Our Country*. New York, 1936, 1937, 1939, 1941, 1942, 1943, 1945.
———. *James G. Blaine: A Political Idol of Other Days*. New York, 1934.
———. *Readings in American History*. New York, 1915, 1921.
———. *The Rise of the New Testament*. London, 1900.
———. *Spiritual Heroes*. New York, 1959.
———, ed. *The Spiritual Franciscans: Prize Essays of the American Historical Association, 1905*. New York, 1907; reprinted Washington, 1914.
———. *The United States of America*. New York, 1922.
———. *Thomas Jefferson*. New York, 1918.
Muzzey, David S. and J. H. Krout, *America: A World Power, 1898–1944*. New York, 1944.
Nathanson, Jerome, ed. *Authoritarian Attempt to Capture Education: Papers from the Second Conference on the Scientific Spirit and Democratic Faith*. New York, 1945.
———. *Forerunners of Freedom*. Washington, 1941.
———. *John Dewey, The Reconstruction of the Democratic Life*. New York, 1951; reissued New York, 1967.
———, ed. *Science for Democracy*. New York, 1946.
———, ed. *Scientific Spirit and the Democratic Faith: Papers from the First Conference on the Scientific Spirit and Democratic Faith*. New York, 1944.
Neumann, Henry. *Drums of Morning*. Boston, 1925.
———. *Education for Moral Growth*. New York, 1923.
———. *Lives in theMaking*. New York, 1932.
———. *Modern Youth and Marriage*. New York, 1928.
———. *Spokesmen for Ethical Religion*. Boston, 1951.
O'Dell, George D. *Public Speaking and Chairmanship: A Book for Propogandists*. London, 1912.
———. *Some Human Contacts*. New York, 1929.
Organized Religion in the United States. Annals of the American Academy of Political and Social Science. March, 1948.
Persons, Stow. *Free Religion*. New Haven, Conn., 1947.
Philipson, David. *The Reform Movement in Judaism*. New York, 1931.

Pierce, Bessie L. *A History of Chicago, 1848–1871*. New York, 1940.

Putzel, Max. *The Man in the Mirror*. Cambridge, Mass., 1963.

Radest, Howard B., ed. *Understanding Ethical Religion*. New York, 1959.

Ratcliffe, S. K. *The Story of South Place*. London, 1955.

Reports of the First and Second Conventions of the Union. Philadelphia, 1888.

Riis, Jacob A. *How the Other Half Lives*. New York, 1890.

––––––. *The Making of An American*. New York, 1925.

Rischin, Moses. *The Promised City*. New York, 1962.

Robertson, John M. *Modern Humanists*. London, 1891.

Rosenfield, Leonora C. *Portrait of a Philosopher: Morris R. Cohen in Life and Letters*. New York, 1962.

Salter, William M. *Anarchy or Government?* New York, 1895.

––––––. *The Basis of the Ethical Movement*. Chicago, 1883.

––––––. *Ethical Religion*, (edited by) the Society of Ethical Propagandists. London, 1900.

––––––. *Ethical Songs*. Philadelphia, 1906.

––––––.*First Steps in Philosophy*. London, 1892.

––––––. *Moral Aspiration and Song: Ethical Addresses*. Philadelphia, 1905.

––––––.*Nietzsche the Thinker*. New York, 1917.

Schmidt, Nathaniel. *The Coming Religion*. New York, 1930.

––––––. *Ecclesiasticus* (Temple Bible). Philadelphia, n. d.

––––––. *Ibn Khaldun: Historian, Sociologist and Philosopher*. New York, 1930.

––––––. *The Messages of the Poets*. New York, 1907.

––––––. *The Prophet of Nazareth*. New York, 1907.

Schneider, Herbert W. *A History of American Philosophy*. New York, 1946.

Sheldon, Walter L. *Citizenship and the Duties of a Citizen*. Philadelphia, 1904.

––––––. *Class Readings in the Bible*. Chicago, 1901.

––––––. *An Ethical Movement*. New York, 1896.

––––––. *An Ethical Sunday School*. New York, 1900.

––––––. *An Ethical Sunday School for the Moral Instruction of the Young*. New York, 1900.

––––––. *A Morning and Evening Wisdom Gem for Every Day in the Year*. 2nd ed. St. Louis, n. d.

––––––. *The Old Testament Bible Stories as a Basis for the Ethical Instruction of the Young*. Chicago, 1902.

––––––. *Scheme for Class Study and Readings in the Bible*. Chicago, 1901.

––––––. *A Sentiment in Verse for Every Day in the Year*. Philadelphia, 1906.

––––––. *The Story of the Bible from the Standpoint of Modern Scholarship*. Chicago, 1899.

Sheldon, Walter L. *Story of the Life of Jesus, for the Young, Told from an Ethical Standpoint.* 2nd ed., Philadelphia, 1909.

———. *Summer Greetings from Japan.* Privately printed. 1905.

Thoughts from the Writings and Addresses of Walter L. Sheldon. St. Louis, 1919.

Sidgwick, Henry. *Practical Ethics.* London, 1898.

Silliman, Vincent, ed. *We Sing of Life: Songs for Children, Young People and Adults.* Boston, 1955. (For the American Ethical Union.)

Simkhovitch, Mary. *Neighborhood, My Story of Greenwich House.* New York, 1938.

Smith, James Ward and A. Leland Jamison, eds. *Religious Perspectives in American Culture,* in *Religion in American Life,* vol. 2. Princeton, N.J., 1961. (Princeton Studies in American Civilization, no. 5.)

———. *The Shaping of American Religion,* in *Religion in American Life,* vol. I. Princeton, N. J., 1961. (Princeton Studies in American Civilization, no. 5.)

Snell, Harry, The Right Hon. Lord. *Britain, America and World Leadership.* London, 1940.

———. *The Mission of the Ethical Movement in Religion.* London, n.d.

Spencer, Anna Garlin. *The Family and its Members.* Philadelphia, 1923.

———. *The History of the Bell Street Chapel Movement.* Providence, 1903.

———. *Orders of Service for Public Worship.* Providence, 1896.

———. *Woman's Share in Social Culture.* Philadelphia, 1925.

The Society of Ethical Propagandists. *Ethics and Religion: A collection of essays by Sir John Seeley, Dr. Felix Adler, Mr. W. M. Salter, Prof. Henry Sidgwick, Prof. G. Von Gizycki, Dr. Bernard Bosanquet, Mr. Leslie Stephen, Dr. Stanton Coit, and Prof. J. H. Muirhead.* London, 1900.

Spetter, Matthew Ies. *Man, the Reluctant Brother.* New York, 1967.

Spiller, Gustav. *The Ethical Movement in Great Britain.* London, 1934.

———, ed. *A Generation of Religious Progress,* for the Union of Ethical Societies and the Rationalist Press Assoc. London, 1916.

———. *Hymns of Love and Duty.* 3rd ed. London, 1903.

———. *The Mind of Man.* London, 1902.

———. *Moral Instruction in 18 Countries,* for the International Union of Ethical Societies. London, 1909.

———. *The Origin and Nature of Man.* London, 1931.

———, ed. *Papers on Inter-Racial Problems.* First Universal Races Congress, 1911, for the World Peace Foundation. Boston, 1911.

———. *Poems of Human Service.* London, 1927.

Sutro, Florentine Scholle. *My First Seventy Years.* New York, 1935.

———. *The Attack on the American Secular School.* Boston, 1951.

Thayer, V. T. *American Education under Fire.* New York, 1944.

Thayer, V. T. *Misinterpretation of Locke as a Formalist in Educational Philosophy.* Madison, Wisconsin, 1921.

————. *The Passing of the Recitation.* Boston, 1928.

————. *Religion in Public Education.* New York, 1947.

————. *Reorganizing Secondary Education.* New York, 1940.

————. *The Role of the School in American Society.* New York, Dodd, 1960.

Tolman, William Howe, and William I. Hull. *Handbook of Sociological Information, New York City,* for the City Vigilance League. New York, 1894.

Tucker, William J. *My Generation.* Boston and New York, 1919.

Twenty Years of the Ethical Movement, 1876–1896. Philadelphia, 1896.

United States Government. *Religious Bodies: Special Reports of the Bureau of The Census,* Washington, D.C., 1926.

Wald, Lillian D. *The House on Henry Street.* New York, 1915.

————. *Windows on Henry Street.* Boston, 1934.

Warren, Sidney. *American Freethought, 1860–1914,* New York, 1943.

Weinstein, Gregory. *The Ardent Eighties and After.* 3rd. ed. New York, 1947.

Weller, Charles F. *World Fellowship.* New York, 1935.

Weston, S. Burns. "Beginning and Development of Ethical Movement," *Ethical Record* (April–May, 1901).

Wiebe, Robert H. *The Search for Order, 1877–1920.* New York, 1967. (The Making of America Series.)

Wise, Stephen. *Challenging Years.* New York, 1949.

Woods, Robert A., and Albert J. Kennedy, eds. *A Handbook of Settlements.* New York, 1911.

————. *The Settlement Horizon.* New York, 1922.

Zueblin, Charles. *The Religion of a Democrat.* New York, 1908.

Pamphlets and Periodicals

Amicus curiae briefs in the religious freedom cases:
  Illinois Released Time Case (McCullum Case), 1946.
  Washington Ethical Society Tax Case, 1956, 1957.
  The Torcaso Case, 1960.
  New York State Regents Prayer Case, 1961.
  Murray-Schempp Case, 1962.
  The Seeger Case, 1965.
The Ethical Addresses, American Ethical Union, 1895–1915.
Ethical Culture Today, American Ethical Union, 1964–1967.

The Ethical Forum, American Ethical Union, 1965–.

The Ethical Frontier Series, New York Society for Ethical Culture.

The Ethical Outlook, American Ethical Union, 1956–1964.

The Ethical Platform, published weekly by the New York Society for Ethical Culture. Jan. 1951–.

The Ethical Record, American Ethical Union, 1888–1890; 1900–1904 1962–1965.

The Index, publication of the Free Religious Association, Boston, 1866–1886.

International Humanism, periodical of the IHEU, published quarterly in the Netherlands. Jan. 1954–.

The International Journal of Ethics, American Ethical Union, 1890–1918; now published by the University of Chicago.

The Plain View, British Ethical Union, London, England. No longer pub.

Proceedings of the Congresses of the International Humanist and Ethical Union:

First: Amsterdam, 1952. The Netherlands, IHEU, 1953.

Second: London, 1957. The Netherlands, IHEU, 1958.

Third: Oslo, 1962. The Netherlands, IHEU, 1963.

Fourth: Paris, 1966. The Netherlands, IHEU, 1966.

70th Anniversary Pamphlet, New York Society for Ethical Culture, 1946.

The Standard, American Ethical Union, 1914–1955.

Thayer, V. T., *The Ethics of Democracy,* Felix Adler Lecture, New York Society for Ethical Culture, 1956.

Woolf, S. J., "Dr. Adler at 80 Develops Man's Advance," *New York Times Magazine,* 1930.

Index

337